THE LYRIC METRES
OF
GREEK DRAMA

THE LYRIC METRES
OF
GREEK DRAMA

BY

A.M.DALE

SECOND EDITION

CAMBRIDGE
AT THE UNIVERSITY PRESS
1968

CAMBRIDGE UNIVERSITY PRESS
Cambridge, New York, Melbourne, Madrid, Cape Town, Singapore,
São Paulo, Delhi, Dubai, Tokyo, Mexico City

Cambridge University Press
The Edinburgh Building, Cambridge CB2 8RU, UK

Published in the United States of America by Cambridge University Press, New York

www.cambridge.org
Information on this title: www.cambridge.org/9780521147569

This edition © Cambridge University Press 1968

First published 1948
Second edition 1968
First paperback printing 2010

A catalogue record for this publication is available from the British Library

Library of Congress Catalogue Card Number: 68–10019

ISBN 978-0-521-06923-6 Hardback
ISBN 978-0-521-14756-9 Paperback

PREFACE TO THE SECOND EDITION

I am grateful to the Cambridge University Press for the opportunity to revise the many errors and shortcomings of the first edition of this book. I have tried to take into account work published in the intervening years, but in the absence of any flood of light comparable to that shed by the great, careless, unorganized book of Wilamowitz the effects of this have been mostly in those smaller details which modify the general picture, and have, I hope, been absorbed in the evolution of my own ideas. I have borne in mind the criticisms made of the first edition, but have rejected those which would have preferred a Handbook of Greek Metric or an exhaustive analysis of all the cantica of drama. It remains a book *about* lyric metres rather than a statement of all varieties.

The revision extends to all chapters, but affects most those on dactylic, dochmiac and aeolo-choriambic, the last of these being considerably expanded.

September 1966   A. M. D.

My wife would, as I now do, have wanted to pay tribute again to the great expertise and courtesy of the Press. The articles to which she refers will be published by the Press in a volume of collected papers. I am very grateful to Miss M. L. Cunningham for reading the first proofs. The errors which remain are mine.

July 1967   T. B. L. W.

PREFACE TO THE FIRST EDITION

This book was half-written by September 1939 and then laid aside for six years. The decision to finish it on the original plan was not made without some misgivings, since in the interval my views on the nature of Greek metric as a whole had undergone some modification. This, however, concerned mainly the relation of dramatic lyric to other forms of choral lyric and monody, and confirmed me in the notion that tragedy and comedy yield a particular kind of lyric metre which can legitimately be treated in some isolation from the rest and lends itself better than, for instance, the Pindaric odes to description within the traditional concepts and terminology. I hope subsequently to publish a more fundamental examination of the rhythmical structure of Greek lyric in its various types, with particular reference to Pindar.

I have not attempted here a complete and systematic study either of the whole body of lyric in the drama or of each metrical category. I have tried to indicate what I take to be the prevailing movement of each type of rhythm and any characteristic uses by particular poets. The problems of classification, and the limits within which classification can be of use, receive special attention.

My thanks are due to Professor Paul Maas and Professor Albert Wifstrand for their kindness in reading the first part of this book and for their many useful criticisms and suggestions. If there is much in the whole with which they would disagree, that is perhaps inevitable in a subject so full of speculation and hazard. I wish also to record my gratitude to my husband, Professor T. B. L. Webster, for his help with each chapter and with proofs and index, and to the University Press for the removal of many blemishes from the text.

Finally, as a small tribute to the scholar to whom in this subject, as in all Greek studies, I owe more than I can ever find words to express, I wish to dedicate this book

TO
GILBERT MURRAY

A. M. D.

CONTENTS

I

INTRODUCTION

Metric a proper subject for study even without a knowledge of music and dance, since these were ancillary, not fundamental—Greek verse rhythm based on quantity alone, with no stress accent—The commonest equation $-\;=\;\cup\cup$, with occasional modifications—Difference of English and French verse rhythms from the structural complexity of Greek—Structural elements of the stanza: colon, with or without metra, colon-compound, minor period, major period—Astrophic ἀπολελυμένα—Problems of a systematic study of lyric metres.

The Athenian spectator of the *Agamemnon* in 458 B.C. saw and heard the choral lyrics as a performance compounded of words, music and dance. An Athenian reading the same play in the next century would at least have the experience of many other performances similar in kind to guide his interpretation of the words on the page before him. We, who have never seen Greek dance nor heard Greek music, can never hope to recreate the living whole. Choral lyric was so elaborate and so delicate a structure that even among the Greeks comprehension waned simultaneously with the art of composition; the 'colometry' or line-division which the great Alexandrian philologists set in their texts is not finally authoritative, and the metrical systems of a later antiquity give an analysis of external phenomena which often ignores and obscures the more essential. The modern reader of Greek choral lyric, not content to interpret the bare meaning of the words but seeking to apprehend them as poetry, has to attempt to elucidate from the words themselves the ordered cadences of rhythm, divorced from melody and visible movement; and the metrical principles thus evolved have in the last resort no other criterion of their substantial accuracy than the text itself.

Such an attempt is justified only if it was possible for a Greek poet himself to write the words of his lyrics following principles of pure metric, upon which music and dance (even though also composed by the poet) supervened as a reinforcement of the rhythm. This assumption has been sometimes questioned. It can be said at once that if dance or music is to be taken as primary we may abandon all attempt at formulating a theory of metric, since too little is known of either art in the classical period to build any system upon them. Probably some ghostly reflection of the dance survives in the traditional terminology, if 'arsis' and 'thesis' echo the lift and fall of the dancers' feet.[1] From a comparison of the metres of the Lesbian poets, sung but not danced, with those of choral lyric, it is not unreasonable to suppose that the complex polymetry of the latter, with its resolutions, contractions and shifting rhythms, was first made possible by the interpretative power of the dance. But that such complexity could make itself heard without dance is clear; the monody of Andromeda chained to her rock is composed of metrical elements of the same kind as those of the songs sung by freely moving choruses.

That music too was ancillary and not basic has been more often denied. The systems of metric reared by scholars of the last century, notably Rossbach and Westphal, upon (as they believed) the doctrines of musical theorists such as Aristoxenus and Aristides Quintilianus were vitiated by the assumptions they borrowed from modern European music with its requirements of 'bar' and 'beat'. More recent work has been of interest for the study of Greek music as a separate branch of knowledge. But most of the evidence, and it is little enough, which can be gathered as to the relation of music to metric is of too late a period to help our understanding of the metres of Greek drama. No material evidence survives from pre-Hellenistic times; and we have only to consider the later plays of Euripides and the parodies of Aristophanes to realize how rapidly the relation of words to music was changing even before the end of the fifth century. The papyrus-fragment[2] which preserves a few dochmiac lines from

---

[1] These terms, obscured as they have been by the varied and contradictory usage of past generations of scholars, can only lead to confusion in a modern system of metric. For some discussion of the subject see ch. XIII.

[2] Published by Wessely, *Papyri Rainer*, 1892; cf. E. G. Turner, *J.H.S.* 76, 1956, 95, who suggests a date *c.* 200 B.C. See below, ch. XIII.

the *Orestes* with musical notation disposes the words in an order somewhat different from that of our accepted text—possibly indeed to be preferred to it. Scholars who have discussed this papyrus, if they accept it as Euripides' own music, would hold it a somewhat uncharacteristic fragment from the fifth century; the *Orestes* belongs to an era of musical experiment, and Euripides notoriously departed from the classical tradition of dramatic lyric. In any case, the written lines of this fragment can be so disposed as to comply with the ordinary laws of dochmiac metre, and the most probable assumption is that they were thus composed before they were 'set to music' and suffered rhythmic modification, so that there is nothing here to discourage us from studying the principles of metric from the written word alone. The best guarantee of the reality of the metrical principles recoverable from the written page is the extreme complexity of the system, which can be built up from observation, tested by its own coherence, and disciplined by intimate relation to textual criticism. It is inconceivable that so elaborate an art of metric should have been evolved if it were regularly overlaid in performance by a further conflicting musical rhythm. Since all Greek metre is based on quantity, the ways in which music might radically affect the metrical structure would be the introduction of 'pause' and 'hold', and the power to alter the apparent quantity of syllables. Certain simple phenomena of pause and hold are readily conceivable; in dimeters and trimeters, for instance, 'syncopated' and 'catalectic' metra may have been audibly equated with full metra—syncopated by means of protraction, catalectic by a pause: thus an apparent cretic − ∪ − or bacchiac ∪ − − may occupy the time of ∪ − ∪ − or − ∪ − ∪.[1] But if musical determination, invisible on the written page, were fundamental to the composition of Greek lyric, the syllabic sequences would

---

[1] Choeroboscus in his commentary on Hephaestion (p. 180 Consb.), written in the sixth century A.D. or perhaps later but drawing on much older material, says the metricians and grammarians know only of the long syllable which is equal to two shorts, but that 'rhythmicians' distinguish longs equal to three or more short syllables. Such trisemes and tetrasemes are readily accounted for by syncopation and catalexis, but we do not know enough of the actual workings of protraction to write in the signs ⌐ and ⌐ in our metrical schemata.

assuredly present an unintelligible chaos instead of their complicated but traceable pattern. A further reassurance is the measure of
likeness, and also the kind of difference, between the metres of
dialogue and recitative[1] on the one hand and those compounded
with song, or song and dance, on the other. The conventional nature
of many metrical principles discernible in the latter, unrelated to the
sense of the words or the rhythms of prose, indicates that here is the
element introduced by music, or at least characteristic of poetry
written to be sung as distinct from spoken poetry. We shall never
know what further modifications the actual music introduced in any
given case, but we can be fairly sure that at least for the greater part
of the fifth century these were merely modifications and not fundamental changes of rhythm. Any new system set on top of the metrical
sequences of longs and shorts would either produce something too
complicated to be intelligible to the spectator or would break up and
re-simplify the elaborate original; neither hypothesis is *a priori*
likely. In conclusion, then, music was, generally speaking, an under-
lining of the quantitative rhythm discernible in the written phrase,
and even where on occasion it introduced more profound modifications there is strong probability that the words were composed in
metre before they were set to music and dance. In either case we are
justified in proceeding, as 'grammarians and metricians', to formu-
late as far as we can a system of Greek metric with no material other
than the quantity—long or short—of the written syllables, deter-
minable by rules of prosody.

If it be true that melodies 'unheard are sweeter', then such must
be our consolation in the study of Greek lyric. Not only is our
aesthetic understanding crippled by the loss of music and dance;
there is the further difficulty of training our ear to appreciate, or even
to hear, a purely quantitative rhythm. Germanic peoples, with their
ear accustomed to poetic and prose rhythm in which stress is the
dominant factor, have here an all but impossible task, and even in

[1] I use the term 'recitative' as the accepted translation of παρακαταλογή,
'near-declamation', παρὰ τὴν κροῦσιν λέγειν as distinct from ᾄδειν. It is
not, of course, the 'recitative' of 'Recitative and Aria' in opera and
oratorio.

languages like French where stress is weak and fluctuating the effect
of lyrics set to music with equidistant beat is to create a similar
demand for 'ictus' as an element in ordered rhythm. There is no
vestige of evidence that dynamic stress had any structural significance in Greek verse rhythm before the imperial period. The spoken
language doubtless had its slight and fluctuating variations of stress,
whether accompanying the pitch-accent or the longer quantities; it
is conceivable also that dance, especially the energetic dancing of a
fairly simple and regular metre (as often in comedy), reinforced the
quantitative rhythm with some kind of dynamic beat. But the basis
of all poetic rhythm was quantity alone. In spoken poetry the pitch-
accent must of course have been audible above the quantitative
rhythm, to which it stood in no kind of regular relation; in sung
poetry also rhythm was independent of word-accent, and it is quite
uncertain how far the melodic pitch took any account of the spoken.[1]
An ear trained to stress-rhythm has often great difficulty in appre-
hending a purely quantitative form as rhythmical at all, and in
reading we almost inevitably falsify the time-relations in our craving
for some kind of equidistant beat. On practical grounds this is not
serious so long as we are aware of using stress as a mere device for
the satisfaction of our ear alone, to give audible shape, as it were, to
the phrases which form the metrical units of Greek lyric; moreover
it is possible with practice to emancipate ourselves in some degree
from its demands. The danger is that we may be influenced, con-
sciously or unconsciously, by such presuppositions in our interpretation of Greek metres.[2] It is the more easy to fall into this error
since quantitative rhythm and stress-rhythm in some ways work

[1] If, as is mostly assumed, strophe and antistrophe were sung to the same
melody, then clearly antistrophic music at least paid no regard to word-
accent. But no absolute principles can be deduced from the musical
fragments in inscriptions or papyri. See the well-balanced summary in
R. P. Winnington-Ingram's survey, *Lustrum*, 3, §3 'Melody and Word-
Accent', see below ch. XIII.

[2] As, for instance, in such aberrations as the invention of the 'cyclic
dactyl', wherein − ∪ ∪ was supposed to occupy the time of − ∪, and
the derivation of the dochmiac ∪ − − ∪ − from an 'iambic tripody'
∪ − (∪) − ∪ −.

alike: thus there is a certain resemblance between the metra of iambic and trochaic verse, with their syncopated and catalectic variations, and the bars of 'common time'; the sense that iambic movement is kept when – – ∪ – replaces ∪ – ∪ – but broken by ∪ – – – is acceptable to our ear on principles of stress-rhythm; the general rule that a phrase in falling rhythm may not be followed by a phrase in rising rhythm without the intervention of a pause[1] corresponds with our own feeling. Probably the reason for this degree of correspondence is the presence of a quantitative *element* in stress-rhythm.

Syllabic quantity was determined by laws of prosody, which remained almost constant throughout the history of Greek lyric, certain modifications being regularly associated with certain types of verse. Prosody distinguished only two categories of quantity, long and short. The exact nature of the time-relation of – to ∪ is a difficult problem. Ancient metricians speak only of – = ∪ ∪, and the common practice of resolution indicates that this was the ordinary convention. The musician Aristoxenus, however, a pupil of Aristotle, in a fragment[2] of his treatise on rhythm says that while the conventional signs demarcate exactly equal 'feet' the art of ῥυθμοποιία recognizes much more varied distinctions of tempo: αἱ δ᾽ ὑπὸ τῆς ῥυθμοποιίας γινόμεναι διαιρέσεις πολλὴν λαμβάνουσι ποικιλίαν. Dion. Hal.[3] also speaks of syllables longer than the normal long and shorter than the normal short, and adds[4] that according to the 'rhythmicians' the long of an epic dactyl was less by an indeterminate amount than the sum of two shorts. Much has been built on this distinction between the science of 'metric' and the science of 'rhythmic', but caution is always necessary in arguing from Greek theory to Greek practice. It is a reasonable assumption that quantity, since it is the basis of Greek poetic rhythm, was more clearly defined and perceptible an element in speech-rhythm also than is the case in most modern

---

[1] Thus a trochaic colon ending in – ∪ – ⌣ may not be followed by iambic ⌣ – ∪ –. Such special exceptions, however, as the dactylic tetrameters of Sophocles so often followed by iambic clausula – ∪ ∪ – ∪ ∪ | × – ∪ – keep us warned of the fallibility of our ear.

[2] § 292 Marq.   [3] *De Comp. Verb.* 15.   [4] *Ibid.* 17.

European languages; but consonantal groups, degrees of emphasis and the inflections of the voice must nevertheless have kept it irregular. Some writers of artistic prose strove to harness this spoken rhythm, with its indefinitely fluctuating quantities, in syllabic sequences measured like those of poetry, especially in the close of their periods. In declaiming such prose, the speaker doubtless steadied its quantities to an audible regularity greater than that of everyday speech; it would be interesting to know how the degree of regularity compared with that of the iambic dialogue of tragedy. It is clear from Dionysius' statement that in recitative, such as the rhapsode used in declaiming the Homeric hexameter, the relative value of longs and shorts was kept remarkably constant. But though Greek theory (witness Dionysius) passes easily from the approximations of prose to the regulated rhythm of poetry, and metricians quite reasonably use the same symbols to 'measure' the quantities of spoken verse and of song, the empirical irregularities of elocution find of course no echo in sung metres. The music defined the quantities, and without this definiteness it would not be possible to apprehend the rhythmical complexity of lyric metres. Our traditional music, rich in harmony, constructive symmetry and melodic grace, is relatively limited in rhythm; the poverty of Greek music in purely musical forms allowed a corresponding wealth of rhythmical expression. The existence of trisemes, tetrasemes and pentasemes, of which the musicians tell us, indicates a definite numerical relation between – and ∪ as the normal, and the variations of this ratio would account for the ποικιλία claimed by Aristoxenus. It is probable that in many places where he considers the metricians' measurement of 'equal feet' inadequate our more scientific system would also reject their analysis; their separation of disyllabic 'feet', for instance, has been recognized as a largely unreal division.[1] Nevertheless, – = ∪ ∪ is to be assumed as the commonest equation

[1] When Aristoxenus speaks (§§293-4) of feet in which the relation of ἄνω to κάτω is neither 1:1 nor 1:2 but something which he does not determine with numerical exactitude between the two, it seems probable that this ἀλογία is such as occurs in e.g. the long *anceps* of an iambic metron ⤬ – ∪ – in relation to the following true long.

in musical μετρητική. The *slight* adjustment of relative values required for audible 'long *anceps*' is a different phenomenon. Though unfortunately such a 'modified long' is not susceptible of proof, yet since bar-free music could quite well follow such niceties of quantity its existence could make sense of our efforts to distinguish different metrical movements in apparently identical phrases; thus, for example, the ambiguous – – – ∪ ∪ – – could be differentiated by musical elocution into ionic, pherecratean or dactylic. The strongest evidence for such determination is of course context, but that is by no means always enough and it is a reasonable conjecture that such *standardized* variations from the normal quantity of 'long' did express the recognized conventional tempo of certain metres, and that they were slight, addressed only to the sensitive perception engendered by quantitative rhythm.

To this accurate hearing of time-values our ear is unaccustomed. Syllabic quantity is indeterminate in the metrical systems of modern European poetry. Taking the classic metres of French and English poetry as representative of two different types, the rhythmical principle of the first is a fixed number of syllables, of the second a fixed number of equidistant stresses, in phrases running in a series and demarcated by pause. Assonance or 'rhyme' often reinforces the rhythmical separation of one phrase from another and groups them in larger units. Differences of quantity are in both, so long as they remain spoken verse, an empirically modifying factor only. Set to music, the syllables assume definite quantity, but this is determined by the musical tempo, not by the inherent quantities of the words. The rhythm of French verse acquires a new structural factor in the stresses given by the musical beat; in English, musical stress is substituted for the spoken, with which it often, but not necessarily, coincides. In both, the delicate art of the spoken rhythm is largely overridden by the music, since the structural principles of verse-rhythm are in each case simple, and rhythmical finesse comes into play only with empirical modifications. This is especially the case with English, where the regulative principle itself, equidistant stress or 'ictus', is subject to modification by its degree of conflict or coincidence with the natural spoken stress of the word or group of words, and is obscured to a greater or less extent by the differences of tempo arising from the varying length of words, the obstruction of consonants, rhetorical pauses and the like. These empirical factors often enter into harmonious co-operation with the sense, as in

> My heart aches, and a drowsy numbness pains
> My sense...

The variety and suppleness of the rhythm lie precisely in the susceptibility of the regulative principle itself to these irregular influences; the actual operation of this principle is a question of *degree*, and it is the simplicity of the principle that makes possible so great a range and delicacy of variation. 'Vers libre' emancipates itself from structural principle and proceeds arbitrarily, with none but empirical elements; the subtlety of its rhythms is not a formal complexity but arises from the fusion of a number of indeterminates, the effect of which again is weakened or annulled by the addition of music. In all this there is nothing of the formal elaboration which makes Greek metric a difficult and involved but systematic study. English verse has an extremely simple metrical structure with infinite degrees of modification reducible to no laws, whereas Greek verse starts from conventionally fixed units, syllables of certain lengths, and achieves its variety by combining these in extremely elaborate patterns, reducible to laws of great complexity. The rhythm of spoken Greek verse was indeed subject to a limited degree of indeterminate modification (in the fluctuations of pitch-accent, the proportion of vowels to consonants and the like), but even the incidence of word-end was largely controlled by law, and in sung poetry the part played by indeterminates was still further diminished. English poetic rhythm achieves its most versatile expression in spoken verse, and therefore its variety lies in the sphere of τὸ ἄπειρον, whereas Greek lyric, composed to be sung and not read, has a variety enormously exceeding that of any known body of verse in any language, but this is a formal and structural variety, based on τὸ πέρας.

The rhythms of stressed verse are often used as illustrations for certain phenomena in Greek metric, and such parallels are useful

pedagogically for the beginner confronted with a bewildering variety
of phenomena and terminology. Generations of young scholars have
been grateful for the poem of 'the wise kangaroos' as a mnemonic
for dochmiacs; in

> singest of summer with full-throated ease

the opening rhythm has an effect like that of 'choriambic anaclasis'
− ∪ ∪ − ∪ − − in the clausula of an iambic period; a simple parallel
for syncopated iambics is given by such a verse as

> Yet, stranger, here from year to year   − − ∪ − | ∪ − ∪ −
> she keeps her shadowy kine.
> O, Keith of Ravelston,   − − | ∪ − ∪ −
> the sorrows of thy line!

But these are rough analogies only, and at a later stage the differences
appear more instructive than the resemblances. The dochmiac is not,
like 'the wise kangaroos', ∪ ⊥ ∧ ⊥ ∪ ⊥, but ∪ − − ∪ −. In 'singest of
summer' the inversion of the first stress is intimately linked with the
melodious assonance of the words 'singest' and 'summer'; the protraction of 'O, Keith' is a device used deliberately for its plangent
effect. Many such modifications, indeed, have no reference beyond
the rhythm itself, but it is, nevertheless, characteristic of English
poetry that rhythmic variation is often, as in these examples, intimately related to the sound and sense of the words. In Greek lyric
such a relation is altogether exceptional. Certain metres are often
associated with certain moods, and the prevailing tempo, slow or
broken, of a song may have a general appropriateness to the sentiment, but it is seldom possible to carry such interpretation into the
detail of rhythmic expression. The movement of the ode to Sleep,
in *Philoctetes* 827 ff., is smooth and dreamy with the repeated
rallentando of its long syllables, but in the line καιρός τοι πάντων
γνώμαν ἴσχων the drawn-out rhythm has no such relation to the
sense of the words as can be heard in

> With how sad steps, O Moon, thou climbst the skies.

Sidney's rhythmic variation is onomatopoeic, and arbitrary;
Sophocles' is a piece of musical-metrical technique, an unusual but

admissible variant of the complex metres in which the passage is written.

It is essential for the understanding of Greek metric to make a clear distinction between the metres spoken or delivered in recitative and those composed to be sung, or sung and danced. The former are 'stichic'—that is, they fall into well-demarcated recurrent 'lines' or στίχοι of equal length and uniform movement—and within each στίχος the rhythm is repetitive, so that the line can be analysed into equivalent units called 'feet' or 'metra'. In lyric the structural units of composition are the phrases or κῶλα, which may be of varying length and movement, and to isolate these elements of the composite whole is our first task; correct 'colometry' is here the basis of metrical science. Some of these cola are composed of two or more repetitions of the same rhythmical sequence, and in such a case they can be represented as dimeters, trimeters and so forth; we also use the name 'dimeter' more loosely for cola which fall into two dissimilar halves and are roughly the same length (i.e. contain four long syllables with the appertaining shorts) as true dimeters. Many cola, however, are single sequences, and analytic division is meaningless, or rests on an unproved assumption of the historical development of the phrase by the fusion of smaller elements. In the complex systems of choral lyric the next step is to observe how these cola combine into larger phrases. A combination of cola which was felt to attain a certain rhythmical roundness or completeness was called a περίοδος. The largest of such περίοδοι is the stanza, which in the drama (with rare exceptions) forms a rhetorical unit also. Within the stanza, unless it is very short, are two, three or more smaller περίοδοι, the end of each being marked by a pause. We cannot always distinguish with certainty where a period ends, but often Pause is betrayed by a curtailed or 'catalectic' phrase, by hiatus, or by certain uses of final *anceps*. A short period may be constituted by a single colon, but usually there are two or more cola to a period. Subordinate or 'minor' periods may again be grouped into larger, 'major' periods, still within the circumference of the outer, all-embracing main period or stanza. The same rhythmical movement may be sustained throughout the stanza; more often it changes, whether once, twice, or repeatedly.

Such a change occurs most often at the end of a period, but even a single period may contain unlike cola. Within the period, the division into cola may be defined by change of rhythm, by clear rhetorical separation, or merely by word-end. Sometimes, however, successive cola are welded more closely together, the junction being spanned, as it were, by a single word; thus in

στένουσι δ' εὖ λέγοντες ἄν-
-δρα τὸν μὲν ὡς μάχης ἴδρις (*Agam.* 445–6)

two iambic dimeters coalesce into a tetrameter, and a whole series of similar cola may by this device of word-overlap run on in a chain or πνῖγος (as in *O.C.* 230–3); such πνίγη are also found without overlap, though they are not always easy to distinguish from a series of minor periods. Again, two phrases of unlike movement may combine in a 'dicolon', the compound, whether held together by an overlapping word or not, being attested by its presence in other, older forms of lyric. There is a special group of metres known as 'dactylo-epitrite' where the fusion of unlike cola, rather than their separation by word-end (diaeresis), is a common and deliberately sought effect. The structural elements are thus the colon, the larger colon-compound, the period, minor and major, and the stanza; but single colon or colon-compound may coincide with period, and occasionally period with stanza.[1] Our attempts at colometry cannot always be conclusive, and sometimes the decision is of small importance; more often, however, the rhythmic sequences are altered in character according to the division chosen. The responsion of strophe and antistrophe is an invaluable guide, and close consideration of the context essential, since the single phrase has no sense except as an element in the whole strophe.

Although 'periodic' construction is rarely symmetrical in the strict sense, and attempts like Schroeder's to make all stanzas show regular numerical patterns based on the number of 'theses' are not successful, there is a unity and shapeliness in the stanza-form, an 'inner responsion' (in varying degree), which even in verses not in strophic correspondence greatly simplifies the task of metrical

[1] See further on this subject ch. XII on Strophic Construction.

interpretation. Lyrical monodies which are 'astrophic' ἀπολελυμένα —not composed in stanzas—set harder problems in colometry, since the metrical phrasing changes more arbitrarily and with less regard for structural symmetry in the whole; it was perhaps easier for one singer than for a choir to control complicated changes of tempo. Even here, however, the types of metrical unit, and many of their combinations and transitions, are the same. Knowledge of the habits of these different types and of the possible variants of each has been gradually accumulated by the labours of different scholars, though conclusions must still often be left provisional and tentative. When we try to assign a given syllabic sequence to its proper metrical type we are not dealing in barren terminology. The essential character of the lyrics of Greek drama is that they are composed of phrase-units, most of them traceable to older forms of lyric, set together in such a way that the whole, however heterogeneous the elements, satisfied the poet's ear as a rhythmical form: he might modify some of the phrases to adjust them to their metrical context, but such variations still observe the idiosyncrasies of their several types. The limited length of each colon serves to keep the rhythmical meaning clear; the 'period' would be too long as a unit of audible comprehension, except where (as in the longer dactylic sequences or πνίγη) the movement is simple and uniform.

The art of Greek metric in its more complex forms ceased to be understood at so early a date that the text of the lyrical passages of drama has often reached us in much worse case than the dialogue. All attempts to carry further the knowledge we possess must continue along the lines set by Hermann and continued by recent scholars[1] who have kept metrical in close relation to textual study; problems become harder through the corruption of our texts, but conclusions are more solidly based where text and metre can be made to contribute to a common solution. The nature of the material, however, makes a certain difference of method appropriate in the study of stichic and of lyric verse respectively. In the former a multitude of patient observations, accumulated statistically in historical relation and author by author, are the *only* right basis for an under-

[1] Notably Wilamowitz and Maas.

standing of the nature of this type of rhythm, since here there is ample material to hand, and the area of possible variation is so relatively small that the slightest modifications may be significant. In this way, for instance, the detailed study of the hexameter's development from Homeric to Byzantine times has shown successive phases in the poets' conception of the nature of dactylic rhythm, determined partly by a nicer sense of its technical possibilities, partly by changes in Greek pronunciation. But in the case of lyric poetry the phenomena are enormously more diverse, more uncertain and more complex, and the problem involves two unknowns, music and dance. It is difficult to find principles of classification which shall not be sterile, or to collect enough instances to establish general laws. Imposing systems have been reared on subjective theories of the nature of Greek verse-rhythm, and the past history of scholarship is cluttered with their ruins. Yet in such material as this observation can scarcely be fruitful without the aid of general hypotheses in which the subjective element, an intuitive feeling for what is rhythmical or unrhythmical, rightly plays a considerable part. But such an intuition must itself be formed from the constant study of our texts (and above all from constant reading with an inner ear trained to quantitative accuracy) for an answer to such questions as: What is a phrase? How are phrases grouped in context? How far has each type of poetry or each poet a characteristic style of metrical composition? In this way even tentative conceptions of the nature of the various rhythms and the manner of composition, though they may collapse on a closer study of the data, or prove too nebulous to stand wear, may yet help to show how and what to observe, and so provide the material for their own revision.

II

CLASSIFICATION AND TERMINOLOGY

Classification to some extent based on Hephaestion—Principal categories of lyric metre: dactylic, anapaestic, iambic, trochaic, cretic-paeonic, dochmiac, ionic, aeolic (*a*) aeolo-choriambic (*b*) prosodiac-enoplian, dactylo-epitrite—Fundamental importance of the colon as structural unit—Unreal problems of terminology: catalectic, brachycatalectic, hypercatalectic, acephalous, anacrusis—Notation.

Hephaestion, in the summary handbook into which he finally compressed his voluminous metrical teaching, our oldest[1] treatise on the subject, classifies his material under the various types of metre—iambic, trochaic, etc., each of these being subdivided in terms of size—dimeter, trimeter, and so on. We owe to him a great deal of our terminology, and his type of classification is the most rational starting-point. But his actual categories need modification, some of his analytic terms (especially the disyllabic 'feet' $\cup -$, $- \cup$, $\cup \cup$) have been fruitful in misconceptions ever since, and for lyric metres such codification is no more than a preliminary; we have next to recognize cross-relations, composite effects, and the ambiguities inherent in any system of classification, with its tendency to make us confuse mere convenience of terminology with objective truth.

The cola or phrase-units in the lyrics of fifth-century drama derive from various antecedents, and like their originals permit of certain characteristic variations or alternative forms. The unit of iambic movement, for instance (once repeated for the commonest lyric colon, the dimeter), can best be stated in alternative form $\triangledown - \cup -$, or in Maas's notation $\times - \cup -$ with $\times$ for the variable or *anceps*; this normal unit or 'metron', again, has other variants, formed by resolution, syncopation (suppression of short or *anceps*) or licence to use a double-short in place of a single. Some of the variants used in dramatic lyric are the same as those found in other forms of poetry, sometimes they are more restricted, sometimes less; and it is often

---

[1] *c.* A.D. 200.

enlightening to compare these modifications. To take the example given: resolution is common to all kinds of iambic verse, though in very different proportions; syncopation is peculiar to lyric; the double-short is almost confined to the comic trimeter.

As a preliminary survey of dramatic lyric: there are four categories of metre which are in a special position, in that they appear also in common and well-established forms κατὰ στίχον which had had a long history and were still in active use in the fifth century. As stichic, these are metres of recitative, and of the simple 'recurrent' type: that is, they have within the στίχος an analytic unit or 'metron' of recurring movement. These metra are the dactylic – ᴗ ᴗ, anapaestic ᴗ ᴗ – or ᴗ ᴗ – ᴗ ᴗ –, iambic ᴗ – ᴗ – and trochaic – ᴗ – ᴗ. The dramatic lyric uses cola based on each of these four kinds of movement; here as elsewhere the phrase-unit or colon is the essential, but the fact that this here constitutes a certain 'length' of recurrent movement—a trochaic 'dimeter' or 'trimeter', a dactylic 'tetrameter'—while the corresponding στίχοι of recitative are also 'lengths' (though often different ones) makes a comparison inevitable, all the more since the prevalent στίχοι clearly influenced the lyric cola and in some cases seem to have been their origin, or are even taken over intact, with their observance of law in the incidence of word-end (as occasionally the iambic trimeter and dactylic hexameter).

Next comes a group of metres which still proceed κατὰ μέτρον but appear to be wholly lyrical, with nothing analogous in recitative. Their tempo is strange to our ear, since each metron contains the equivalent of five χρόνοι (χρόνος being the musical term for a single short quantity). These are the cretic – ᴗ –, with its resolved form the paeon – ᴗ ᴗ or ᴗ ᴗ –, and the bacchiac ᴗ – –. It is not always possible to distinguish these from syncopated forms of iambic and trochaic metra, but in some cases the difference of movement is unmistakable, and they clearly had an independent origin.

The multifarious dochmiac, of which the standard form is usually reckoned as ᴗ – – ᴗ –, can conveniently be taken next, since it has curious affinities with both cretics and iambics. It does not move κατὰ μέτρον in quite the same way (though cola composed of a double dochmiac are common), since it may combine with alien metra to form a colon, and not infrequently stands by itself as an independent colon.

The ionic metron ∪ ∪ – – has a different (though still obscure) history, and some of its cola merge with other metrical types to an extent which mocks all attempts at systematic classification. Here the ionic begins to break loose from the metron, and thus establishes an uncertain alliance with the next category, for which the label aeolic is often used, since a number of the cola grouped under it appear in the Lesbian poets. Aeolic cola are in this book subdivided into aeolo-choriambic and prosodiac-enoplian.[1] In the former the choriamb – ∪ ∪ – is an isolable ingredient of the colon; the latter contain no smaller analytic unit but run through to a close in mixed double and single-short movement, the prosodiac in 'falling' movement starting from a long syllable, as, for instance, in the 'alcaic decasyllable' – ∪ ∪ – ∪ ∪ – ∪ – –, the enoplian in 'rising' movement taking off from short or *anceps* to long as in ⊻ – ∪ ∪ – ∪ ∪ – ∪ – –. Again the border-line of these two classes of aeolic is confused, but in some forms they are distinct, and the former still retains some link with the κατὰ μέτρον categories in that the choriamb is a recognizable analytic element which occasionally repeats itself – ∪ ∪ – – ∪ ∪ –.

Finally, there is a large group of metres of which the type called dactylo-epitrite is the most readily comprehensible. It is of the essence of these to progress throughout in compound cola, so that the ear has to carry much longer phrases than in the former categories. The ingredients of the compound are often dissimilar; thus a colon of double-short or 'dactylic' movement is mostly compounded with one of single-short. The length of these colon-ingredients differs considerably, and the compound may be double, treble and even quadruple. This metrical type is peculiar to choral lyric, and here perhaps more than in any other our inability to imagine a *performance* is fatal to any real understanding. The problem was long confused by an ingenious attempt, carried furthest by Schroeder, to interpret

---

[1] The terms prosodiac and enoplian have been used from antiquity downwards for so many different phenomena that they have become almost a *commune bonum*, which I have appropriated for use in this sense.

DLM

these rhythms in terms of mainly tetrasyllabic metra (of an extremely erratic nature) instead of starting from the colon. It cannot be too often emphasized that in *all* Greek lyric the colon is the really effective unit, even in those metres where an audible effect of rhythmic repetition, and the existence of stichic parallels, justify us in analysing further and disengaging a smaller structural unit or metron. The attempt to apply any simple yardstick to other types as well can only end in idle play with pencil and paper.[1]

To grasp the colon's fundamental importance is also to dispel a host of unreal problems which have gathered round such terms as catalectic, brachycatalectic, hypercatalectic, acephalous, anacrusis. The great majority of the cola with which the fifth-century dramatist operates are ready-made units of rhythm, bequeathed him by poetic tradition, or established in the early days of the drama. Some of these are already found in association, but for the most part the combination in polymetric stanzas and sequences is his own; he may also invent new variants or modifications, even on occasion coin a new syllabic sequence hard to refer to any recognized category. The phenomena are multifarious, and the metrician has to subsume them under genus and species, and to recognize which are mere variants. He has also to be able to refer to them in speech and writing, and adopts as far as possible the traditional names. Some of these— glyconic, pherecratean—are derived from poets who made special use of the verse in question; others describe the line in terms of a certain length of its particular type—iambic dimeter, trochaic tetrameter. And in this latter class Hephaestion has a set of terms to describe lines which end a syllable short of the full dimeter, trimeter or tetrameter length: $\cup - \cup - \cup - -$, for instance, he calls an 'iambic

---

[1] In all analyses, from Hephaestion downwards, the intention fluctuates between mere practical μετρητική and interpretation of principles. But it is obvious how easily the former passes into the latter, and in any case exerts a strong influence on it. Schroeder's claims to be full interpretation, among other things of the nature of responsion. The problems which his method of analysis raised are of the utmost importance, and their examination (by Maas, above all) has led to a considerable advance in our understanding of complex lyric metres; especially has it set these in a fruitful relation to textual criticism.

in mixed company also, and with no clausular function, that it is more appropriate to have them labelled with an independent name and merely recognize their catalectic relation to a context where it occurs; mostly, in fact, for the sake of noting the close of a period, of which catalexis is the commonest sign. The pherecratean in the form $-\,-\,-\,\cup\,\cup\,-\,-$ may have relations with ionics, dactyls, and anapaests, and in none of these is it a catalectic colon.

Of more dubious propriety is the use of the term brachycatalexis in Hephaestion and the metrical scholia, to imply that a colon is two syllables short of the norm. The term seems to have been invented in order to fit refractory lengths into the κατὰ μέτρον scheme; thus he makes a 'trochaic dimeter brachycatalectic' of the short colon known as the 'ithyphallic' from its use in old processional songs, $-\,\cup\,-\,\cup\,-\,-.$[1] It is true there are occasional instances of a phrase $\cup\,-\,\cup\,-\,|\,-\,-$ which from its context appears to be iambic (e.g. ὕπεστί μοι θάρσος, Soph. *El.* 479), and on the analogy of this the ithyphallic might be sometimes treated as a trochaic dimeter with both shorts suppressed in the second metron. But there are many contexts where it might more appropriately be analysed as a syncopated iambic dimeter catalectic $-\,\cup\,-\,|\,\cup\,-\,-.$ In default of musical data such questions are merely theoretical. The colon is an old one, used by Archilochus, and is best accepted as it stands, as a common clausula both for trochaic and iambic periods (to say nothing of its other metrical contexts, notably the dactylo-epitrite); and there is no harm in recognizing that in the former case it stands in 'brachycatalectic' relation to the commonest colon, the dimeter. It may equally well stand in catalectic relation to a lekythion.

Hephaestion (or his source) went further and coined a new specimen of terminology, 'hypercatalectic', to denote a phrase which overran a recognized length of metre by a syllable or syllables. Combined with catalexis and brachycatalexis, this enabled any number of syllables to be fitted into the tetrasyllabic construction κατὰ μέτρον.[2] But the suggestion of a standard 'length' of metre and a

---

[1] $-\,\cup\,-\,\cup\,|\,-\,\cup\,\wedge\,\wedge$ as above (p. 19, n. 1).

[2] It was left for his later commentators to run the term to death, see ΣB *passim*.

variant is here most misleading if it be taken to imply anything as to the formation or origin of the cola themselves. The form of aeolic enneasyllable named after Hipponax, for instance, − × − ∪ ∪ − ∪ − − may in the odes of drama follow the glyconic − × − ∪ ∪ − ∪ − and close a period, since overrun is an alternative to catalexis as a clausular device; it provides the same contrast of a pendant after a blunt close, and we naturally hear it in 'hypercatalectic' relation to the shorter preceding colon. But whereas it is conceivable that the pherecratean actually *originated* in popular refrains as a catalectic appendage to the glyconic (though with our insufficient evidence all theories about the origins and derivation of Greek metres are highly speculative), the hipponactean has too many affinities with other enneasyllables and various phrases from Lesbian lyric for its 'hypercatalectic' relation to the glyconic to be taken as primary, though naturally their similarity of movement makes of the two a harmonious sequence.

To turn to the beginning of the colon, the terms 'acephalous' and the much-vexed 'anacrusis' present the same kind of artificial problem. A colon constructed κατὰ μέτρον may have the first metron syncopated, as in νῦν ἄχαλκος ἀσπίδων − ∪ − | ∪ − ∪ −, and thus appear headless, but this is only the same kind of phenomenon as syncopation in the middle of a trimeter, e.g. ∪ − ∪ − | − ∪ − | ∪ − −, and it is better to use the same term 'syncopated' to cover both, so long as we are analysing them in iambic terms. The colon named after the poetess Telesilla ⊻ − ∪ ∪ − ∪ − is acephalous in relation to the glyconic, and so the 'reizianum'[1] ⊻ − ∪ ∪ − − to the pherecratean; there is a strong probability that when Aristophanes writes simple stanzas of telesilleans with reizianum clausulae he is composing in the style of old popular refrains, though the reizianum as used in the drama in general has many other relations than that implied in 'catalectic telesillean'. But the acephalous relation is purely contextual. In *O.T.* 1189–95

τίς γάρ, τίς ἀνὴρ πλέον	tel.
τᾶς εὐδαιμονίας φέρει	glyc.
ἢ τοσοῦτον ὅσον δοκεῖν	glyc.
καὶ δόξαντ' ἀποκλῖναι; ‖	pher.

[1] See below, p. 138, n. 1.

τὸ σόν τοι παράδειγμ' ἔχων, glyc.
τὸν σὸν δαίμονα, τὸν σόν, ὦ glyc.
τλᾶμον Οἰδιπόδα, βροτῶν glyc.
οὐδὲν μακαρίζω reiz.

the aeolo-choriambic strophe falls into two periods, of which the first closes with the pherecratean, the second with the reizianum, a foreshortened echo of the same rhythm, which thus in its turn picks up the first colon or telesillean, foreshortened in relation to the following glyconics. The rhythmic shape of the whole is therewith rounded off. Sophocles has not snipped off heads and tails from certain lengths of metre, but selected existing cola of similar movement and combined them into a shapely whole.

Hephaestion always began his measurements from the first syllable and counted out his feet or his tetrasyllabic metra from that. In the first great attempt of modern scholarship to achieve some understanding of the principles of lyric versification as a whole, Hermann invented a term 'anacrusis' to indicate a kind of 'up-beat' at the opening of certain metres, a prelude to the first 'ictus' or 'arsis'; and the word is still used by many modern scholars rightly concerned to emphasize the relation between certain kinds of rhythm in their general movement, in spite of a difference in opening. But in itself the term is misleading with its suggestion of a preluding syllable or syllables which we are entitled to deduct in order to arrive at the essential cadence of a line.[1] There is no such *principle* in Greek metric, though in our struggles to evolve an adequate terminology we may speak of an 'extra' syllable fore or aft in order to explain the *de facto* relation of one colon to another, especially when the longer one is rare and we have no label ready to hand. Thus, for instance, the colon (a variety of enoplian) *P.V.* 135 σύθην δ' ἀπέδιλος ὄχῳ πτερωτῷ ⏑ – ⏑ ⏑ – ⏑ ⏑ – ⏑ – – has no generally accepted name, and we can ap-

---

[1] The essential point in such lines is that they are in 'rising' metre, i.e. there is a preliminary syllable or disyllable before the first (true) long is reached. Such is the regular structural principle of e.g. iambic or anapaestic verse. But what sounds to our ear most like an up-beat is when an aeolic line starts off × – ⏑ ⏑ . . . like *P.V.* 135 quoted above, and it is *possible* that such rhythms originated in a kind of 'aeolic base' which had one syllable instead of the more usual two.

prehend it most readily here in relation to its context, where the alcaic decasyllable κραιπνόφοροι δέ μ᾽ἔπεμψαν αὖραι – ∪ ∪ – ∪ ∪ – ∪ – – has preceded it (l. 131). But its independent identity is established by its use in Bacchylides and in other dramatic contexts, e.g. Aesch. *Supp.* 526 where it appears in relation to the preceding enoplian:

> μακάρτατε καὶ τελέων   ∪ – ∪ ∪ – ∪ ∪ –
> τελειότατον κράτος ὄλβιε Ζεῦ. ∪ – ∪ ∪ – ∪ ∪ – ∪ – –

Here it is the opening movement which is the same, and the close which is prolonged; the 'Vorschlag' and 'Zusatz', in fact, are terms of a purely relative analysis. The unity of the colon as a piece of rhythm must be respected, only we have to amplify and complete our analytic concept of it by observing all its various associations and affinities, its use in composition.

Notation

To make reading easier I frequently use the following signs:

× *anceps.*

$\underset{x}{}$ long *anceps,* e.g. in iambic $\underset{x}{}$ – ∪ –. The syllable has slightly less than the value of true long, and cannot be resolved.

But long *anceps* before Pause is always unmarked, since Pause automatically gives it the value of true long. It is also left unmarked where on occasion the poet seems deliberately to blur the distinction between long and long *anceps,* cf. p. 106, n. 2 on the dochmiac – ∪ ∪ – ∪ –.

⸚ contracted long, in dactyls, anapaests or choriambs, to show – ⸚ – as a contraction of – ∪∪ –.

This is however ignored in straightforward 'spondaic' dactyls or anapaests mingled with uncontracted.

⌢ resolved long, e.g. in iambic resolution ∪ ⌢ ∪ ⌢.

‿ *brevis in longo* (*syllaba brevis in elemento longo*), at blunt colon-end before Pause, where a short can stand for a long.

But where there is no ambiguity such a syllable may correctly be left as long.

‖ period-close with Pause (where it is certain, and important).

III

DACTYLIC[1]

Modifications of some stichic conventions in lyric cola, especially in the close—Rules for final *anceps*—Method of delivery: analysis of some doubtful cases—Lyric hexameters often have an effect of subdivision, determined by the context—Other lyric cola: analyses—Distinction between A-type and B-type cola—Colometry in πνίγη: ἐπιπλοκή—Ambiguities of classification—Contracted rhythms and the 'alien base'.

The epic hexameter is the oldest form of dactylic rhythm of which we have any knowledge. It is uncertain how far this stichic metre and the dactyls of lyric are to be considered parallel developments of an originally identical rhythm and how far the similarity is due to the influence of the former upon the latter. In both the only forms of metron allowed are the pure dactyl – ∪ ∪ and its contracted or spondaic form – –.[2] Correption of a long vowel (i.e. its shortening

---

[1] For a fuller discussion of this metre see 'Observations on Dactylic', *Wien. Stud.* 77, 1964.

[2] There are two instances of resolution ∪ ∪ ∪ ∪ in non-dramatic lyric where there is no reason to doubt the text: Ibyc. 16 ἅλικας ἰσοκεφάλους ἐνιγυίους, and Pind. *Isth.* IV, 45 ἔρνεϊ Τελεσιάδα. The latter is in dactylo-epitrites, and one of the many instances where a proper name is made the occasion of an altogether exceptional licence, the former apparently a sudden whim of the poet's. In tragedy Eur. *Andr.* 490 is probably corrupt. Wilamowitz (*G.V.* p. 577) would introduce (by emendation) two resolutions into *Bacch.* 135, but a passage where both text and metre as a whole are so uncertain cannot be used as evidence for a double abnormality of so striking a kind. In comedy Ar. *Eccl.* 1169ff. introduces a whole string of resolutions for deliberately grotesque effect into his monstrous Word. The only other apparent instance is *Av.* 1752 διὰ σὲ τὰ πάντα κρατήσας. E. Fraenkel ('Lyrische Daktylen', in *Rhein. Mus.* 72, p. 178) points out that διὰ σέ is here a 'feste Formel', but there is much to be said for the theory that the preposition διά was susceptible of some alternative form of pronunciation which made of it a long monosyllable. It is at any rate curious that this same word should be involved in a similar unexpected licence in three other kinds of metre also, viz. Aesch. *Pers.* 1007 διαπρέπον οἶον δέδορκεν ἄτα where the iambo-

before a following vowel), so frequent in the Homeric hexameter, is more common in dactyls than in any other lyric metre. Hexameter-lengths are not unusual in lyric, and perhaps it is partly to break up the length, partly from the sheer familiarity of the rhythm and the natural adaptability of the vocabulary, that the penthemimeral caesura is so frequent in such lyric hexameters, though it has, of course, not the same kind of structural function as in the stichic.

Finally, there is the frequent marking off of cola by spondaic end: lyric cola with final dactyl exist in all lengths side by side with the forms with final spondee, but the two are in each case distinct and parallel forms, not interchangeable variations. No colon with final dactyl, not even the dimeter and tetrameter, which (see below, pp. 36ff.) constitute a peculiar category, can ever close a period, since it is a principle of Greek metric that no στίχος and no period can end on a pure short syllable. A true long, whether in blunt or pendant close, has always the privilege of becoming 'final *anceps*' before Pause, i.e. at the end of a στίχος or of a lyric period, and in a blunt close is then properly known as *brevis in longo*, written ⏑.[1] In cola which end pendant ... ⏑ – –, however, such as occur in dactylic or aeolic or dactylo-epitrite, the last syllable though usually written – is not true long but long *anceps*, so that the strict formula should be ... ⏑ – ×, and the last syllable may be short without *necessarily* implying Pause in a lyric stanza. But since in practice the vast majority of these cola prefer to end in long *anceps* ... ⏑ – ⤬ with its greater steadying-power, and since in lyric a pendant close is more often than not period-close with Pause, it is usual to write simply ... ⏑ – –.

Similarly, at the beginning of a colon initial long taking off on to a

choriambic trimeter – ⏑ ⏑ – – – ⏑ – ⏑ – – is unmistakable in the anti-strophe 1013 δυσπόλεμον δὴ γένος τὸ Περσᾶν, Ar. *Nub.* 916 διὰ σὲ δὲ φοιτᾶν in regular recitative anapaests where we should expect – ⏑ ⏑ – –, and Eur. *Or.* 1483 τότε δὴ τότε διαπρέπεις where the enoplian ⏑ ⏑ – ⏑ ⏑ – ⏑ – would be quite intelligible, while the resolution is so strange that it has tempted to emendation.

[1] The name and notation are best kept for the blunt close ... ⏑ ⌣, though strictly speaking they could also apply to clausulae in a bacchiac or ionic series with two recurring true longs, ⏑ – ⌣ or ⏑ ⏑ – ⌣ (which in practice are very rare).

short (the double short of resolution does not count here) is never *anceps*, but initial long followed by long is normally *anceps* $\overline{\underline{x}}$ -, though not, of course, if it is formed by contraction of double short ('biceps' in Maas's terminology) $\underline{\underline{-}}$ - as in anapaests.¹ There are a few irrational exceptions, as where the opening of the aeolic telesillean – – ◡ ◡ – ◡ – and of the enoplian – – ◡ ◡ – ◡ – – is also treated as $\underline{\underline{-}}$ -, so that the responsion may be ◡◡ – though never ◡◡ –.²

It is thus possible to read the comminatory string of epithets in A. *Ag.* 153–5 without the unwelcome Pause usually assumed:

μίμνει γὰρ φοβερὰ παλίνορτος   dact. tetram. – ◡
οἰκονόμος δολία μνάμων μῆνις τεκνόποινος   hexam. – –

So too in 158–9:

τοῖς δ' ὁμόφωνον   dim. – ◡
αἴλινον αἴλινον εἰπέ, τὸ δ' εὖ νικάτω

the pentameter refrain is this time, unlike 121 and 139, in metrical and grammatical synaphea with the preceding colon. Again, in Ar. *Pax* 114ff., where four tetrams. are followed by hexam. (or tetram.+adonean):

ὦ πάτερ ὦ πάτερ ἆρ' ἔτυμός γε
δώμασιν ἡμετέροις φάτις ἥκει,
ὡς σὺ μετ' ὀρνίθων προλιπὼν ἐμὲ
ἐς κόρακας βαδιεῖ μεταμώνιος;
ἔστι τι τῶνδ' ἐτύμως; εἴπ' ὦ πάτερ εἴ τι φιλεῖς με,

ἔτυμός γε is a pendant *anceps* like the two above, ἥκει is an ordinary period-close with hiatus, while ἐμὲ | ἐς is a case of hiatus at colon-end without period-close, such as occurs in dactyls Eur. *Supp.* 278;³ the lines thus divide into two dissimilar pairs of lyric tetrameters, rounded off into a major period by the following hexameter.

¹ We group the forms ◡ – ◡ ◡ – ◡ ◡ – – and ◡ ◡ – ◡ ◡ – ◡ ◡ – – together under the name 'paroemiac', but they are really two different, though related, cola, as is clear from the fact that the forms with initial ◡ – and ◡ ◡ – are never allowed in responsion.
² See below, pp. 134, n. 1; 137, n 1.
³ See below, pp. 29f.

The stichic hexameter is occasionally used in comedy[1] as a metre of ordinary dialogue, sometimes (e.g. *Lys.* 770ff.) with ἀντιλαβή, i.e. change of speakers, occurring freely at any point in the line. The method of delivery would naturally be recitative, as in all dialogue-metres other than the trimeter. In tragedy, Soph. *Phil.* 839–42 is a passage of four such στίχοι delivered, probably in recitative, by Neoptolemus between strophe and antistrophe of the chorus; in Eur. *Phaeth.* (773, 66ff.) a herald speaks four hexameters, and passes in the middle of a sentence into two iambic trimeters; so too the riddle of the Sphinx is quoted as four hexameters in the middle of an iambic speech (Eur. *Oed.* P. Oxy. 27, 2459). The close of Ar. *Ran.*, delivered by the Coryphaeus, is of the same solemn recitative kind. There are other passages hard to assign unambiguously to either stichic or lyric class: such is Soph. *Tr.* 1010 ff., where there are three groups of five hexameters, of which the first and last group are antistrophic, part of Heracles' own lament, the rest of which is in lyric measures, while the middle group is divided between the two onlookers, ἀντιλαβή occurring at the hephthemimeral caesura. The lines admit final *anceps* and hiatus freely, and the proportion and irregular distribution of spondees are also of stichic character; it is probable therefore that these too were delivered in recitative. In Eur. *Hel.* 164–6 Helen has two dactylic hexameters followed by a pentameter as an introduction to an antistrophic κομμός sung by herself and the chorus alternately, an arrangement which in spite of the shorter colon still suggests recitative.

There are, further, two passages in which the problem is harder, though perhaps the one may throw some light on the other. In Eur. *Tro.* 595 ff. a lyric lament for two voices is followed by a series of eight hexameters[2] (to l. 602), all with penthemimeral caesura and all pure dactylic except for the final spondee. They are distinguished from epic hexameters only by their greater regularity and the

---

[1] Possibly, to judge by the fragments, rather more commonly by some of the other comedians, especially Pherecrates and Hermippus, than by Aristophanes; some at least are by way of parody.

[2] Probably to be assigned to the respective speakers as in Wilamowitz's translation, i.e. 595–600 Andr., 601–2 Chorus, 602ff. Hec.

heightened lyricism of their tone and content. In the remaining lines Wilamowitz is almost certainly right in rejecting responsion, which postulates serious disturbance in the text not warranted by deficiencies of sense; Hecuba begins with another hexameter, but οἷος ἰάλεμος οἷά τε πένθη[1] rings genuine as a tetrameter rhythm, which if shifted to the end of a hexameter after a lacuna of – ∪ ∪ – – (following Seidler) would produce a line of wholly different type from the preceding ones. Another tetrameter follows in δάκρυά τ᾽ ἐκ δακρύων καταλείβεται, and the rest looks like a hexameter (in synaphea, καταλείβετᾱι | ἀμετέροισι) of the same rhythm as all the rest, ἀδάκρυτος being deleted as an obvious gloss.[2] The last four lines would thus be a sung passage of lyric dactyls, two tetrameters enclosed between two hexameters, following eight recitative hexameters.

Next, in Eur. *Supp.* 271 ff. the Chorus breaks off an iambic speech and proceeds in dactyls, of which the first four and the last four lines appear to form corresponding groups (rhetorically distinct also) of stichic hexameters with *anceps* and occasional spondees; there is, however, no true caesura in the last line of the first group (274) and the first of the second (282), irregularities which should not be emended away. Between the two groups lies a corrupt passage which, however reconstituted, is clearly a departure from stichic hexameters. If the unintelligible 275–6 be deleted (so most editors), we are left with four lines which look as if they were dactylic:

πρός ⟨σε⟩ γενειάδος, ὦ φίλος, ὦ δοκιμώτατος Ἑλλάδι,
ἄντομαι ἀμφιπίτνουσα τὸ σὸν γόνυ καὶ χέρα δειλαία.[3]
οἴκτισαι ἀμφὶ τέκνων μ᾽ ἱκέταν †ἤ τιν᾽ ἀλάταν†
οἰκτρὸν ἰήλεμον οἰκτρὸν ἱεῖσαν.

---

[1] Wilamowitz (*G.V.* p. 353, n.) would read πένθεα, unnecessarily.
[2] I cannot follow Wilamowitz in his arrangement of 606 as
ἀμετέροισι δόμοις· ὁ θανὼν δ᾽ ἐπι- tetram.
λάθεται ἀλγέων ἀδάκρυτος. – ∪ ∪ – ∪ | – ∪ ∪ – – double adonean.
Neither the whole colon-compound nor the *anceps* of the first adonean in the middle of a word seems to me tolerable.
[3] Markland's σε and Hermann's emendation of δειλαίαν are necessary for the sense. The shortening of the diphthong syllable of δείλαιος and γεραιός is well attested in drama.

Wilamowitz[1] would take the first two lines as 'aeolic' dactyls,[2] i.e. both with cretic close – ∪ ⌣, the final *anceps* and hiatus showing that they are used κατὰ στίχον, as in the Lesbian poets. But the length of the cola would be quite without parallel for this metrical type,[3] and it is more probable that both lines are lyric hexameters ending in pure dactyls, Ἑλλάδι, | ἄντομαι being a hiatus of the type already noticed Ar. *Pax* 116, and supported by rhetorical pause,[4] and δειλαίᾳ. | οἴκτισαι in synaphea. The next line is clearly corrupt; possibly we should delete ἤ τιν' ἀλάταν and so leave a tetram. cat., or again with the omission of a syllable the line may have been a pentameter with spondaic close; the following line is unmistakably a tetrameter of the same rhythm as *Tro.* 604 οἷς ἰάλεμος οἷά τε πένθη. The whole passage would thus form a lyric 'inset' of four dactylic cola between the two groups of four recitative hexameters.

The hexameter is also found sporadically in lyric stanzas of varied dactylic cola or mixed metres. Where, as in Eur. *Supp.* 808 = 821, it detaches itself from its context by change of speaker and by final *anceps* or hiatus, it cannot be distinguished from an epic στίχος, and the mode of delivery is still uncertain, just as we often cannot be sure how a similarly isolated iambic trimeter was treated. Less disconnected are the hexameter cola in Eur. *Andr.* 117ff. I quote the first antistrophe:

γνῶθι τύχαν, λόγισαι τὸ παρὸν κακὸν εἰς ὅπερ ἥκεις.	hexam.
δεσπόταις ἁμιλλᾷ	ithyph.
Ἰλιὰς οὖσα κόρα Λακεδαίμονος ἐγγενέτῃσιν;	hexam.
λεῖπε δεξίμηλον	ithyph.
δόμον τᾶς ποντίας θεοῦ. τί σοι	sync. iamb. trim.
καιρὸς ἀτυζομένᾳ δέμας αἰκέλιον καταλείβειν	hexam.
δεσποτῶν ἀνάγκαις;	ithyph.
τὸ κρατοῦν δέ σ' ἔπεισι. τί μόχθον	∪ ∪ paroemiac ∪
οὐδὲν οὖσα μοχθεῖς;	ithyph.

---

[1] *Die Ilias und Homer*, p. 351. Cf. also E. Fraenkel, 'Lyrische Daktylen', *Rhein Mus.* 72, p. 177.   [2] See below, pp. 117, 157, n. 1.
[3] Eur. *Med.* 135–6, quoted as analogous by Fraenkel, are shorter, and in any case the text is probably wrong, see p. 25, n. 1.
[4] Cf. the examples of hiatus quoted by Schroeder, *Ar. Cant.*, loc. cit. It may be noted that according to Σ the passage from Ar. *Pax* is adapted from Eur. *Aeolus*.

Here are probably four periods, each closed by an ithyphallic; the first three contain hexameters (pure dactylic except for the final spondee), the last the colon called paroemiac,[1] corresponding to the section of a hexameter which falls after the penthemimeral caesura. It will be noted that this caesura occurs in each hexameter, subdividing the long colon and bringing it into relation with the shorter paroemiac in the context. In the next strophe, similarly, the opening hexameter is taken up after a lekythion by a colon, δμωὶς ἐπ' ἀλλοτρίας – ∪ ∪ – ∪ ∪ –, which corresponds to its first section up to the caesura. (The colon is usually called a 'hemiepes', i.e. epic half-line, as being equivalent to μῆνιν ἄειδε, θεά.) This effect of subdivision is common, and the point in the line where it occurs depends upon the cola in the context; another favourite break is after the fourth metron (the 'bucolic diaeresis' of epic) so that the line falls into tetrameter+adonean, cf. *O.T.* 151 ff.

ὦ Διὸς ἁδυεπὲς φάτι, τίς ποτε | τᾶς πολυχρύσου
Πυθῶνος ἀγλαὰς ἔβας   iamb. dim.
Θήβας; ἐκτέταμαι φοβερὰν φρένα | δείματι πάλλων.
ἰήιε Δάλιε Παιάν,   paroem.
ἀμφὶ σοὶ ἁζόμενος τί μοι ἢ νέον   dact. tetram. ∪ ∪
ἢ περιτελλομέναις ὥραις πάλιν   dact. tetram. ∪ ∪
ἐξανύσεις χρέος.   dact. dim. ∪ ∪
εἰπέ μοι, ὦ χρυσέας τέκνον Ἐλπίδος, | ἄμβροτε Φάμα.

The effect of the diaereses and the separate tetrameters and dimeter of the context is to make of the longer lines a compound rather than a simple colon. The same division is found again Eur. *Hcld.* 608 ff.

Such hexameters are of course purely lyrical, and sung. There are other lyric 'lengths', from dimeter to octameter; colometry in a continuous dactylic passage or πνῖγος is sometimes a little uncertain, and becomes almost a matter of taste, the appearance of the printed page emphasizing one aspect or another of the rhythmical sequence. The proportion of pure dactyls is generally higher than in stichic lines, and the incidence of contraction is emphasized by the frequency with which such a spondaic metron is contained in a single word, instead

---

[1] See below, pp. 33, 48 ff.

of being mostly cut across by caesura or part of a longer word as in epic. Such a rhythm, for instance, as in Aeschylus's pentameter *Ag.* 125, πομπούς τ' ἀρχάς· οὕτω δ' εἶπε τεράζων would be impossible in stichic dactyls. In antistrophic stanzas the correspondence of dactyls and spondees is rarely broken. Uniformly dactylic stanzas, without admixture of other metres, are found only in Euripides of the tragedians, as *Hcld.* 608 ff. and the mixed stichic and lyric passages quoted. In *Hel.* 375–85 and apparently *Andr.* 1173 ff. (a corrupt passage) only the clausula is alien. *Phoen.* 784 ff. is uniform except for a remarkable variation in the strophe, l. 796. The first part contains hexameters and tetrameters, one dimeter and one pentameter, and then (794 ff.) continues:

> Ἰσμηνοῖο θοάζεις,
> Ἀργείοις ἐπιπνεύσας | Σπαρτῶν γένναν   (cf. *Ag.* 125 above)
> 796 ἀσπιδοφέρμονα θίασον ἔνοπλον
> ἀντίπαλον κατὰ λάινα τείχεα
> χαλκῷ κοσμήσας.
> ἦ δεινά τις Ἔρις θεός, ἃ τάδε
> μήσατο πήματα γᾶς βασιλεῦσιν,
> Λαβδακίδαις πολυμόχθοις.

The first and last lines are trimeters; the colon is a common one, with many other besides dactylic relations; it is the pendant form of the hemiepes, – ∪ ∪ – ∪ ∪ – –. χαλκῷ κοσμήσας is a rare contracted form of the blunt hemiepes – ∪ ∪ – ∪ ∪ –, and corresponds to οὐδ' οἱ μὴ νόμιμοι in the antistrophe, where only one dactyl is contracted. The third line with its surprising 'tribrachs' θίασον ἔνοπλον corresponds to l. 813 Οἰδιπόδα κατὰ δώματα καὶ πόλιν, which is the tetrameter we should expect here. The phenomenon is discussed below, p. 66.

Ar. *Nub.* 275 ff. is a dactylic stanza with very little alien admixture:

> ἀέναοι Νεφέλαι
> ἀρθῶμεν φανεραὶ δροσερὰν φύσιν | εὐάγητον,
> πατρὸς ἀπ' Ὠκεανοῦ βαρυαχέος
> ὑψηλῶν ὀρέων κορυφὰς ἐπὶ | δενδροκόμους, ἵνα |
> τηλεφανεῖς σκοπιὰς ἀφορώμεθα
> καρπούς τ' ἀρδομέναν ἱερὰν χθόνα
> καὶ ποταμῶν ζαθέων κελαδήματα
> καὶ πόντον κελάδοντα βαρύβρομον.

ὄμμα γὰρ αἰθέρος ἀκάματον σελαγεῖται
μαρμαρέαις ἐν αὐγαῖς,
ἀλλ᾽ ἀποσεισάμεναι νέφος ὄμβριον
ἀθανάτας ἰδέας ἐπιδώμεθα
τηλεσκόπῳ ὄμματι γαῖαν.

The introductory hemiepes is in both strophe and antistrophe separated from the following line by hiatus, and hence can reasonably be analysed as a catalectic trimeter. In both, again, the dimeters are given a half-detached effect by diaeresis and the recurrent tetrameter-lengths of the context, so that the second and fourth cola become compounds, tetram.+dim. and tetram.+dim.+tetram. respectively.[1] Periods are difficult to discern, though it is highly probable that one closes with the non-dactylic μαρμαρέαις ἐν αὐγαῖς – ∪ ∪ – ∪ – – (the aeolo-choriambic 'aristophanean'). The last period is then of two tetrameters, with a paroemiac as final clausula. This is a colon often introduced among dactyls, though independent of dactylic relations; the example quoted above (Eur. *Andr.* 133) is the related form with initial double-short; the monosyllabic opening (*anceps*, in accordance with the principle stated p. 27) is commoner.[2]

It may be noted that in the antistrophe the end of the pentameter θαλίαι τε shows again the pendant *anceps*. The tetrameters all have final dactyl, and it is in this form of the metre that the difference between stichic and lyric dactyls is most striking. This has led many metricians[3] to postulate a fundamental distinction between dactyls measured κατὰ πόδα – ∪ ∪ and κατὰ μέτρον or κατὰ συζυγίαν – ∪ ∪ – ∪ ∪, taking the former as exemplified by the epic hexameter (which would thus more accurately be termed a hexapody) and some of its stichic descendants in drama, and the latter as the typically lyric form; thus what have here been described as 'tetrameters' are from Alcman downwards called 'dimeters' in such classification. It may be doubted whether the confusion of terminology and of thought which

[1] Cf. Ar. *Ran.* 1338-9.
[2] Heph. allows the name 'παροιμιακός' under protest; he quotes the old παροιμίαι as examples: πότε δ᾽ Ἄρτεμις οὐκ ἐχόρευσεν and καὶ κόρκορος ἐν λαχάνοισιν, but objects that there were also proverbs in other metres.
[3] E.g. Wilamowitz, Schroeder, Maas, White and many others.

D L M

has resulted makes the distinction in this form a profitable one.[1] The analogy with other 'metra', iambic, trochaic and anapaestic, which all contain two invariable longs, would thus be neater, and the reversal of iambic ⤫ – ∪ – into trochaic – ∪ – ⤫ acquire a parallel in anapaestic ∪ ∪ – ∪ ∪ – and dactylic – ∪ ∪ – ∪ ∪. But even on grounds of neatness it is an awkward objection that – ∪ ∪ – ∪ ∪ is actually an alternative form of lyric *anapaestic* metron, while there is, as we shall see,[2] a kind of anapaest (or whatever name we choose to call it by) which does not move κατὰ συ3υγίαν either; the rising movement with double-short ∪ ∪ – ∪ ∪ – ∪ ∪ –, etc., is all that can be disengaged as the structural principle.

To come to more objective grounds of argument: the numerous dactylic cola with an odd number of 'feet' raise a difficulty. There are no analogous iambic or trochaic 'tripodies' and 'pentapodies', whereas even if the dactylic 'tripody' be argued away as a special colon of different origin—a hemiepes[3]—pentapodies and heptapodies, complete and catalectic, remain obstinately numerous, their movement absolutely indistinguishable from that of other lengths with spondaic close, while there is nothing in diaeresis or responsion to justify cutting them up into smaller lengths to fit an artificial theory; it is, for instance, a mere evasion when Schroeder calls Eur. *Phaeth.* 773, 53 λισσομένα προσέβαν ὑμέναιον ἀεῖσαι a choriambic+paroemiac, or when White divides *Nub.* 309 εὐστέφανοί τε θε-|-ῶν θυσίαι θαλίαι τε monometer+brachycatalectic dimeter. The only way round the difficulty is to assume, as Wilamowitz does, two sorts of *lyric* dactyls, one which goes κατὰ πόδα and one which goes κατὰ μέτρον.

In itself, the division of lyric dactyls into two classes is fully justified. The one type—we might call it 'A'—has like the stichic form no other structural unit than the simple – ∪ ∪. The term 'metron' is so firmly attached to this unit by the traditional name 'hexameter'

---

[1] Passing references in ancient metrical theory are of no great importance to the argument either way; neither the affirmative of Aristides Quintilianus and Marius Victorinus nor the denial of Hephaestion and his commentators need influence us.   [2] See below, pp. 56 and 60.
[3] To call it a 'brachycatalectic dimeter' is merely playing with words.

that it is unpractical to insist on calling it a 'foot', and so confusing it with e.g. the unreal iambic 'foot' ∪ –. 'Metron' as a term meaning unit of recurring movement or structural element is an intelligible concept, and in this sense – ∪ ∪ is the metron of the A-type of dactylic colon precisely as × – ∪ – is the metron of an iambic. But in dactylic metre, as in one kind of anapaestic, the shortness of the structural unit makes it less self-sufficient than the longer units × – ∪ –, – ∪ – × and ∪ ∪ – ∪ ∪ –. The minimum *self-sufficient* dactylic length is the dimeter, and a single – ∪ ∪ should not even be reckoned as an analytic ingredient in a mixed compound; we must not, for instance, analyse – ∪ ∪ – ∪ – ∪ – – as dactyl+ithyphallic. But longer dactylic lengths of A-type are structurally multiples not of the dimeter but of the single metron, and hence are found in all lengths, odd-numbered as well as even. These cola normally have final spondee, and the two shortest have other affinities besides dactylic: the adonean – ∪ ∪ – –, which owes its name to the ritual cry ὦ τὸν Ἄδωνιν, is probably an old form of 'colarion'[1] (i.e. not a 'length' of anything) of now untraceable origin, and has connections with the choriambics; the pendant hemiepes – ∪ ∪ – ∪ ∪ – – is a dactylo-epitrite ingredient no less than a dactylic trimeter. The tetrameter – ∪ ∪ – ∪ ∪ – ∪ ∪ – – according to Hephaestion was first used by Archilochus, and adopted by Anacreon for whole poems. The remaining lengths, pentameters, hexameters, heptameters, octameters, are longer than average lyric cola, but for special reasons the hexameter, as we have seen, is nevertheless common. Catalectic forms—with blunt close, therefore—occur in most of these lengths (see below, p. 42). Any of them, except perhaps the rare heptameter, may also occasionally appear with final dactyl, but such a form is clearly distinguished from the spondaic in that (1) the two are never found in responsion, (2) the pure dactylic is only used where the metre continues dactylic in the following colon, so that the whole forms either a compound or an asynartete πνῖγος,[2] and the separate

---

[1] The 'Kurzvers' of German metricians.

[2] I use the term 'asynartete πνῖγος' of a chain of cola in uniform metre separated by diaeresis; 'synartete πνῖγος' where cases of word-overlap occur in the chain.

cola are not always unambiguously discernible; they run out finally in the normal spondaic or blunt end.[1]

Dactylic cola of B-type are confined to dimeters and tetrameters, so that there is some ground for here disengaging a unit $- \cup \cup - \cup \cup$, which is, however, a συ3υγία or 'pair' rather than a simple unit, so that κατὰ συ3υγίαν is a better term for this movement than κατὰ μέτρον; it might in fact be described as κατὰ δίμετρον. The δίμετρον has some analogies with the anapaestic syzygy $\cup \cup - \cup \cup -$, but this latter is welded much more into an effective unity by the normal practice of diaeresis between one syzygy and the next; there is no such regulation of the dactylic B-tetrameter (though diaeresis at dimeter-end is *somewhat* commoner than in A-type), so that the simple unit, the metron, remains effective as it were under the paired movement. The dactylic syzygy thus shares with iambic and trochaic metra the characteristic of possessing two true longs and not practising diaeresis, but there is this cardinal difference, that the regular *anceps* of iambic and trochaic forbids analysis into any smaller unit of recurring movement; a metron is not a pair of 'feet', since all variations of iambic rhythm are relative to the *minimum* length $\times - \cup -$, and the common description of a trimeter in our handbooks of verse-composition as a 'line of six iambic feet with

---

[1] It is possible that two passages in Euripides should be accounted exceptions to this rule. *El.* 456 and 459 ~ 468 and 471 give dactylic trimeters $- \cup \cup - \cup \cup - \cup \cup$ which cannot be treated as ibyceans $- \cup \cup - \cup \cup - \cup -$ with final *brevis in longo*, since (*a*) a short syllable in all four places would be too much of a coincidence, (*b*) the prepositional ending of 459 rules out Pause. 456–7 ~ 468–9 is therefore a compound $- \cup \cup - \cup \cup - \cup \cup \mid \underline{\cup}\widehat{\cup\cup} \cup - -$ (three dact. and resolved iambo-trochaic colarion, see below, p. 71) and 459 ~ 471 introduces a synartete period of dact. trim. + three choriambic cola, ending in an enneasyllable -σχεῖν Διὸς ἀγγέλῳ σὺν Ἑρμᾷ, and followed by another enneasyllable (hipponactean) as final clausula. The curious compound 456–7 probably gives the clue to *Phoen.* 1580–1,

ὦ πάτερ, ἀμετέροισι δόμοισιν ἄχη θεὸς | ὃς τάδε τελευτᾷ,

five dact. + the same colarion $\underline{\times}\widehat{\cup\cup} \cup - -$. Eur. seems in fact here to end trim. and pentam. with a phrase of iambic rhythm, as Soph. so often does his B-tetrams. (see below).

spondees allowed in the first, third and fifth place' is a rigmarole descended from a faulty tradition.

It is characteristic of cola of B-type that the last metron is open – ∪ ∪ (we might say that this last metron, like any earlier in the line, may occasionally be spondaic,[1] but if so responsion is normally strict, and the colon ceases to be distinguishable from A-type dimeters and tetrameters). Thus, unlike A-cola, B-tetrameters frequently pass straight from the pure dactylic ending into other metres, or again continue in a chain of unambiguously discernible cola; the only thing they may not do (see above p. 26) is to close a period. The B-dimeter – ∪ ∪ – ∪ ∪ is frequently (as in *O.T.* 151 ff., Ar. *Nub.* 280 quoted above) only semi-detached from its surroundings—indistinguishable, then, from an A-dimeter of this form—but *O.C.* 235–6 is a clear case where a dimeter too passes out into a following iambic clausula. The tetrameter, however, is the normal length of B-type colon; it appears first in Alcman,[2] and is the prevailing type of dactylic rhythm in later Sophocles,[3] who often forms a period of a series of these with iambic clausula. Ar. *Nub.* 275 ff. (see above, p. 32) is largely constructed of such tetrameters, and cf. *Av.* 1748 ff.

ὦ μέγα χρύσεον ἀστεροπῆς φάος,	B-tetram.
ὦ Διὸς ἄμβροτον ἔγχος πυρφόρον,	B-tetram.
ὦ χθόνιαι βαρυαχέες	A-trim. – ∪ ∪
ὀμβροφόροι θ' ἅμα βρονταί,	A-trim. (= pendant hemiepes)
αἷς ὅδε νῦν χθόνα σείει.	A-trim. (= pendant hemiepes)
διὰ σὲ τὰ πάντα κρατήσας	A-trim. (= pendant hemiepes)
καὶ πάρεδρον Βασίλειαν ἔχει Διός,	B-tetram.
'Υμὴν ὦ 'Υμέναι' ὦ.	pherecratean

The A-trimeter ὦ χθόνιαι βαρυαχέες might be run up into the following line as a hexameter (see above, p. 36), but the diaeresis and surrounding colon-lengths make the colometry here given reasonable. The B-tetrameters are unambiguous, and the last ushers in the alien clausula. It is important to note how freely A- and B-types of

---

[1] E.g. Soph. *Phil.* 1198–1200. For abnormal responsion see on *Phil.* 827 ~ 843, p. 117.

[2] Page, *P.M.G.* 27.

[3] Cf. the article referred to p. 25, n. 1.

colon intermingle,[1] since over-emphasis on B-types as in some sense *the* lyric form of dactylic rhythm, and an exaggeration of the structural difference between these and A-types, have led to much artificial division of cola in a mistaken effort to secure even numbers of metra on every possible occasion. Thus Wilamowitz[2] on *Nub.* 275 ff. endeavours to carry through uniformity, 'da die Daktylen κατὰ συζυγίαν gebaut sind', by getting rid of the awkward pentameter 285 = 309, and transfers -γεῖται and -αι τε to the following colon. Genuine tetrameters of B-type are an unusually distinct form of colon. The κομμός of Electra and the Chorus, Soph. *El.* 121–250, may be taken as illustration. In the first strophe

Χο. ὦ παῖ παῖ δυστανοτάτας
   Ἠλέκτρα ματρός, τίν' ἀεὶ τάκεις
   ὧδ' ἀκόρεστον οἰμωγὰν
   τὸν πάλαι ἐκ δολερᾶς ἀθεώτατα
   ματρὸς ἁλόντ' ἀπάταις Ἀγαμέμνονα
   κακᾷ τε χειρὶ πρόδοτον; ὡς ὁ τάδε πορὼν
   ὄλοιτ', εἰ μοι θέμις τάδ' αὐδᾶν.
Ηλ. ὦ γενέθλα γενναίων,
   ἥκετ' ἐμῶν καμάτων παραμύθιον ·
   οἶδά τε καὶ ξυνίημι τάδ', οὐ τί με
   φυγγάνει, οὐδ' ἐθέλω προλιπεῖν τόδε,
   μὴ οὐ τὸν ἐμὸν στενάχειν πατέρ' ἄθλιον.
   ἀλλ' ὦ παντοί-|-ας φιλότητος ἀμειβόμεναι χάριν,
   ἐᾶτέ μ' ὧδ' ἀλύειν,
   αἰαῖ, ἱκνοῦμαι

after a choriambic opening (three cola) two tetrameters are followed by iambics. Electra's first phrase is a contracted hemiepes,[3] then come four tetrameters and a compound of spondaic (i.e. dactylic) dim.+ tetram. (cf. Ar. *Nub.* 277), closing once more in iambics. In the

[1] Cf. Fraenkel, 'Lyrische Daktylen', *Rhein. Mus.* 72, 191.
[2] *G.V.* p. 249, n. But Wilamowitz does in general make a clear distinction between two types of lyric dactyls.
[3] The text is uncertain; if LA be accepted here, the antistrophe must have a lacuna, and the line is an anapaestic dimeter without metron-diaeresis. The same problem occurs in the epode, where I should interpret 238 as a contracted dactylic tetrameter, followed by four anap. dims. ending in *brevis in longo* (πτέρυγᾱς) and an aeolic clausula.

next strophe again 162 is a single tetrameter with following iambic close, 167–70 a series of four with final clausula iambic. In the third strophe the penultimate[1] colon is a single tetrameter with iambic clausula, and the epode contains three (236–8), of which the last is heavily contracted, among anapaests. The colon ἀλλ' ὦ παντοίας κτλ. could be taken alternatively as a B-hexameter, but in any case the tetrameter-section is clearly marked off from the initial spondees by the release into the 'pure' rhythm of all the surrounding tetrameters. Hence a series of tetrameters where word-end continually runs counter to colon-end may be suspected of false colometry, if the passage is antistrophic and in both verses the natural pauses suggest a different division; thus in Eur. *Hcld.* 615–17 = 626–8 the cola are clearly trim.+trim.+pentam. in spite of the preceding tetrameters. In non-antistrophic stanzas, and especially in astrophic ἀπολελυ-μένα, colometry is often more uncertain, but it is important to take the natural rhetorical rhythm as a guide wherever possible, since it is characteristic of such passages, above all in Euripides and the later plays of Sophocles, that rhetorical pause and metrical colon are becoming more often coincident. Thus in *Bacch.* 165–7 (φοιτάσιν κτλ.) the dactylic metra should be divided up as 3+2+4+5.

There are, however, passages, such as *O.C.* 229ff. (astrophic) and Eur. *Hypsipyle*, pap. frag. 1, cols. 2 and 3 (antistrophic, cf. especially the antistrophe, ll. 11–15), where a chain of tetrameters ignores colon-diaeresis, and in the latter case the test of responsion (the strophe carries through diaeresis) shows clearly that no alternative colometry is in question. The passages are in fact synartete πνίγη. Here the distinction between A- and B-types of cola is beginning to disappear. The only remaining link with B-type is the even number of metra; the chains 'work out', so to speak, in tetrameter-lengths, we have no analogies for so long-protracted a chain in any but tetrameter-lengths, and the strophe of the *Hyps.* passage shows that such in fact was the measurement here. But of construction κατὰ δίμετρον no trace remains; there is nothing but the simple dactylic movement

---

[1] The penultimate is a favourite place for a sporadic piece of dactylic rhythm in both Soph. and Aesch., cf. *Phil.* 142, *Ant.* 339–40, *Ag.* 165, *Cho.* 592, *Eum.* 395 *et al. mult.*

‒ ᴗ ᴗ in a long series. In *Hyps.* the πνῖγος runs out in a blunt hemiepes, followed by ithyphallic clausula: in *O.C.*

> οὐδενὶ μοιριδία τίσις ἔρχεται
> ὦν προπάθῃ τὸ τίνειν· ἀπάτα δ' ἀπά-
> -ταις ἑτέραις ἑτέρα παραβαλλομέ-
> -να πόνον, οὐ χάριν, ἀντιδίδωσιν ἔ-
> -χειν. σὺ δὲ τῶνδ' ἐδράνων πάλιν ἔκτοπος
> αὖτις ἄφορμος ἐμᾶς χθονὸς ἔκθορε
> μή τι πέρα χρέος
> ἐμᾷ πόλει προσάψῃς

it recovers into a B-tetrameter with diaeresis l. 234, followed by a B-dimeter and iambic clausula.

It is not always easy to determine how best to set out a πνῖγος on the printed page. In antistrophic verse, however, a careful study of responsion is of extreme importance; and a passage like Aesch. *Pers.* 882–6 = 891–5 shows quite unmistakably an interesting type of πνῖγος of which our generally accepted colometry often takes no account:

> οἶα Λέσβος ἐλαιόφυτός τε Σάμος
> Χίος ἠδὲ Πάρος
> Νάξος Μύκονος Τήνῳ τε συνάπτουσ'
> ᾿Ανδρος ἀγχιγείτων,

and in the antistrophe:

> καὶ ῾Ρόδον ἠδὲ Κνίδον Κυπρίας τε πόλεις,
> Πάφον ἠδὲ Σόλους
> Σαλαμῖνά τε, τᾶς νῦν ματρόπολις τῶνδ'
> αἰτία στεναγμῶν.

The exact correspondence of diaeresis and rhetorical phrasing leaves it beyond doubt that this (Murray's) colometry reflects something essential in the delivery of this πνῖγος which the more mechanical division into two tetrams.+trim. (adopted e.g. by Wilamowitz and Mazon) merely serves to obscure. The phenomenon is of importance for the understanding of Greek metric. The dactylic rhythm is continuous, in the sense that where one phrase ends ᴗ ᴗ ‒ the next begins ‒‒ ‒ ᴗ ᴗ,[1] but the new segments which emerge may some-

---

[1] This is a different phenomenon from so-called 'rising dactyls' or dactyls with anacrusis, for which see below, p. 67, s.v. 'dactylo-anapaests'.

times have the shape and length of familiar cola in rising double-short rhythm, i.e. anapaestic or enoplian (as here ∪ ∪ – ∪ ∪ –). This form of close sequence of phrases of what first appear to be antithetical metres, without change of tempo, I believe to be an occasional phenomenon in Greek metric for which one might adopt the name ἐπιπλοκή from the ancient metricians.[1] Where we lack the guide of responsion it is hardly more than a matter of taste whether we choose to emphasize the rhetorical pauses or the numerical sequence of metra; thus Eur. *Phoen.* 1488ff. might be shown as two A-tetrams.+ pentam. cat.:

> αἰδομένα φέρομαι βάκχα νεκύ-
> -ων, κράδεμνα δικοῦσα κόμας ἀπ' ἐ-
> -μᾶς, στολίδος κροκόεσσαν ἀνεῖσα τρυφάν,

or with ἐπιπλοκή:

> αἰδομένα φέρομαι βάκχα νεκύων,
> κράδεμνα δικοῦσα κόμας ἀπ' ἐμᾶς,
> στολίδος κροκόεσσαν ἀνεῖσα τρυφάν.[2]

[1] They were simply concerned with the fact that, e.g. in the same infinite series × – ∪ – × – ∪ – × – ∪......, it is possible to mark off both iambic and trochaic segments, in ∪ ∪ – ∪ ∪ – ∪ ∪ – ∪ ∪...... dactylic and anapaestic, and so on.

[2] S. *Phil.* 1202ff. I am now inclined to leave in its regular colometry. 1202 may be better left as an extreme case of broken diaeresis, with ἄρθρον ἀπῶσαι. ἀλλ' apparently forming an adonean among tetrameters. (If so, the vehemence of the singer's passion must be the defence of the unparalleled synaloephe.) But there is much to be said for Erfurdt's excision of ἀλλ' (cf. below, p. 116 on S. *El.* 1239), and the case must remain open. 1203–7 then continue with five dact. tetram. B (still agitated, with change of speaker in the middle of 1204 and hiatus at the end of 1205); in 1206 read Hermann's ⟨δή⟩, with clausula 1209 ∪ – ∪ – ∪ ∪ – –, an aeolo-choriambic enoplian in rising rhythm. 1210–12 and 1214 syncopated iambic; 1213 aeolo-choriambic *either* ⨯͡∪ – ∪ – ∪ ∪ – like Ἰκαρίων δ' ὑπὲρ πελαγέων *Aj.* 702 (see below, p. 136, n. 1) *or*, more simply and effectively (with Gleditsch), ὦ πόλις, πόλις πατρία – ∪ – ∪ – ∪ ∪ –; for 1215 Pearson's colometry ὅς γε σὰν λιπὼν ἱερὰν λιβάδ' – ∪ – ∪ – ∪ ∪ – ∪ ∪ is the most organic, though the colon is nameless: it starts like 1213 (Gleditsch) but ends with open dactyl like the tetrams., followed by 1216 ⨯͜ – ∪ – ∪ ∪ – in rising rhythm, a catalectic version of 1209. The final clausula ∪ – ∪ ∪ – ∪ – – is an

B-tetrameters, especially in a series and with alien clausula in rising rhythm, are the prevailing type of dactyl in later Sophocles; Euripides and Aristophanes use more A-cola, and these are favoured by Aeschylus above all, especially the longer ones. Often the closing spondee ends a run of two, or three, 'pure' cola (which thus give the effect of a compound), as Eur. *Hcld.* 613–14 tetram. ⁻◡◡+tetram. ⁻⁻, 615–17 trim. ⁻◡◡+trim. ⁻◡◡+pentam. ⁻⁻, Ar. *Nub.* 569–70 tetram. ⁻◡◡+pentam. ⁻⁻. Sometimes such a run is checked by catalexis; thus Eur. *El.* 157–8

λουτρὰ πανύσταθ᾽ ὑδρανάμενον χροῒ
κοίτᾳ ἐν οἰκτροτάτᾳ θανάτου

(tetram. ⁻◡◡+tetram. cat.), and *Hel.* 383–4

καλλοσύνας ἕνεκεν · τὸ δ᾽ ἐμὸν δέμας
ὤλεσεν ὤλεσε πέργαμα Δαρδανίας

(tetram. ⁻◡◡+pent. cat.). There are in fact certain common types of cola which from the context may sometimes conveniently be reckoned as catalectic lengths of dactyl, though most of them have other connections too, notably with the dactylo-epitrite and prosodiac groups. Commonest of these is the blunt hemiepes – ◡ ◡ – ◡ ◡ –, and next the tetrameter, but longer forms occur also, as pentam. cat. *Eum.* 534 δυσσεβίας μὲν ὕβρις τέκος ὡς ἐτύμως (cf. Eur. *El.* 482, *Hel.* 384, Soph. *Aj.* 225). Some of these longer cola, however, really belong to another category: thus Eur. *Hipp.* 121 Ὠκεανοῦ τις ὕδωρ στάζουσα πέτρα λέγεται is really a compound of double hemiepes (pendant+blunt) called 'choerilean', see below, p. 175 ; and Eur. *Andr.* 274

ἦ μεγάλων ἀχέων ἄρ᾽ ὑπῆρξεν, ὅτ᾽ Ἰδαίαν

with antistrophe

ταὶ δ᾽ ἐπεὶ ὑλόκομον νάπος ἤλυθον οὐρειᾶν

enoplian variant of 1209. Thus the whole eloquent epodic passage 1169–1217 is an intricate mixture—intricate to describe but straightforward in delivery—of iambic, ionic (below, p. 130) and aeolo-choriambic down to 1195, then a climax of passion in the open dactylics, dying away into despair as it returns to iambic and aeolo-choriambic.

(the same isolation of the last word as a molossus − − − being found again Ar. *Pax*, 789 = 810) is a form of prosodiac (see below, ch. x). Shorter lengths with a similar contraction in the closing rhythm propound similar ambiguities of classification: thus *Rhes*. 27 ἁρμόσατε ψαλίοις ἵππους, following a dactylic tetram. ‾‿‿, has a clear effect of tetram. cat., but *Or*. 1257 πήματα πήμασιν ἐξεύρῃ is from its context better taken as a form of prosodiac (see below, p. 168); again, apparent trim. cat. − ‿ ‿ − − − is most often a form of dochmiac.[1] Still more is there an open question when spondaic contraction opens a short dactylic colon; but *Eum*. 1037 εὐφαμεῖτε δὲ πανδαμεί − ⸚ − ‿ ‿ − ⸚ − may be taken as tetram. cat. in view of 1042 λαμπάδι τερπόμεναι καθ᾽ ὁδόν, and in the same way − − − ‿ ‿ − − and − − − ‿ ‿ − may sometimes be contracted hemiepes, though in the majority of cases they connect with the choriambic group. This ambiguity affords opportunity for transition from one category of rhythm to another; thus in *Pers*. 576ff. (the exclamations are *extra metrum*)

γναπτόμενοι δ᾽ ἁλὶ δεινᾷ φεῦ	− ‿ ‿ − ‿ ‿ − −
σκύλλονται πρὸς ἀναύδων ἠέ	− − − ‿ ‿ − −
παίδων τᾶς ἀμιάντου, ὀᾶ	− − − ‿ ‿ − −
πενθεῖ δ᾽ ἄνδρα δόμος στερη-	− − − ‿ ‿ − ‿ −
-θείς, τοκέης δ᾽ ἄπαιδες	− ‿ ‿ − ‿ − −

the uncontracted hemiepes is followed by two with spondaic opening, which may equally well be pherecrateans; these make an easy transition to the following priapean,[2] a form of choriambic dicolon.

Spondaic introduction with the spondee contained in a single word gives a specially stately effect to some of Aeschylus's long dactylic cola: repeatedly thus in the enumeration of Darius's conquests *Pers*. 864–906, where the rhetorical period overflows the ends of the strophes and the dactylic period 883ff. rolls in a πνῖγος into a trochaic close like an immensely prolonged dactylo-epitrite compound

[1] Where the context is unambiguous this colon can be differentiated by notation: − ‿ ‿ − ⊼ − aeolo-choriambic hexasyll. (see p. 139)
⊼͡‿ − ⊼ − dochmiac (see p. 106);
− ‿ ‿ − ⸚ − contracted hemiepes.
[2] See below, p. 134. Cf. the next strophe 584 ff.

colon. Of the distinguishable cola the heptameter is seven times repeated:

λίμνας τ' ἔκτοθεν αἱ κατὰ χέρσον ἐληλαμέναι περὶ πύργον
τοῦδ' ἄνακτος ἄϊον,
Ἕλλας τ' ἀμφὶ πόρον πλατὺν εὐχόμεναι, μυχία τε Προποντίς,
καὶ στόμωμα Πόντου.

Ag. 151 shows the same colon, and Euripides in his derisive cento *Ran.* 1274 selects yet another from the Ἱέρειαι (though here without diaeresis after the spondee):

εὐφαμεῖτε μελισσονόμοι δόμον Ἀρτεμίδος πέλας οἴγειν.

Ran. 1266 (like *Pers.* 879) is a hexameter in the same rhythm, and this makes it the more likely that Aristophanes in his curious monostrophic ode 814ff. with the introductory hexameter each time − − | − ∪ ∪ − ∪ ∪ − ∪ ∪ − − is adopting the Aeschylean manner. The lekythion clausula ῥήμαθ' ἱπποβάμονα recalls the passage from *Pers.* again (see the stanza quoted, with lekythion 866 and ithyphallic, i.e. catalectic lekythion, clausula). The mixture of dactylic and trochaic cola is typical for Aeschylus,[1] and it is noteworthy that here (*Pers.*) there is a kind of transition from mixed dactylic and trochaic to dactylo-epitrite, in the behaviour of the successive clausulae; thus 870 = 877 are separate ithyphallic cola, 886 = 896 are ithyphallics half-connected by elision (weak colon-diaeresis) with the dactylic πνῖγος, while in the epode 906 -γαῖσι ποντίαισιν has joined indissolubly with the pendant hemiepes δμαθέντες μεγάλως πλα- in a typical dactylo-epitrite compound. Such interplay of dactylo-epitrite rhythms with separate dactylic and trochaic cola is common (cf. Aesch. *Supp.* 40ff., Soph. *Aj.* 172ff., Ar. *Pax* 775ff., *Av.* 737ff.), and these categories have in fact quite indeterminate boundaries.

The incidence of spondees so markedly modifies the rhythm that it is only rarely that strict responsion is broken in this respect (as *Ag.* 104 = 122, *Eum.* 1042 = 1046). A double spondee is even more striking, as in Aeschylus's refrain αἴλινον αἴλινον εἰπέ, τὸ δ' εὖ νικάτω, or with diaeresis *Ag.* 144 τούτων αἰτεῖ σύμβολα κρᾶναι, and *Ag.* 106 = 125 three consecutively. The effect of a series of dactyls

[1] Cf. *Ag.* 160ff., *Eum.* 347ff., 526ff., 956ff.

following initial spondee or spondees is to isolate the latter as a kind of 'base', and in certain circumstances (cf. Soph. *El.* 134 quoted above) the longer form of this base may be so far detached as to become rather an ingredient in a colon-compound. It is one step further than this when Aeschylus introduces (e.g. *Ag.* 104ff. among plain dactylic and iambic cola) dactylic phrases with an alien base in the form of an iambic metron. This is in each case welded on to the dactylic segment by word-overlap ('synartete', in Hephaestion's terminology):

ὅπως Ἀχαι-|-ῶν δίθρονον κράτος Ἑλλάδος ἥβας,

so that the *words* (ὅπως Ἀχαιῶν) which stand isolated by diaeresis at the beginning of the line form an 'iambic colarion' ⏑ – ⏑ – –, just as in an iambic trimeter with penthemimeral caesura, only that the last syllable must always be long.[1] In *Ag.* 109 and 116, and in Aristophanes' excerpts *Ran.* 1264 (from *Myrmidons*) and *Ran.* 1291 (*incert.*), the colon is iamb.+four dact., but *Ran.* 1270 (from *Telephus*)

κύδιστ' Ἀχαιῶν Ἀτρέως πολυκοίρανε μάνθανέ μου παῖ

runs into five dact. It is evidently Aeschylus who makes most characteristic use of these synartetes, but Sophocles has a colon of the kind *O.T.* 174 = 186

ἄλλον δ' ἂν ἄλλῳ προσίδοις ἅπερ εὔπτερον ὄρνιν

in a context of iambic, dactylic, paroemiac and iambo-paroemiac cola; and again Eur. *Hipp.* 1102ff. is a stanza composed of similar elements:

ἦ μέγα μοι τὰ θεῶν μελεδήμαθ', ὅταν φρένας ἔλθῃ
λύπας παραιρεῖ· ξύνεσιν δέ τιν' ἐλπίδα κεύθων
λείπομαι ἔν τε τύχαις θνατῶν καὶ ἐν ἔργμασι λεύσσων·
ἄλλα γὰρ ἄλλοθεν | ἀμείβεται· | μετὰ δ' ἵσταται ἀνδράσιν αἰὼν
πολυπλάνητος ἀεί,

dact. hexam., iambo-dact. (=*Ag.* 109), dact. hexam., a compound

---

[1] The type of synartete thus produced has some analogies with dactylo-epitrites and with a group of metres found especially in *P.V.*, see below, pp. 129f.

of two dact.+iamb. metron – ∪ ∪ – ∪ ∪ ∪ – ∪ – +⏑⏑ paroem.,¹
iamb. dim. cat. The second strophe continues with the same cola,
dactylic, iambic and paroemiac, here uncompounded.²
Eur. *Cycl.* 608ff. is a gay stanza of syncopated trochaics and
iambics mixed with dactyls, in which the metra – ∪ – and – –
appear as the 'base' of dactylic cola.

λήψεται τὸν τράχηλον   – ∪ – – ∪ – ∪
ἐντόνως ὁ καρκίνος   – ∪ – ∪ – ∪ –
τοῦ ξενοδαιτυμόνος· πυρὶ γὰρ τάχα   – ∪ ∪ – ∪ ∪ – ∪ ∪ – ∪ ∪ |
φωσφόρους ὀλεῖ κόρας.   – ∪ – ∪ – ∪ –
ἤδη δαλὸς ἠνθρακωμένος   – – – ∪ – ∪ – ∪ –
κρύπτεται ἐς σποδιάν, δρυὸς ἄσπετον   – ∪ ∪ – ∪ ∪ – ∪ ∪ – ∪ ∪ |
ἔρνος· ἀλλ' ἴτω Μάρων,   – ∪ – ∪ – ∪ –
πρασσέτω, μαινομένου 'ξελέτω βλέφαρον   – ∪ – – ∪ ∪ – ∪ ∪ – ∪ ∪ – |
Κύκλωπος, ὡς πίῃ κακῶς.   ∪ – ∪ – ∪ – ∪ –
κἀγὼ τὸν φιλοκισσοφόρον Βρόμιον   – – – ∪ ∪ – ∪ ∪ – ∪ ∪ – |
ποθεινὸν εἰσιδεῖν θέλω,   ∪ – ∪ – ∪ – ∪ –
Κύκλωπος λιπὼν ἐρημίαν·   – – – ∪ – ∪ – ∪ –
ἆρ' ἐς τοσόνδ' ἀφίξομαι ;   ⨯ – ∪ – ∪ – ∪ –

¹ The colometry is uncertain here. If the division is made after ἀμείβεται,
we have a curious colon, recalling Soph.'s – ∪ – ∪ | – ∪ ∪ – ∪ ∪ *Phil.*
1215, see above, p. 41, n. 2. But it could also divide: ἄλλα γὰρ ἄλλοθεν
dact. dim. B-type, ἀμείβεται· μετὰ δ' ἵσταται ἀνδράσιν αἰών iambo-
paroemiac = Soph. *O.T.* 173 ἰηίων καμάτων ἀνέχουσι γυναῖκες. In
either case I regard it as a compound, i.e. the choice is of more theoretical
than rhythmical significance.
² For so-called 'aeolic dactyls' see under 'Prosodiacs', ch. x.

IV

ANAPAESTIC

Characteristics of the recitative anapaestic 'system'—Modifications of these in melic anapaests—Melic anapaests usually in long, fairly homogeneous periods—Anapaests in comedy: proceleusmatics and association with cretic-paeonic—Solo-arias in Euripides: association of anapaests with dochmiacs: cola of all lengths from four to eight long syllables—Some anomalous cola—Dactylo-anapaests.

Anapaests in the drama fall into two main classes: those written in the same 'attic' as the dialogue and delivered in recitative, and melic anapaests, which in tragedy use the ordinary lyric dialect that for convenience may be termed 'doric'. These latter must have been sung when mixed with other metres; the case is less certain where they appear unmixed in astrophic form, especially in long sequences. Only melic anapaests come under the head of lyric metres properly speaking, and with the tetrameters of comic dialogue and parabasis this inquiry is not concerned; the anapaest of the long dimeter-systems must, however, be briefly considered, because of the strong influence its familiar rhythm exerted over its melic kindred.

The anapaest ∪ ∪ − is a reversed dactyl, but all the evidence points to a difference in origin and nature between dactyls and the recitative type of anapaest. The latter is frequently used as a marching metre in the drama, and the existence of Spartan ἐμβατήρια[1] in a kindred rhythm suggests that this may have been the origin of anapaestic movement. The tramp of soldiers' feet then gives us the normal anapaestic tempo—left, right to ∪ ∪ −, i.e. an even stress[2] with no

[1] See below, p. 55.
[2] Marching anapaests have been brought as evidence to support a theory of metrical ictus in Greek, but it is difficult to believe that soldiers on the march could gabble them so fast as to set down their feet on the long syllables only. (There may of course have been a *de facto* stress imposed by the step on the first short as against the second.) The movement of an entering chorus, however, may well have been slower, with the foot raised in arsis ∪ ∪ and set down on thesis −.

[47]

'arsis' and 'thesis' of feet, literally speaking, to differentiate shorts and long, a rather slow enunciation, and an exact equivalence of one long or two shorts; and here at any rate a catalectic line, the equivalent of seven longs instead of eight, must have left a pause of the length of the amputated syllable. The even time-relation of − = ∪ ∪ would differentiate the rhythm from the dactylic as given by Dionysius,[1] and would account for the fact that for ∪ ∪ − can be substituted not only ∺ − but also ∺ ᴐᴑ. A still wider cleft between the two movements, however, is the grouping of recitative anapaests into pairs, so that the effective unit of movement is not ∪ ∪ − but ∪ ∪ − ∪ ∪ −, and this latter is rightly counted the 'metron' of anapaests of this type. In the overwhelming majority of dimeters there is diaeresis between the two metra, monometers also occur, and there is a perceptible relation of variants to this unit of length in the incidence of 'dactylic' inversion; thus − ∪ ∪ − − and − ∪ ∪ − ∪ ∪ are common, while ᴓᴑ − − ∪ ∪ is very rare. The anapaestic metron is, nevertheless, felt as a 'syzygy' or pair, in contrast to the iambic or trochaic metron, since it has no *anceps* and the two halves are exactly balanced; this tendency is exaggerated in comic πνίγη, where in the frequently recurring lists of one sort and another each word often forms a single anapaest:

κύρβις κρόταλον κίναδος τρύμη.

The dimeters of these systems follow one another in strict synaphea, and weak colon-diaeresis (by elision) is not uncommon. They are grouped into irregular periods known as 'systems', rounded off by catalectic clausulae usually of the form ᴓᴑ − ᴓᴑ − ∪ ∪ − − and thus identical with one form of the paroemiac.[2] There is no regular diaeresis after the first metron in this clausula, the penultimate is never resolved and the ante-penultimate ∪ ∪ rarely contracted, and final *anceps* is common; in other words, this line is not so much a double metron as an indivisible colon with pendant close, effectively the same as when it appears in dactylic contexts. Within the period occasional monometers occur among the dimeters, and as metron-diaeresis is so regular we are sometimes aware only of having an odd

---

[1] See above, p. 6.   [2] See above, pp. 27, n. 1, 33, n. 2.

number of metra to set down, the particular metron selected for isolation being a matter of taste.[1] It is not true, however, that the division into dimeters in our editions is an artificial arrangement which originated in hellenistic times for the mere convenience of spacing on the written page, as Wilamowitz says.[2] The reality of the dimeter as the normal anapaestic phrase-length is proved by such exceptions to the rule of metron-diaeresis as *Aj.* 146 ἥπερ δορίληπ-|-τος ἔτ᾽ ἦν λοιπή (the commonest variant) and *P.V.* 172 καί μ᾽ οὔτι μελι-|-γλώσσοις πειθοῦς, while at the end of the dimeter such a caesura is never allowed;[3] by the frequency of such anaphora as

Tro. 102   πλεῖ κατὰ πορθμόν, πλεῖ κατὰ δαίμονα;

and by the existence of the indivisible paroemiac as a catalectic clausula. Synaphea is, nevertheless, so strictly regarded that the junction of one dimeter and the next is subject to the same rules as the junction of the two metra within it: thus, as a sequence of four short syllables is avoided,[4] a dimeter ending with an inversion – ∪ ∪ may not be followed by ∪ ∪ – at the beginning of the next. A resolved anapaest ∪ ∪ ⌒, called by Hephaestion a proceleusmatic, is never found in tragedy in these recitative sequences, and is very rare in comedy (cf. *Eq.* 503 ὑμεῖς δ᾽ ἡμῖν προσέχετε τὸν νοῦν—significantly, all in one word; Bentley's πρόσσχετε would of course be an easy emendation). On the whole, Aeschylus has the least regular anapaestic systems of all the dramatists; thus, for instance, *Supp.* 5–7

χθόνα σύγχορτον Συρίᾳ φεύγομεν
οὔτιν᾽ ἐφ᾽ αἵματι δημηλασίαν
ψήφῳ πόλεως γνωσθεῖσαι

have a most unusual rhythm, with the metron ∪ ∪ – – ∪ ∪ in the first line, and a contracted ante-penult ≏ – ∪ ∪ – ≏ – – in the

---

[1] Cf. Eur. *Med.* 1081–9, where the papyrus-fragment published *Cl. Rev.* XLIX, 1, 1935 shows that εὕροις ἂν ἴσως (in the penultimate position) was the monometer in this version of the text instead of 1081 πολλάκις ἤδη.

[2] *Einl. i. d. gr. Tr.* p. 129.

[3] The only exception, presumably for comic effect, is Ar. *Vesp.* 753–4.

[4] The only exception I have been able to find in recitative anapaests is Eur. *Hec.* 145 ἴζ᾽ Ἀγαμέμνονος ἱκέτις γονάτων – ∪ ∪ – ∪ ∪ | ∪ ∪ – ∪ ∪ –, where the proper name would account for the licence.

clausula. Inversions at the end of a dimeter, not uncommon in tragedy, are rare in comedy, whereas wholly spondaic dimeters, avoided in tragedy, are fairly common in comic authors, especially in the patter-πνίγη.

Such then in outline are the regular systems of recitative anapaests. Melic anapaests are of several different kinds, varying in their degree of approximation to recitative anapaests, and often following immediately upon a recitative system or even mingling with it. Thus in the anapaestic opening of *I.A.* Agamemnon and the Old Man begin a dialogue in attic anapaests, but from 115 to 142 Agamemnon's become melic,[1] while the Old Man continues in attic, then to 163 all is recitative again. The change appears to mark a greater intensity of emotion. In *Med.* 96–104 the Nurse speaks attic anapaests, Medea off stage has anapaests of exactly the same type except that they are in doric, and the Chorus sings polymetric stanzas with opening anapaestic periods. *Ag.* 1448–1577 is an exchange between Clytaemnestra and the Chorus in which Clytaemnestra chants her defiance in three strophes and antistrophes of recitative attic anapaests, each time of a different pattern but formed of the regular ingredients (cf. Menelaus in a similar frame of mind *Andr.* 515–22 ~ 537–44); the Chorus's antistrophic stanzas are in other metres, while their three ephymnia start with anapaestic periods of the same type but with doric ᾱ.[2] In *O.C.* 117ff. passages of recitative anapaestic dialogue, not here in responsion, are sandwiched between the songs of the Chorus, of which str. and ant. α′ end with an anapaestic period, str. and ant. β′ begin with one. *Pers.* 908ff., Soph. *El.* 86ff., and Eur. *Tro.* 98ff. all show recitative anapaests taken up by melic, in both strophic and astrophic form. *Ion* 219ff.

[1] And contain licences elsewhere unparalleled in drama: 119 a dimeter ending with πρός, and 123 a paroemiac of the form ⏓ – ⏓ ⏔ ∪ ∪ – –, whereas elsewhere the sequence ⏓ ⏔ ∪ ∪ – in the catalectic line is confined to the opening, as in ὤφελεν ἐλάταν πομπαίαν. In view of the strange position of γὰρ δή 122 I am inclined to believe in Verrall's transposition of ὥρας, giving εἰς ἄλλας γὰρ δὴ παιδός | δαίσομεν ὥρας ὑμεναίους.

[2] It must be admitted that the textual tradition is full of uncertainties and fluctuations in the transmission of 'attic' and 'doric' in anapaests.

presents a curious arrangement, with the antistrophe (only) of the Chorus broken at irregular intervals by Ion's anapaestic replies and questions, of varying length. These are all in attic monometers or acatalectic dimeters, with diaeresis but no clausulae, and in one case (226 εἰ μὲν ἐθύσατε πέλανον πρὸ δόμων) the melic rhythm – ∪ ∪ – ∪ ∪ | ∪ ∪ – ∪ ∪ –. Synaphea is observed between the end of Ion's anapaests and the next phrase of the Chorus; thus the 'inverted' ends – ∪ ∪ of 222, 224, 228 and 232 are kept short by the opening syllables of the Chorus.

It has been remarked that some melic anapaests represent only a very slight modification of the recitative type. In general, melic are differentiated by one or more of the following characteristics: by 'dialect'; by a greater freedom of contraction and resolution, so that they often appear in wholly spondaic form or with occasional proceleusmatics and sequences of the form – ∪ ∪ ∪ ∪ –; by an admixture of other metres, whereas recitative systems (except for a rare patch of melic) are strictly uniform; and by a licence to ignore the pair-unit whether in diaeresis or in the form of their variants, so that the single anapaest ∪ ∪ – becomes in effect more the unit of movement than the syzygy ∪ ∪ – ∪ ∪ –. The familiar movement κατὰ συζυγίαν often prevails in practice, and the normal phrase-lengths are still the 'dimeter' and paroemiac, but sometimes emancipation from the pair-unit is carried so far that other lengths, not reducible to pairs, are found. The paroemiac, though still generally felt as catalectic,[1] has ceased to have merely clausular function and occurs with great frequency, even two or three in succession: moreover, the clausula need not be a paroemiac at all; the series may end on an acatalectic dimeter. Melic anapaests are found in uniform sequences like the recitative systems, in stanzas, whether uniformly anapaestic or containing anapaestic periods, and in astrophic ἀπολελυμένα with a greater or smaller admixture of other metres.

---

[1] Cf. the relative frequency of final *anceps* (very rare in full dimeters) and the extreme rarity of weak diaeresis (elision) and proclitic words at the end of the colon. The only cases I have found are *Tro.* 129 (elision between two consecutive paroemiacs) and *Pers.* 935, where τάν is generally assumed to be either misplaced or corrupt.

When a character sings (or recites) melic anapaests in contrast to the recitative systems of the Chorus (as in *Hec.* 59ff.) or of a minor character (as in *I.A.* and *Med.*), the effect is to isolate the melic singer on a higher emotional level. The difference may lie merely in the dialect, as in *Med.*;[1] or in dialect and the admission of spondaic paroemiacs, as *I.A.*; or may extend to the admixture of other metres, as *Hec.*[2] In Soph. *El.* 86–120 the dialect is attic, and most of the chant is of the ordinary recitative type, except for two consecutive spondaic paroemiacs 88–9

πολλὰς μὲν θρήνων ᾠδάς,
πολλὰς δ' ἀντήρεις ἤσθου

and again (with one resolution) 105–6. In comedy, naturally, doric is never a distinguishing feature of the melic type, except in Euripidean parody, as *Thesm.* 776–84.

Sporadic anapaestic cola in polymetric stanzas are not very common. In Aeschylus all acatalectic dimeters that occur thus observe metron-diaeresis (as *Ag.* 1455–6, *Pers.* 959–60, 979). Sophocles *O.T.* 469–70 ~ 479–80 has two dimeters that move κατὰ συζυγίαν, but *Trach.* 959 ~ 968 does not, and his spondaic cola, unlike those of Aeschylus, break away completely from the metron, cf. *El.* 850–1:

κἀγὼ τοῦδ' ἴστωρ ὑπερίστωρ
πανσύρτῳ παμμήνῳ πολλῶν.

Euripides has even one case (*Hcld.* 775 ~ 782) of an anapaestic dimeter without diaeresis which is linked by word-overlap to an iambic syncopated trimeter:

ὀλολύγματα παννυχίοις ὑπὸ παρ-
-θένων ἰαχεῖ ποδῶν κρότοισιν.[3]

[1] And possibly the absence of a paroemiac clausula 167, cf. *Hec.* 215.

[2] It is probable that here as elsewhere the fluctuation between attic and doric in Hecuba's song is due to faulty textual transmission. The whole passage in any case appears to be corrupt and full of interpolations.

[3] The metre here is really a lengthy specimen of the class of compounds dealt with under 'Dactylo-Epitrites', see below, ch. XI. Overlap nowhere occurs between two consecutive anapaestic dimeters in a uniformly anapaestic passage. The creation of two such linked dimeters at *Hipp.* 1374–5 by the emendations of Wilamowitz and Markland is therefore open to grave suspicion, see below, p. 67, n. 2.

But more characteristic than these isolated outcrops are the longer periods, whether entirely or only predominantly anapaestic, of stanzas which as already mentioned follow on anapaestic systems. Soph. *El.* 193–200

οἰκτρὰ μὲν νόστοις αὐδά, ||
οἰκτρὰ δ' ἐν κοίταις πατρῴαις
ὅτε οἱ παγχάλκων ἀνταία
γενύων ὡρμάθη πλαγά. ||
δόλος ἦν ὁ φράσας, | ἔρος ὁ κτείνας,
δεινὰν δεινῶς | προφυτεύσαντες
μορφάν· εἴτ' οὖν | θεὸς εἴτε βροτῶν
ἦν ὁ ταῦτα πράσσων

shows (*a*) a spondaic paroemiac as colon-period, (*b*) two spondaic dimeters without diaeresis + a spondaic paroemiac, (*c*) three more un-contracted dimeters with diaeresis + an ithyphallic clausula. The exact correspondence of the antistrophe shows that this change of ana-paestic rhythm in the middle is deliberate. In the frequently returning anapaestic movement of this κομμός there are some ambiguous cola; it is impossible to tell from the written text whether they are in-verted anapaests or dactylic tetrameters—whether, that is, in actual performance some difference in tempo or foot-movement indicated a transition of rhythm at any point in the following (236–43):

καὶ τί μέτρον κακότατος ἔφυ; φέρε   — ∪ ∪ — ∪ ∪ — ∪ ∪ — ∪ ∪
πῶς ἐπὶ τοῖς φθιμένοις ἀμελεῖν καλόν;   — ∪ ∪ — ∪ ∪ — ∪ ∪ — ∪ ∪
ἐν τίνι τοῦτ' ἔβλαστ' ἀνθρώπων;   — ∪ ∪ — — — — — —
μήτ' εἴην ἔντιμος τούτοις   — — — — — — — —
μήτ' εἴ τῳ πρόσκειμαι χρηστῷ   — — — — — — — —
ξυνναίοιμ' εὔκηλος, γονέων   — — — — — ∪ ∪ —
ἐκτίμους ἴσχουσα πτέρυγας   — — — — — ∪ ∪ ◡
ὀξυτόνων γόων.   — ∪ ∪ — ∪ —

The dochmiac final clausula is of course alien, like the ithyphallic 200. (The next period continues in dochmiacs.) The rare *anceps* at the end of the last acatalectic dimeter is noteworthy.[1] It is conceivable that we have here four minor periods: (*a*) three dact., (*b*) two anap., (*c*) two anap. with final uncontracted metron, (*d*) dochmiac *coda* binding the whole into a single major period.

---

[1] Cf. *Ion* 167, *I.T.* 231, in both cases followed by anapaestic cola.

Aesch. *Pers.* 908ff. shows another ambiguous transition. Xerxes and the Chorus have each a period of recitative anapaests, and then the Chorus changes to doric and sings a period of nine anapaestic cola, with regular movement κατὰ συζυγίαν but with a clausula 930 of the form – – – – | ⏑ ⏑ ⏑ ⏑ ⏑ ⏑ – αἰνῶς αἰνῶς ἐπὶ γόνυ κέκλιται.

This last metron (identical with one form of dochmiac) is repeated in the following stanzas, first by itself as a period-close 933 κακὸν ἄρ᾽ ἐγενόμαν, then twice as a dimeter κακοφατίδα βοάν, κακομέλετον ἰάν, and in the final clausula 942 as in 930 πέμψω πέμψω πολύδακρυν ἰαχάν. Here all appears straightforwardly anapaestic, but in the antistrophe the most probable emendation of the corrupt 945 is λᾱοπαθέα σέβων ἀλίτυπά τε βάρη, where the lengthening of the first syllable is permissible in a dochmiac but not of course in a proceleusmatic anapaest. The same dochmiac recurs 976 (cf. 986) and 1075 ἰὴ ἰὴ βάρισιν ὀλόμενοι – – – – | ⌣ ⌒ ⌒ ⏑ –, making the case stronger for its appearance here. It occurs similarly in the middle of an anapaestic period Soph. *El.* 205

> ὦ νύξ, ὦ δείπνων ἀρρήτων
> ἔκπαγλ᾽ ἄχθη · | τοὺς ἐμὸς ἴδε πατὴρ |
> θανάτους αἰκεῖς διδύμαιν χειροῖν.

Comedy also has stanzas wholly or predominantly anapaestic, with certain characteristically comic modifications. The rhythm tends to be simplified and more homogeneous: thus *Ran.* 371 ff. is wholly spondaic, except for one resolution in a proper name in the antistrophe:

> χώρει νυν πᾶς ἀνδρείως
> ἐς τοὺς εὐανθεῖς κόλπους
> λειμώνων ἐγκρούων
> κἀπισκώπτων
> καὶ παίζων καὶ χλευάζων,
> ἠρίστηται δ᾽ ἐξαρκούντως.

The third colon here has been variously accounted for as a 'double molossus', as 'two catalectic monometers', or as a 'brachycatalectic' dimeter. It is true that the diaereses here and in the antistrophe (τῇ φωνῇ μολπάζων) might seem to suggest two groups of three syllables, and recall Ion's ritual cry (125–7)

ὦ Παιὰν ὦ Παιάν,
εὐαίων εὐαίων
εἴης ὦ Λατοῦς παῖ.

This last line, however, does not so divide, and we shall see good reason to suppose that there is a type of anapaestic colon of this length—and indeed, with the virtual disappearance of the metronunit, there is no reason why there should not be. Here in the *Frogs* it has in its context the effect of a catalectic version of the preceding paroemiacs.

The song just quoted is sung as the procession of Mystae gets under way; it is in fact a marching rhythm recalling the old Spartan ἐμβατήρια such as that attributed to Tyrtaeus: ἄγετ᾽ ὦ Σπάρτας εὔανδροι κτλ., in paroemiacs κατὰ στίχον. Similar to these, though less spondaic, is the entrance-song of the Chorus in Cratinus᾽ ᾽Οδυσσῆς:

σιγάν νυν ἅπας ἔχε σιγάν,
καὶ πάντα λόγον τάχα πεύσει·
ἡμῖν δ᾽ ᾽Ιθάκη πατρὶς ἐστίν,
πλέομεν δ᾽ ἅμ᾽ ᾽Οδυσσέϊ θείῳ.

A different type of anapaestic movement, and one peculiar to comedy, has frequent proceleusmatic resolutions and no inversions. Hephaestion quotes a line from an unnamed play of Aristophanes (698 Kock)

τίς ὄρεα βαθύκομα τάδ᾽ ἐπέσυτο βροτῶν; ᵕ ᵕ ෆ ᵕ ᵕ ෆ ᵕ ᵕ ෆ ᵕ ᵕ –

which is typical of this pattering kind of rhythm, with its syllable-groups emphasizing the division into feet or metra, and the anapaest giving the effect of a contracted proceleusmatic as much as the proceleusmatic of a resolved anapaest. It is significant that this is so often found in combination with cretic-paeonic[1] rhythm, where there is the same kind of prevailing diaeresis and the same ambiguity as to whether – ᵕ – is contracted – ᵕ ෆ or the paeon a resolved cretic. A fragment of the Ταγηνισταί (506 Kock) begins with curious syzygies of proceleusmatic+spondee ᵕ ᵕ ෆ ⸚ –

ἅλις ἀφύης μοι· παρατέταμαι γὰρ τὰ λιπαρὰ κάπτων,

[1] See below, ch. vi.

and continues in cretic-paeonic tetrameters. *Lys.* 476–83 ~ 541–7 opens with an uncertain text, but some at least of the first period is cretic-paeonic; it continues:

> τόδε τοι τὸ πάθος μετ᾽ ἐμοῦ ‖
> ὅ τι βουλόμεναί ποτε τὴν
> Κραναὰν κατέλαβον, ἔφ᾽ ὅ τί τε
> μεγαλόπετρον ἄβατον ἀκρόπολιν
> ἱερὸν τέμενος.

Here the hiatus at the end of the first colon isolates it unmistakably as a 'tripody',[1] and though what remains is clearly a πνῖγος the division into further phrases of the same length rather than into Wilamowitz's amorphous 'dimeters' (with word-overlap) is justified by the balanced unity of 545 ἕνι φύσις ἕνι χάρις ἕνι θράσος. Of construction κατὰ συζυγίαν there is not a trace. We need therefore have no hesitation on these grounds in accepting the notorious

> σὲ μὲν οὖν καταλεύσομεν ὦ μιαρὰ κεφαλή

(*Ach.* 285 ~ 336) as an 'anapaestic pentapody', unparalleled though this length is.[2]

Av. 1058 ff. mixes spondaic anapaests with cretic-paeonic periods; and in 327 ff. both types, the spondaic and the proceleusmatic, occur, the latter again in tripodies,[3] while the last period presents an unexampled *responsion* of proceleusmatics to paeons, the correspondence in number of syllables being allowed to obscure the quantitative discrepancy:

> ἔα ἔα,
> προδεδόμεθ᾽ ἀνόσιά τ᾽ ἐπάθομεν·
> ὃς γὰρ φίλος ἦν ὁμότροφά θ᾽ ἡμῖν
> ἐνέμετο πεδία παρ᾽ ἡμῖν,
> παρέβη μὲν θεσμοὺς ἀρχαίους,
> παρέβη δ᾽ ὅρκους ὀρνίθων·
> ἐς δὲ δόλον ἐκάλεσε
> παρέβαλέ τ᾽ ἐμὲ παρὰ

---

[1] Wilamowitz unjustifiably emends, to get rid of this unorthodox length.

[2] Cf. however, below, pp. 168 ff.

[3] The arrangement into dimeters, obstinately carried through by some editors, damages the natural rhythm, even if the hiatus 345–6 παντᾷ | ἐπίβαλε (cf. *Lys.* 479 quoted above) be emended away.

γένος ἀνόσιον ὅπερ
ἐξότ' ἐγένετ' ἐμοί[1]
πολέμιον ἐτράφη.

The phrasing in this last period gives five groups of eight syllables, or seven syllables with a final contraction, and an opening long syllable (i.e. a paeonic) in the first and fourth groups. In the antistrophe it is cretic-paeonic throughout, with corresponding phrase-groups:

οὔτε γὰρ ὄρος σκιερὸν
οὔτε νέφος αἰθέριον
οὔτε πολιὸν πέλαγος
ἔστιν ὅ τι δέξεται
τώδ' ἀποφυγόντε με.[2]

The association of anapaests with cretic-paeonics is, like the particular type of anapaest in question, confined to comedy. Association becomes a more acute and complicated problem in tragedy, at least in Euripides, who develops and extends the use of melic anapaests far beyond the practice of the other dramatists. It is his long sequences which are characteristic, particularly in the form of a solo-aria; these figure most prominently in four plays, *Hec.*, *Ion*, *Tro.* and *I.T.* They are mostly astrophic ἀπολελυμένα, and where they are arranged in corresponding strophes, as *Tro.* 153–229 (two pairs), the case is merely like that of Clytaemnestra's recitative anapaests in *Ag.* 1448 ff.: the precise pattern corresponds, but the ingredients are the same as in the astrophic sequences. In this passage, as a matter of fact, the anapaests approach more nearly to recitative regularity than in the preceding ἄστροφα 122–52 sung by Hecuba; there is a good

---

[1] The MS reading is hard to accept here. ἐξότ' ἐγένετ' ἐπ' ἐμοί would mean that the metre on changing to paeonic resolves a cretic – ∪ ∪ ∪ ⌣ ∪ – in an unprecedented position, and also loses the syllabic correspondence with the antistrophe.

[2] Cf. precisely the same licence of responsion (clumsily emended in our texts) Ar. *Vesp.* 339 ~ 370 τίνα πρόφασιν ἔχων ∪ ∪⌣ ∪ ∪ – ~ ἀλλ' ἔπαγε τὴν γνάθον – ∪⌣ – ∪ –. Schroeder's analysis of the anapaestic pentameter σὲ μὲν οὖν κτλ. indicates that he explains this too as a series of foreshortened cretics ∪ ∪ – for – ∪ – as ἐτράφη above ~ -όντε με. It is true that the context is partly cretic-paeonic, but to my ear at least it requires a much more artificial effort to hear the rhythm in this way.

deal of spondaic contraction, but the paroemiacs are all clausular except for the pair 209–10 ~ 224–5. Of Hecuba's preceding lament the last part (143–52) is regular too; the earlier lines are more typical of the Euripidean ἀπολελυμένα.

	πρῷραι ναῶν ὠκείαις	paroem.
	Ἴλιον ἱερὰν αἷ κώπαις	paroem.
	δι' ἅλα πορφυροειδέα καὶ	⌒ ∪ – ∪ ∪ – ∪ ∪ –
125	λιμένας Ἑλλάδος εὐόρμους	⌒ ∪ – ∪ ∪ – x̄ –
	αὐλῶν παιᾶνι στυγνῷ	paroem.
	συρίγγων τ' εὐφθόγγων φωνᾷ	– – – – – – – –
	βαίνουσαι πλεκτὰν Αἰγύπτου	– – – – – – – –
	παιδείαν ἐξηρτήσασθ',	paroem.
130	αἰαῖ, Τροίας ἐν κόλποις	paroem.
	τὰν Μενελάου μετανισόμεναι	– ∪ ∪ – – | ∪ ∪ – ∪ ∪ –
	στυγνὰν ἄλοχον, Κάστορι λώβαν	– – ∪ ∪ – | – ∪ ∪ – –
	τῷ τ' Εὐρώτᾳ δυσκλείαν,	paroem.
	ἃ σφάζει μὲν	– – – –
135	τὸν πεντήκοντ' ἀροτῆρα τέκνων	– – – – | ∪ ∪ – ∪ ∪ –
	Πρίαμον ἐμέ τε μελέαν Ἑκάβαν	∪ ∪ ∪ ∪ ∪ ∪ | ∪ ∪ – ∪ ∪ –
	ἐς τάνδ' ἐξώκειλ' ἄταν.	paroem.
	ὤμοι θάκους οἵους θάσσω,	– – – – | – – – –
	σκηναῖς ἐφέδρους Ἀγαμεμνονίαις.	– – ∪ ∪ – | ∪ ∪ – ∪ ∪ –
140	δούλα δ' ἄγομαι	– – ∪ ∪ –
	γραῦς ἐξ οἴκων πενθήρη	paroem.
	κρᾶτ' ἐκπορθηθεῖσ' οἰκτρῶς.	paroem.

The frequent pair-grouping in these lines is noteworthy, even to the presence or absence of metron-diaeresis in the acatalectic cola (cf. *I.A.* 1319–29). This may give a clue to the puzzling 136, discussion of which may be postponed for the moment. It also supports the text of 124–5, difficult of analysis though these cola are. They appear to be a free form of glyconic.[1] The standard pattern of this colon is – ∪ – ∪ ∪ – ∪ –, with much latitude (including resolution) allowed in the first two syllables and an occasional licence to lengthen the penult. Such a 'dragged close', as here in 125, assimilates the colon more nearly to anapaestic rhythm; 124 may be a freak glyconic[2]

---

[1] See below, ch. IX.

[2] In the context this is the most likely explanation. The termination -έα might possibly be a single long syllable by synizesis, but the glyconic with word-end at a long penult (cf. ch. IX, Additional note, p. 154) is

like *El.* 439 ~ 449 κοῦφον ἅλμα ποδῶν Ἀχιλῆ, thus again approximating to the surrounding anapaests. Consecutive glyconics are often linked by word-overlap, as here (by καί). This is clearly a case of the association of an alien metre, only partially assimilated to anapaestic rhythm; the cola cannot be represented as freak forms of anapaest. Glyconics are not elsewhere so used, but in stanzas are often contiguous with anapaests, cf. *Ion* 504–8, *El.* 112ff.; and the kindred choriambic dimeter,[1] especially in the forms – x̄ – x̄ – ∪ ∪ – or x̄ – x̄ – ∪ ∪ –, mixes still more easily, cf. *Cycl.* 41–81.

The commonest associated metre is the dochmiac. This we have already met in Aeschylus and Sophocles, both in the compatible form ∪ ∪ ∪ ∪ ∪ ∪ – and from this passing over to the incompatible – ∪ ∪ ∪ ∪ ∪ –. Euripides favours other variants,[2] notably the 'dragged' – – – – – and – ∪ ∪ – – –. These are obviously consonant with anapaestic rhythm, though of unorthodox length; they form in effect an anapaestic 'colarion', but less tractable variants are also found. Thus in *Hec.* 177–96 regular anapaestic lengths are punctuated by dochmiacs: 182 αἰαῖ σᾶς ψυχᾶς, 190 Πηλείᾳ γέννᾳ, 193 μάνυσον μᾶτερ,[3] all as it were 'anapaestic' dochmiacs, and one 185 τί ποτ' ἀναστένεις ∪ ∪ ∪ – ∪ – of incompatible rhythm. The assimilable variants make possible a transition to the discrepant. The forms – ∪ ∪ – – – and the resolved ∪ ∪ ∪ ∪ – – – make up a period in succeeding pairs *Ion* 148–50

> ἂν ἀποχεύονται
> Κασταλίας δῖναι,
> νοτερὸν ὕδωρ βάλλων
> ὅσιος ἀπ' εὐνᾶς ὤν[4]

not at all probable, nor is a third paroem. followed by the rare aeolic enneasyll. καὶ λιμένας κτλ. (*Hipp.* 525, *Bacch.* 877 are both opening gambits). ¹ See below, ch. ix.

[2] The proceleusmatic, as *Ion* 883 κέρασιν ἐν ἀψύχοις ἀχεῖ ∪ ∪ ⌢ ≏ – ≏ – –, is rare in Eur.: *Hipp.* 1371 μέθετέ με τάλανα is a good example of its deliberate use in an outburst of physical anguish, cut off as it also is by *brevis in longo* from the surrounding cola.
[3] 187 is probably a monometer (like 180): τί τόδ' ἀγγέλλεις;
[4] The natural rhythm of these paired phrases disappears in Wilamowitz's mechanical grouping, *G.V.* p. 368, n. 2.

and in 894–6 are associated with the discrepant ∪ ∪ ∪ – ∪ –

θεὸς ὁμευνέτας   ∪ ∪ ∪ – ∪ –
ἄγες ἀναιδείᾳ   – ∪ ∪ – – –
Κύπριδι χάριν πράσσων.   ∪ ∪ ∪ ∪ – – –

Euripides treats the dragged dochmiac – – – – – with the effect of a short paroemiac: thus it can be clausular, as in the passage from *Hec.*, quoted above, and *Ion* 178 ναοί θ' οἱ Φοίβου; it occurs in pairs, as *I.T.* 126–7

ὦ παῖ τᾶς Λατοῦς
Δίκτυνν' οὐρεία;

and in *Hec.* 200–1 it follows a 'tripody' with catalectic effect

ἐχθίσταν ἀρρήταν τ'
ὦρσέν τις δαίμων

as a paroemiac follows a dimeter. There is in fact some justification for representing melic anapaestic rhythm in this form (spondaic with occasional resolution) as having cola of all lengths from four to eight long syllables or the equivalent.[1] And just as the 'pentamakron' forms a transition to the dochmiac class of metres, so the 'hexamakron' links up with a metre of the choriambic group, the pherecratean.

In the first place, the existence of the hexamakron cannot reasonably be called in question. There are many more examples than the five already quoted in this chapter, e.g. *Tro.* 144 καὶ κοῦραι δύσνυμφοι, *Hec.* 158 τᾶς οὐ φερτᾶς, οἴμοι,[2] *I.T.* 150 ζωᾶς οἵαν ἰδόμαν and 154 οἴμοι φροῦδος γέννα, *Ion* 891 λευκοῖς τ' ἐμφὺς καρποῖς.[3] Some of these

---

[1] This may give a clue to the phrasing of the lyric fragment ascribed (probably wrongly) to Terpander by Clem. Alex. (fr. 1 D.):

Ζεῦ πάντων ἀρχά,
πάντων ἀγήτωρ,
Ζεῦ σοὶ πέμπω
ταύταν ὕμνων ἀρχάν.

It was 'sung to the Dorian mode'.

[2] Probably 154–76 should not be forced into responsion with 197–215; too much arbitrary emendation is required. There is only a general similarity in the two passages.

[3] Also *Ion* 904, 912 quoted presently.

are easily enough emended, but as there are so many, including some which resist emendation, the more logical course is to let them all stand. *Ion* 902–15 gives an illustration of the intermingling of the shorter with the longer cola of this melic type:

	οἴμοι μοι· καὶ νῦν ἔρρει	paroem.
	πτανοῖς ἁρπασθεὶς θοίνα	paroem.
	παῖς μοι καὶ σὸς τλάμων·	hex.
905	σὺ δὲ κιθάρᾳ κλάζεις	pent.
	παιᾶνας μέλπων.	pent.
	ὠή, τὸν Λατοῦς ⟨σ'⟩ αὐδῶ,	paroem. (for hiatus cf. 860)
	ὅστ' ὀμφὰν κληροῖς	pent.
	πρὸς χρυσέους θάκους	pent.
910	καὶ γαίας μεσσήρεις ἕδρας,	oct.
	εἰς οὓς αὐδὰν καρύξω·	paroem.
	Ἰὼ κακὸς εὐνάτωρ	hex.
	ὃς τῷ μὲν ἐμῷ νυμφεύτᾳ	paroem.
	χάριν οὐ προλαβὼν	tetr.
915	παῖδ' εἰς οἴκους οἰκίζεις.	paroem.

Among the choriambic group of metres there is a colon often used as a catalectic clausula to glyconics − ∪ − ∪ ∪ − −, and like the glyconic having a considerable freedom in the first two syllables, so that in one of its forms it is compatible with anapaests − − − ∪ ∪ − −. To this the ancient metricians gave the name 'pherecratean' from the comic poet Pherecrates, whose connection with the colon is based not on its ordinary use as a choriambic colon but on a 'new invention' by which he gave a series of anapaestic 'hexamakra' κατὰ στίχον the form of pherecrateans:[1]

ἄνδρες πρόσσχετε τὸν νοῦν
ἐξευρήματι καινῷ,
συμπτύκτοις ἀναπαίστοις.[2]

---

[1] Cf. p. 43 for the assimilation of pherecrateans to dactylic rhythm. In all these 'assimilated' aeolics long *anceps* is regularized into true long.

[2] We need not trouble about Heph's. fancy description of the line (15. 106) as an 'antispastic dimeter dicatalectic', i.e. − − − ∪ | ∪ − − ∧ *bis*. Nor does it matter that he thus reckoned a double colon (ἄνδρες... καινῷ), since in any case there was diaeresis after each pherecratean length. For a slightly different interpretation see Koster, 'De Glyconei et Pherecratei

The word σύμπτυκτος in ancient metrical theory is used of a contracted 'foot', such as a spondee in dactyls or anapaests. Obviously it was no 'new invention' of Pherecrates to contract an anapaest, and the most probable explanation seems to be that instead of ordinary anapaestic cola with irregular incidence of spondees he uses hexamakra with resolutions and contractions so regularized that each line 'folds up' into a pherecratean. It is noteworthy that in *Ion* 490ff.

Euripides takes up another choriambic colon nearly related to the pherecratean (in effect a headless form of it), the 'reizianum' − − ∪ ∪ − −, and plays on its compatibility with anapaests:

μετὰ δὲ κτεάνων μετρίων βιοτᾶς   anap. dim.
εὔπαιδος ἐχοίμαν,   reiz.

mixing it with dragged dochmiacs of which it is as it were a resolved form

συρίζεις ὦ Πὰν   − − − − −
τοῖς σοῖσιν ἐν ἄντροις,   − − ∪ ∪ − −

and resolving its first syllable to make it still more anapaestic in movement

θηρσί τε φοινίαν δαῖτα, πικρῶν γάμων   2 doch. (choriambic)
ὕβριν· οὔτ᾽ ἐπὶ κερκίσιν οὔτε λόγοις   2 anap. 'dims.'
φάτιν ἄιον εὐτυχίας μετέχειν   (or tetrapodies)
θεόθεν τέκνα θνατοῖς.   reiz. ∪ ∪ − ∪ ∪ − −

There remain a few puzzling lines in the long monody of Creusa (*Ion* 859ff.) and the κομμός (*I.T.* 123ff.), passages otherwise straightforwardly anapaestic with dochmiac transitions in the manner described. These have variously exercised the ingenuity of editors, who obelize or emend or seek a metrical explanation of some while abandoning others. The lines are:

   (1) *I.T.* 220 ἄγαμος ἄτεκνος ἄπολις ἄφιλος
   (2) *Ion*   889 κρόκεα πέταλα φάρεσιν ἔδρεπον

Origine', *Philol.* 80. It has also been held that the lines refer to 'anapaests' which follow next (i.e. the parabasis), as Ar. *Av.* 684 ἄρχου τῶν ἀναπαίστων. In that case there would be anapaestic cola following, presumably of ordinary length for a parabasis but spondaic (σύμπτυκτοι). But it is difficult to see how Heph. could have reckoned in double cola if he had these three pherecrateans and no more before him.

(3)   900   ἵνα με λέχεσι μελέαν μελέοις
(4) *I.T.* 130   πόδα παρθένιον ὅσιον ὁσίας
(5)   213   ἔτεκεν ἔτρεφεν εὐκταίαν
(6)   232   ἔτι βρέφος ἔτι νέον ἔτι θάλος
(7)   197   φόνος ἐπὶ φόνῳ ἄχεα ἄχεσιν.

Each of these, with the possible exception of the last, which follows a deeply corrupt passage, is entirely unobjectionable in its context except on the grounds of its metrical peculiarity, and the presumption is therefore strong that we should seek to interpret rather than to emend. (6) to begin with need cause no difficulty except to stubborn upholders of the metron-syzygy. It is three proceleusmatics like Aristophanes' ἔνι φύσις ἔνι χάρις ἔνι θράσος. The uncommonness of the resolutions (in tragedy) serves, as in *Hipp.* 1371 μέθετέ με τάλανα, to underline the emotional stress, and the line is further isolated by the rare *brevis in longo* at the end of the preceding acatalectic colon. By counting syllables, the same interpretation could be given of (1) and (2), both of which are followed, like (6), by lines beginning with a vowel. This may be the right explanation, but I believe the audible *effect* of the lines to have been wholly different. We have seen how neatly proceleusmatics, at least if they occur in a series, tend to coincide with the word-lengths, and editors who explain (1), (2) and (6) as iambic or trochaic dimeters are treating the diaereses of (1) and (2) with due respect; but in (6), away from any iambic or trochaic context, such an intrusive rhythm could scarcely have been made audibly intelligible. Moreover, the occurrence of isolated iambic or trochaic cola in the middle of melic anapaests is difficult to accept; no phenomenon of metrical 'transition' such as we have hitherto observed leads us to expect this abrupt dissonance. It becomes still more awkward when we are asked to accept (5) as iambic metron+molossus, (3) as iambic+anapaestic metron and (4) as anapaestic+iambic metron πόδα παρθένιον ὅ- σιον ὁσίας ∪ ∪ – ∪ ∪ ⌒ ∪ ⌒ ∪ – (so Schroeder). Such schemes may work out on paper but could not mean anything in terms of the actual delivery of the lines in a melic anapaestic series. Another explanation makes these lines paroemiacs with resolution of the penultimate long. It is otherwise an unbroken rule of Greek metric that the penult in a pendant close can never resolve; would it be possible to assume that Euripides is in these cola breaking off all relations, as it were, with the ordinary paroemiac – – ∪ ∪ – ∪ ∪ – – and treating the colon as if it were a long form of dragged dochmiac, which *can* resolve its penult, just as we have seen him treating the dochmiac as a short form of paroemiac? There would perhaps be most ground for interpreting (3) and (4) thus, since they appear sandwiched between ordinary spondaic paroemiacs which might set the rhythm of the context with sufficient clearness:

ναῶν χρυσήρεις θριγκούς
πόδα παρθένιον ὅσιον ὁσίας   ∪ ∪ – ∪ ∪〰 ∪ ∪〰 –
κληδούχου δούλα πέμπω.

(1) and (2), however, resist such treatment more vigorously:

ἄγαμος ἄτεκνος ἄπολις ἄφιλος   ∪ ∪〰 ∷〰 ∪ ∪〰 ‿
κρόκεα πέταλα φάρεσιν ἔδρεπον   ∪ ∪〰 ∪ ∪ – ∪ ∪〰 ‿

and the *brevis* at the end of both is a suspicious coincidence. Nor does the explanation give any help with the remaining lines.

The trouble with all these interpretations is that they take no account of the difficulty of conveying such fancy rhythms in actual performance. We may succeed in making the scheme audible to ourselves by the aid of a thumping 'ictus', but it is most significant that in Greek a clear rhythmical context is provided to keep departures from the norm intelligible, and that where a great deal of resolution is in question the aid of diaeresis is so often invoked.[1] I venture here to put forward what is no more than a very tentative hypothesis which would, if accepted as a principle, account for all these difficult cola. It is this: that on occasion Euripides deliberately abandons quantity and substitutes diaeresis, syllable-grouping, for it, probably with extra pauses to keep the quantitative tempo correct. It is possible that in these lines the noticeably symmetrical pitch-accents came through in the melody and emphasized the word-division, perhaps giving an effect not unlike that of inverted anapaests – ∪ ∪. But this, if it happened at all, I should regard as a mere reinforcement of the

[1] Cf. Wifstrand, *Grekisk Metrik*, p. 20.

diaereses and not indispensable. Thus (1) and (2) would each run into four light anapaests, (3) into two light+two normal, in (4) the middle two would be light, (5) would of course be a paroemiac with two light opening feet. If the text of (7) is correct,[1] the extra pauses would make the hiatuses intelligible—more intelligible, at least, than the correption of φόνῳ in iambics which Schroeder postulates. The same explanation would account also for *Tro.* 136 (see above, p. 58) Πρίαμον ἐμέ τε μελέαν Ἑκάβαν, which would thus be on the same model as (3), and would pair with the preceding line as an acatalectic 'dimeter' with metron-diaeresis.

So unorthodox a departure from quantitative determination may be felt hard to swallow, but there are kindred phenomena elsewhere in Greek metric.[2] In comedy the responsion of paeons to proceleusmatics already mentioned is similar in principle; Aristophanes also mixes paeons and trochees in irrational responsion,[3] $- \cup \cup \cup \sim - \cup - \cup$. *Thesm.* 437 ∼ 525 looks like a similar case of the irrational lengthening of resolved trochees to dactylic rhythm:[4] the antistrophe is normal:

κατὰ τὸ φανερὸν ὧδ' ἀναιδῶς ⌒ ∪⌒ ∪ | − ∪ − −

while the strophe has

πάντα δ' ἐβάστασε[ν] φρενὶ πυκνῶς τε − ∪ ∪ − ∪ ∪ | ⌒ ∪ − ∪

in syllabic but not quantitative responsion. It is highly probable, too, that Ar. *Av.* 242 τριοτό· τριοτό· τοτοβρίξ is by the Euripidean licence the equivalent of an anapaestic tripody, cf. 260–2 where proceleusmatic anapaests again occur mixed with cretics:

τοροτορο τοροτορο τίξ	anap. trip. cat.
κικκαβαῦ κικκαβαῦ	2 cret.
τοροτορο τοροτορο λιλιλίξ.[5]	anap. trip.

[1] The opening of the line would here have to be the equivalent of − ∪ ∪ ∪ ∪ − with the first syllable 'lightened'. Possibly we should read, with Barnes, ἀχεά ⟨τ'⟩.
[2] See further on this subject, pp. 78 f.
[3] See below, p. 89.   [4] See below, p. 90.
[5] Could Aesch. *Eum.* 130 λάβε λάβε λάβε λάβε φράζου be such an anapaestic tripody, and not after all *extra metrum*?

It is true that such licences are more easily conceivable in comedy, with its vigorous dancing able sometimes to impose a 'beat' on the rhythm, than in tragedy. Yet the principle is really the same in that most exclusively tragic of all metres the dochmiac, with its equations of $\cup - - \cup -$ with $\bar{\times} - - \bar{\times} -$, and of $\cup \frown \frown \cup \frown$ with $\bar{\times} \frown \frown \cup \frown$.[1] Moreover, there are one or two other passages in Euripides where an application of this same principle would defend the traditional text. Reference was made earlier[2] to the strange appearance of 'tribrachs' among dactyls, *Phoen.* 796

ἀσπιδοφέρμονα θίασον ἔνοπλον

in responsion to a normal dactylic tetrameter 813

Οἰδιπόδα κατὰ δώματα καὶ πόλιν,

and Wilamowitz (*G.V.* p. 360) has called attention to the impropriety of disturbing the trisyllabic groups by the ugly emendation ἐνόπλιον, which by creating a resolved dactyl (θίασον ἐ- νόπλιον) merely substitutes a still stranger anomaly. It would be possible to read εὔοπλον, though even so there is no parallel for the quantity θίασον. Again, in l. 1557 of the same play the anapaestic monometer ξίφεσιν βρίθων is highly obtrusive among the dactyls, whereas ξίφεσι βρίθων, the reading of all the MSS but one, would give a 'light' adonean $\cup \cup \cup - -$, with again the accent and word-end to help the rhythm.[3] It must be admitted, however, that the whole theory of this type of metrical anomaly cannot be urged as any more than a hypothesis which perhaps covers more of the puzzling phenomena than any hitherto advanced. And as applied to the metres where it appears only sporadically it remains an anomaly, an occasional metrical licence which cannot be taken as affecting the general principles on which they work.

One further type of metre may be discussed here which forms a

---

[1] See below, p. 105.

[2] See above, p. 32.

[3] Possibly too 1498 τίνα προσῳδόν (among regular dactyls), though this might be taken as a genuine trochaic metron used as a gambit to dactyls. The effect in delivery would be the same in either case.

link between anapaests and dactyls without strictly belonging to either category. Fraenkel (*loc. cit.*), who traces their origin from Stesichorus, calls these 'steigende Daktylen'; I prefer the name dactylo-anapaests. They start in rising movement ∪∪ – and end in falling – ∪∪;[1] they do not move κατὰ μέτρον but merely in a continuous single-long double-short series, wherein the longs may not resolve. They are found in dactylic, anapaestic, or 'dactylo-epitrite' contexts; so *P.V.* 559

ἰότατι γάμων ὅτε τὰν ὁμοπάτριον ἔδνοις,

which is the length of a headless hexameter. A shorter length appears in a context of mixed ἀπολελυμένα *I.T.* 886 θανάτῳ πελάσεις ἄρα βάρβαρα φῦλα and 895 τίς ἂν οὖν τάδ' ἂν ἦ θεὸς ἦ βροτὸς ἦ τί, and the paroemiac with opening ∪∪ is itself in effect a colon of this type, one size smaller still. Final resolution usually means that the next colon opens dactylic, as *P.V.* 166–7

πρὶν ἂν ἦ κορέσῃ κέαρ ἦ παλάμᾳ τινὶ
τὰν δυσάλωτον ἕλῃ τις ἀρχάν,

where the 'alcaic decasyllable' clausula picks up as if in a πνῖγος. Eur. *H.F.* 1055, however,

ἦ δέσμ' ἀνεγειρόμενος χαλάσας ἀπολεῖ πόλιν,

is continued in dochmiacs, and *Hipp.* 1374, if the text is sound,[2]

[1] I do not include here, as Fraenkel does, lines which end blunt ∪ ∪ –; the much vexed κύκλοι or κύκλιοι of Dion. Hal. (*Comp. Verb.* 17), to which the 'rhythmicians' attributed a rhythm ἀντίστροφος to the dactylic, I should regard as melic anapaests which have no regular metron-diaeresis and are therefore 'distinct from anapaests' of the recognized systematic type. But such anapaests admittedly do appear, together with dactylo-anapaests, in 'dactylo-epitrite' contexts, and the issue is more one of terminology than of a real difference of opinion.

[2] The emendations of Wilamowitz and Markland, commonly adopted, as was pointed out (see above, p. 52, n. 3) only substitute another anomaly. The position of μ' in *codd.* is certainly more natural, and the simple verb ὄλλυτε gives a better rhythm from diaeresis than προσαπόλλυτ' ἀπόλλυτε τὸν δυσδαίμονά μ'. In *codd.*, of course, the metre here breaks away from anapaestic, as presently again l. 1379.

strikingly presents an uncompromising hiatus after the resolved close:

προσαπόλλυτέ μ' ὄλλυτε τὸν δυσδαίμονα·
ἀμφιτόμου λόγχας ἔραμαι.

Dactylo-anapaests are no more than an occasional phenomenon in the drama, though we shall meet a kindred rhythm among cola of the dactylo-epitrite group.

V

IAMBIC, TROCHAIC AND IAMBO-TROCHAIC

Fundamental unity of iambo-trochaic movement underlying iambic and trochaic—Lyric syncopation.

Iambic: simplest forms of unsyncopated iambic lyric found in comedy, in dimeter series divided into periods by catalexis—Similarity to stichic leads to question of delivery—Comic syncopation limited and simple— Comic iambics in mixed metres and dicola—Iambics in Aeschylus: syncopation and clausulae—Iambics in Sophocles—Iambics in Euripides— Delivery of iambic trimeters in lyric.

Trochaic: dimeter series in comedy—Association with cretic-paeonic: various comic licences—Comparative rarity in tragedy—Special trochaic type in four plays of Euripides.

Iambo-trochaic: mixture of iambics and trochaics characteristic of tragedy—Ambiguous cola.

Just as in double-short movement there proved to be grounds for distinguishing dactyls, anapaests and an intermediate class of dactylo-anapaests, so in single-short there are the polar species, iambic and trochaic, and a third kind which moves ambiguously between the two. These iambo-trochaics, however, are a much larger and more important class than dactylo-anapaests, and the border-lines on either side are more fluctuating and difficult to draw. The extremes of plain iambic and trochaic movement are perfectly distinct, and the Greeks explicitly recognized a difference in character between the two. Doubtless when Aristotle[1] speaks of the iambic as μάλιστα λεκτικὸν τῶν μέτρων, and the trochaic as κορδακικώτερος because τροχερός, he was influenced partly by the actual use of the two metres, partly by the apparent etymology of the name τροχαῖος;[2] it is not always easy to determine in such judgements which was primary, the inherent appropriateness of the metre to the style or the long *de facto* association of style and metre. Perhaps, however,

---

[1] *Poet.* 1449a24, *Rhet.* III, 8. 4.

[2] For which χορεῖος was used as a significant alternative.

it is not too fanciful to assume a real tendency in the delivery of
'falling' metre to move a shade more quickly off an initial long on
to a following short than in the corresponding places when the line
starts in rising movement; and in a metre which has a long early
history as recitative this slight empirical shortening of the long
quantities may have been decisive for its later use and accepted
tempo. (This would account also for the faintly hurried quantity
of dactylic longs mentioned by Dionysius.) But even in the straightforward stichic species of iambic and trochaic there is no such
fundamental difference of origin and modification as that which
separates dactyls and anapaests, and here, if anywhere, the ancient
commentators were justified in their idea of an infinite series in
ἐπιπλοκή...∪ – × – ∪ – × – ∪...as a sort of matrix from
which you could hack out iambic or trochaic segments according to
whether you began with *anceps* or following long and ended with
anceps or preceding long. The iambic is the rising, blunt metron, the
trochaic the falling and pendant; but it is significant that the earliest
and commonest trochaic length of which we know anything is a
'tetrameter *catalectic*', which begins falling and ends blunt—that is,
there is here already some iambo-trochaic character. In fact the
unsyncopated trochaic cannot reach a pause without a blunt end,
since even in lyric, with the rarest exceptions, its clausulae must be
blunt. Its case is the precise opposite of the anapaest, which must
always run to a pendant final close. The lekythion corresponds in
function and frequency to the paroemiac; the one – ∪ – × – ∪ – is
as it were a form of closed, blunt ἐπιπλοκή in single-short, the other
∪∪ – ∪∪ – ∪ ∪ – – of open, pendant ἐπιπλοκή in double-short.
Open, pendant ἐπιπλοκή in single-short produces the third line of the
alcaic stanza × – ∪ – × – ∪ – × ; this iambo-trochaic enneasyllable,
though not common in drama, occurs *Trach.* 102 εἴπ' ὦ κρατιστεύων
κατ' ὄμμα as a clausula (by 'overrun') to iambic dimeters.[1] The

---

[1] The notion of a segment of iambo-trochaic matrix emerges clearly in
this enneasyllable and pentasyllable as more appropriate than that of
construction κατὰ μέτρον. The lekythion *can* of course always be
analysed as dimeter, whether catalectic trochaic or syncopated iambic;
but in dactylo-epitrites, at least, the relation of this colon to other types

shorter colarion of similar formation × – ∪ – × is very common, but usually as an element in a compound, especially in dactylo-epitrites. It appears independently, Soph. *El.* 136, and, resolved to ⊻ ⌢ ∪ – –, Eur. *El.* 457.

It is important to grasp this fundamental unity of iambo-trochaic movement which underlies the unsyncopated iambic and trochaic, not only because it is the most rational explanation of the 'epitrite' element in the large class of compounds called dactylo-epitrite and enables us to dispense with awkward concepts such as 'hyper-catalectic' metra, but also because even where the στίχοι and cola can be labelled unequivocally one thing or the other they are modified internally, some more, some less, by the introduction of the opposite factor. This applies most to the stichic metres, where the incidence of word-end is of paramount importance, and the more and the less modified are, respectively, the στίχοι of the tragedians and iambographers and those of the comedians. In general, the effect of the regulation of word-end in the former is to prevent the line from splitting up into separately audible metra; thus the lines

καὶ δὸς κύσαι | καὖθις κύσον | καί μοι φράσον

and

καὶ Πλαταιᾶς | εὐθὺς εἶναι | κἀντὶ δούλων | δεσπότας

have an unchecked iambic or trochaic movement which would be improper in tragedy. The tragic line must divide (by word-end) into two segments with contrasted close, pendant and blunt respectively. As the heavier *anceps* ∪ – ⤫ | is more noticeable than the lighter ∪ – ∪ |, care must be taken that the former never occurs elsewhere than at the cardinal mid-line point (the 'penthemimeral caesura' of the iambic trimeter and the 'middle diaeresis' of the trochaic tetrameter); hence 'Porson's Canon' and, in the trochaic tetrameter, the rule against starting – ∪ – ⤫ |. Thus both iambic and trochaic στίχοι in their severer, tragic forms contain the *same* rhythmic antiphony, mid-verse pendant—end blunt; and the

of epitrite is best seen by thinking of it too as such a segment, cf. below, pp. 184 ff. For the use of iambo-trochaic in early lyric poets, especially Alcman, cf. 'Stichos and Stanza', *C.Q.* 56, 1963, 46.

distinctness of the two movements is thereby reduced.[1] Naturally, there remains the difference of character effected by their rising or falling start and by the inequality and variation in length of the two segments of the iambic trimeter as against the regularity of the trochaic break, dimeter+dimeter catalectic. It should be noted, however, that this difference is not reflected in subject matter in Archilochus or early tragedy; it is not till the later plays that trochaic dialogue is an indication of accelerated pace and excitement.

Turning to lyric metres, we find the ambiguity of iambic and trochaic movement further complicated by the practice of syncopation, that is, the omission of the *anceps* or the short, giving iambic metra of the form ∧ – ∪ – (cretic) or ∪ – ∧ – (bacchiac), and as trochaic metra – ∪ – ∧ or – ∧ – ∪ (palimbacchiac). Occasionally the elimination of both *anceps* and short leaves an apparent spondee – –. The palimbacchiac, a forward-leaning rhythm, is never clausular, though it is occasionally found at the end of a colon when paired – – ∪ | – – ∪ or following a cretic ∪͜∪ ∪ – | – – ∪. The bacchiac appears most often as the last metron of a colon with an effect of catalexis; it may, however, open a colon ∪ – – | ∪ – ∪ – or ∪ – – | – ∪ –, or again be paired ∪ – – | ∪ – –. It is practically never found succeeding an iambic metron of the form – ∪ – or × – ∪ – except with following Pause;[2] once it has been hung on to such a metron the minor period closes. Thus such analyses as that of Wilamowitz (*G.V.* p. 525) at *O.C.* 1725 ∼ 1739

– ∪ ∪ ∪͞∪ | ∪ – – | ͞∪͞∪ ∪ – | ∪ – ∪ –
ἵμερος ἔχει μέ τις τὰν χθόνιον ἑστίαν ἰδεῖν,
καὶ πάρος ἀπεφύγετον τὰ σφῶν τὸ μὴ πίτνειν κακῶς,

making an 'iambic tetrameter', are illegitimate; the 'tetrameters'

---

[1] I have argued in *C.Q.* 56, 1963, 46 for the probable priority of the tetrameter, and the subsequent development of the trimeter from it.
[2] The single exception I have been able to find is Ar. *Thesm.* 1034-5, a quotation, possibly parodied, from the *Andromeda*:

γαμηλίῳ μὲν οὐ ξὺν
παιῶνι δεσμίῳ δέ

where, of course, no pause is possible after the preposition. The pairing of the twin cola legitimizes the unusual effect.

would fall apart into the impossible sequence dim. cat., dim., each time with an article in catalexis. There should be colon-division after τις, giving a dochmiac[1]+full iambic dimeter.

Where it is the short syllable that is suppressed, the *anceps* with rare exceptions takes the short form, lest the nature of the movement be obscured by strings of long syllables. The apparent 'molossus' is, however, permitted as an opening metron in place of a bacchiac: σῶν ὦ δυστυχεστάτα $\underset{\times}{}$ − − | ∪ − ∪ −.

It has been pointed out already[2] how often syncopation, in the absence of any knowledge of the musical accompaniment, forces us to shelve questions of iambic and trochaic labelling. A further problem arises from the existence of cretic-paeonic measure, where each metron, according to the ancient metricians, contains five χρόνοι; how do we know when a cretic is a 'true' cretic and when it is a syncopated iambic or trochaic metron (which should contain six χρόνοι), and is there such a thing as a 'true' bacchiac? Is syncopation always shown by a pause equivalent to one χρόνος or by protraction of a long syllable − = ∪ ∪ to a triseme ⌐ = ∪ ∪ ∪, and in the latter case which long was protracted, ⌐ ∪ − or − ∪ ⌐, ∪ ⌐ − or ∪ − ⌐? These questions are taken up again in the next chapter; here, while admitting the speculative and somewhat arbitrary nature of the whole argument, I would merely put forward certain suggestions which seem to me probable: (1) That, while there is no instance of a long syllable in antistrophe corresponding to more than two shorts (no ⌣⌣⌣), there are notable differences in the practice of resolution in cretic-paeonic and in syncopated iambic or trochaic, and therefore there was a real difference, however indicated, in the tempo of the metra in these two classes of movement. In a 'true' cretic series the final long readily resolves, and − ∪ ∪ ∪ − ∪ − may correspond to − ∪ − − ∪ −. But in syncopated iambic or trochaic cola there is no instance where resolution unmistakably precedes syncopation:[3] thus, for instance, the colon τέκνον ἄχος ἐφάνη βροτῶν can be analysed ∧ ⌒ ∪ ⌒ | ∪ − ∪ − if it is iambic and ⌒ ∪ ⌒ ∪ | − ∪ − ∧ if it

[1] See below, p. 116.   [2] Ch. II, pp. 19 ff.
[3] *Lys.* 1279, if the text is sound, is an exceptional case where the colon falls into two separate metra with a pause between, see below, p. 90.

is trochaic; and such a colon as τόδ' ἄχος ἐφάνη βροτῶν or τῶνδε δ' ἐφάνη βροτῶν is never found in iambic or trochaic metre. The inference would seem to be that cretic syncopation was indicated in some audible way, and that it would cease to be audible if a resolution preceded the suppressed syllable. (2) That, similarly, the bacchiac was never allowed to resolve into ∪ ⌣⌣ – (there is no instance in tragedy where this sequence of syllables cannot be taken as a resolved cretic ⌣⌣ ∪ –). It may be doubted, however, whether the bacchiac as a *final* metron in the close of an iambic period was distinguished from other pendant closes by a special form of protraction. The penultimate long of a pendant close is always inviolable, for obvious reasons: in a rhythm based on quantity and not on ictus the essential character of the close would disappear if it were broken up into ∪ ⌣⌣ ⌴. Resolution of the second long in a bacchiac metron (except of course at the close of a period) was permissible and not infrequent, as in Eur. *Tro.* 564, where in the middle of a series of cola ∪ – – ∪ – ∪ – occurs καράτομος ἐρημία ∪ – ⌣⌣ | ∪ – ∪ –.[1] Soph. *Tr.* 218 shows the catalectic form of this colon: ἰδού μ' ἀναταράσσει ∪ – ⌣⌣ | ∪ – –.[2] (3) That protraction or some modification of the delivery could distinguish a trochaic dimeter – – ∪ | – ∪ – ⌴ from an iambic catalectic – – ∪ – | ∪ – ⌒, since this would enable us to introduce more metrical coherence and intelligibility into some choruses of Euripides (see below, p. 92). It is significant that in every such instance the first syllable is long; had the colon been iambic the *anceps* might have been expected to take the short form occasionally.

[1] This argues against Koster's view that the *invariable* (as distinct from the usual) form of bacchiac protraction was ∪ – ⌊—.

[2] In view of Soph.'s fondness for repeating unusual metrical effects in the same stanza, l. 205 is quite possibly another instance:

ἀνολολυξάτω δόμος   ⌣⌣ ∪ – | ∪ – ⌣⌣
ἐφεστίοις ἀλαλαγαῖς.   ∪ – ∪ – | ⌣⌣ ∪ –.

The transposition of *Sept.* 964 and 965 (Hartung and Wilamowitz) is a bad one. The two resolved bacchiacs ἴτω γόος ἴτω δάκρυ ∪ – ⌣⌣ | ∪ – ⌣⌣ should be left in the penultimate position before the unresolved pair πρόκεισαι κατακτάς, and not treated as iambic metra out of synaphea ∪ – ∪ ⌣ | ∪ – ∪ ⌣; cf. the echo 994 ἰὼ πόνος ἰὼ κακά.

Finally, a colon ending in a full trochaic metron can never be
followed by an initial full iambic or bacchiac metron: in other words,
iambic and trochaic movement are so far a unity that the final *anceps*
of a trochaic is never contiguous with the initial *anceps* of an iambic,
nor can Pause (period-close) be postulated in such a position. Thus,
for example, the colometry given by Wilamowitz (*G.V.* p. 609) for
Soph. *Tr.* 894–5 ἃ νέορτος ἅδε νύμφα | δόμοισι τοῖσδ' 'Ερινύν
– ∪ – ∪ – ∪ – x̄ | x̆ – ∪ – ∪ – – is inadmissible: the first colon
must begin, as in Pearson's text, at νέορτος so as to leave a syncopated second metron -δε νύμφα ∪ – –. So long as there is no syncopation or catalexis, iambo-trochaic movement must proceed in a
single series or πνῖγος irrespective of colon-end.[1]

IAMBIC

The simplest and most uniform systems of unsyncopated iambics are
to be found in comedy. The commonest phrase-unit is the dimeter,
and there are stanzas built up solely of these, divided into periods
by catalexis. The relation of this elementary type of lyric to stichic

---

[1] G. Zuntz, *Inquiry into the transmission of the plays of Euripides*, pp. 65–6,
seems to me to have essentially solved the problem at E. *Supp.* 76–7 ∼
84–5; in the strophe LP is correct (ὄνυχι λευκὸν αἱματοῦτε χρῶτα φόνιον,
'scratch the white cheek bloody'), and Triclinius both misunderstood
the grammar and created a *versus-non* by adding τε (with the meaningless ὄνυχα 76), which was meant to accommodate the metre to the antistrophe including ἒ ἔ. Zuntz makes a trochaic dimeter in ant. too by
simply transposing to πάθος πέφυκε—but with ἒ ἔ (in 85 only) *extra
metrum*. He thus assumes Pause between 77–8 ∼ 85–6. Here I cannot
follow him, because I know of no other iambo-trochaic context where
(as at 77 here) – ∪ – x is followed, even with rhetorical break, by
x – ∪ –. The full trochaic metron, with no preceding syncopation,
before Pause is in any case extremely rare. I would supply ἒ ἔ (scanned,
and possibly spelt, as αἰαῖ, cf. *Hel.* 166) in 77 too; it is rare to have such
interjections with nothing corresponding: thus we get a syncopated
troch. trim. in str. and ant.

77 αἱματοῦτε χρῶτα φόνιον· αἰαῖ – ∪ – ∪ – ∪ ∪̆∪̆ ∪ – – ||
85 ἐς γόους πάθος πέφυκεν· αἰαῖ

after which the clausula, ia. sync. trim., follows as a coda.

metre is easily seen: the tetrameter catalectic in which whole scenes of dialogue are written is itself like a primitive form of stanza— dim.+dim. cat.; the next stage is to wind up such a scene with a πνῖγος of full dimeters closing in a single catalexis. Exactly the same form is found in anapaestic and trochaic scenes, and an iambic monometer occasionally appears, like an anapaestic, in the penultimate place, as *Nub.* 1450. *Plut.* 290ff. after a tetrameter dialogue continues with a vulgar little song composed of three tetrams. (i.e. dim.+dim. cat.) and three dims.+dim. cat. *Ran.* 386ff. has a stanza of four dims.+dim. cat., *Ach.* 1008ff. is an ἀμοιβαῖον of Dicaeopolis and Chorus in the form two dims.+dim. cat., dim.+dim. cat. *bis*, two dims.+dim. cat. Such pure dimeter-stanzas, however, are less common in iambic than in trochaic measure; it is more usual to have an admixture of trimeters, full or catalectic, or an occasional monometer thrown in. *Ran.* 420ff. is a string of eight little stanzas formed of two dims. cat. (pendant)+trim. acat. as a blunt clausula:

> βούλεσθε δῆτα κοινῇ
> σκώψωμεν Ἀρχέδημον ;
> ὃς ἑπτέτης ὢν οὐκ ἔφυσε φράτερας.

This song represents the old rustic ἰαμβισμός or γεφυρισμός, the 'lampooning at the bridge', which was probably the most primitive form of the popular metre. It is preceded by a κλητικὸς ὕμνος to Iacchus in three stanzas of slightly less simple pattern:

Ἴακχε πολυτίμητε, μέλος ἑορτῆς	trim. cat.
ἥδιστον εὑρών, δεῦρο συνακολούθει	trim. cat.
πρὸς τὴν θεόν,	monom.
καὶ δεῖξον ὡς ἄνευ πόνου	dim.
πολλὴν ὁδὸν περαίνεις.	dim. cat.
Ἴακχε φιλοχορευτὰ συμπρόπεμπέ με.	trim. (refrain)

The resolutions are slightly varied in responsion. The phallic song intoned by Dicaeopolis, *Ach.* 263ff., is again obviously a genuine rural type:

> Φαλῆς ἑταῖρε Βακχίου
> ξύγκωμε νυκτοπεριπλάνη-
> -τε μοιχὲ παιδεραστά,

ἕκτῳ σ' ἔτει προσεῖπον ἐς
τὸν δῆμον ἐλθὼν ἄσμενος,
σπονδὰς ποιησάμενος ἐμαυ-
-τῷ, πραγμάτων τε καὶ μαχῶν
καὶ Λαμάχων ἀπαλλαγείς.
πολλῷ γάρ ἐσθ' ἥδιον, ὦ Φαλῆς Φαλῆς,
κλέπτουσαν εὑρόνθ' ὡρικὴν ὑληφόρον
τὴν Στρυμοδώρου Θρᾷτταν ἐκ τοῦ Φελλέως
μέσην λαβόντ' ἄραντα καταβαλόντα καταγιγαρτίσ'
ὦ Φαλῆς Φαλῆς.
ἐὰν μεθ' ἡμῶν ξυμπίῃς, ἐκ κραιπάλης
ἕωθεν εἰρήνης ῥοφήσει τρύβλιον·
ἡ δ' ἀσπὶς ἐν τῷ φεψάλῳ κρεμήσεται.

Two dims.+dim. cat. give the invocative address in a clearly marked period; then follows a πνῖγος of five dims. The second part has two groups of three trims. separated by a frisky pentameter; note the penultimate *brevis in longo* leaving the rhetorical contrast of the last line distinct.

It is impossible to be certain what modifications of delivery were made in these simple types of lyric as compared with the similar dialogue-metres among which they appear. We do not even know when, and in what type of composition, the iambic trimeter was first treated differently from other στίχοι and spoken without musical accompaniment. It is difficult to believe that Archilochus made any distinction of the kind between his iambic trimeters and trochaic tetrameters, whether they were both accompanied or both unaccompanied, and there are no *a priori* grounds for imagining a difference between them in Aeschylus at any rate among the tragedians, or in the comedies of Epicharmus. Probably both alike were in early drama spoken unaccompanied, though in a more rhythmically formal style of elocution than any to which we are accustomed on the stage. But the comic trimeter in Aristophanes and later comedians stands out so sharply from all other types of stichic dialogue by its metrical licence that it is natural to assume a radical distinction here; probably this alone in Attic comedy was freely spoken as we speak verse-dialogue, while all others, iambic, trochaic or anapaestic, were delivered with much greater regularity.

Of the licences of the comic trimeter, the most startling, the substitution of double-short for single-short, occasionally spreads to other iambic στίχοι, cf. *Ran.* 937

οὐχ ἱππαλεκτρυόνας μὰ Δί᾽ οὐδὲ τραγελάφους ἅπερ σύ,

where the second metron has the form ◡ ◡ – ◡ ◡ –. The resolution of *anceps* into two shorts is found occasionally at the opening of other cola, as for instance in the tragic trimeter, but the responsion of single-short to double-short in mid-verse appears to flout a fundamental principle of Greek metric. The account commonly given of this by modern scholars is that popular and freer forms of versification are indifferent to the number of short syllables—one or two—which fall between two longs, rather like

Hére we go roúnd the múlberry búsh.

It is natural that the phenomenon should present itself in this way to an ear trained to stress-rhythm, but in Greek the anomalous 'Doppelsenkung' is a phenomenon of comic speech or near-speech, not of song or of high poetry. The rare examples in sung lyric might more easily be regarded as yet another case where syllable-counting is allowed to prevail against the strict quantitative principle, so that the anapaest would be as it were a misused tribrach

–-τρυόνας μὰ Δι᾽ οὐ- above would be a modification of -τρυονα μα Δια. This would at least mean that the anomaly was brought into line with others found in comic metres, such as the equation of paeons to resolved anapaests – ◡ ◡ ◡ ≡ ◡ ◡ ◡ ◡ or – ◡ – ≡ ◡ ◡ –, and of trochaic to paeonic metra – ◡ – ◡ ≡ – ◡ ◡ ◡.[1] Whatever the

[1] Cf. above, p. 65. An interesting parallel in sung iambics occurs, *Lys.* 262–3 ~ 277–8, in a stanza of iambic dimeters with ithyphallic clausula. The strophe has regular tribrachic resolution:

κατὰ μὲν ἅγιον ἔχειν βρέτας   ◡◠ ◡◠ | ◡ – ◡ –
κατὰ δ᾽ ἀκρόπολιν ἐμὰν λαβεῖν

while the antistrophe gives

ᾤχετο θὤπλα παραδοὺς ἐμοὶ   x̄◠ x̄◠ | ◡ – ◡ –
σμικρὸν ἔχων πάνυ τριβώνιον.

The genuineness of the phenomenon is defended by its repetition in consecutive lines. Here the syllable-counting equation has produced x̄◠ for ◡◠, an inversion of the usual ◡ ◡ –. (Eur. *Hipp.* 1108 ἄλλα explanation, it is clear that in sung iambics syllable-counting is not a regularly admitted principle but merely a rare licence as in other metres, and almost all these exceptions occur precisely in passages where the relation to stichic metres is closest, as *Ran.* 980ff., *Ach.* 1040, *Nub.* 1450—all in contexts which might be described as half stichic. This is a slight piece of evidence that the delivery of such passages may have approximated to that of the surrounding recitative-dialogue, though perhaps with an accompaniment of dancing or skipping about. Certainly the trimeters of the Phales-song are iambics of the same type as its dimeters and show none of the irregularities of spoken trimeters.[1]

Syncopation in comic iambics is confined to simple and obvious patterns. Commonest is the insertion of lekythia among full dimeters, or the use of ithyphallics instead of catalectic dimeters as final clausulae. The *Birds* ends with a series of dicola formed of dim.+lek.:

> ἔπεσθε νῦν γάμοισιν ὦ
> φῦλα πάντα συννόμων,

and the similar dicolon dim.+ithyph.

> ἐγὼ δὲ σὺν ταῖσιν κόραις | εἶμι καὶ γυναιξίν

is even used κατὰ στίχον in dialogue. Strepsiades' little ἐγκώμιον (*Nub.* 1206–12) has a less regular but easily perceptible pattern after an ionic opening colon:

᾽μάκαρ ὦ Στρεψίαδες,	∪∪−−∣∪∪⌣‖
αὐτός τ᾽ ἔφυς ὡς σοφὸς	x̱−∪−∣−∪−
χοῖον τὸν υἱὸν τρέφεις᾽	x̱−∪−∣−∪−
φήσουσι δή μ᾽ οἱ φίλοι	x̱−∪−∣−∪−
χοἰ δημόται	x̱−∪−
ζηλοῦντες ἡνίκ᾽ ἂν σὺ νι-	x̱−∪−∣∪−∪−
-κᾷς λέγων τὰς δίκας,	−∪−∣−∪−
ἀλλ᾽ εἰσάγων σὲ βούλομαι	x̱−∪−∣∪−∪−
πρῶτον ἐστιᾶσαι.	−∪−∣∪−−

γὰρ ἄλλοθεν ἀμείβεται − ∪ ∪ − ∪ ∪ ∣ ∪ − ∪ − is shown by the context to be dact.+ia.—possibly the dact. dim. should be a separate colon— and cannot be regarded as parallel.)

[1] Cf., however, *Vesp.* 886 προλελεγμένων: evidently these first two trimeters were close to spoken tempo, though in the strophe there is no rhetorical pause at 869 before the following lyric cola.

The iambic exchange between the Hoopoe and the Chorus beginning ἰὼ ἔποψ σέ τοι καλῶ (*Av.* 406–26) has a cretic patch in the middle, and unlike other comic lyrics keeps to the short *anceps* throughout (409 ξένω Dindorf), obviously to give a light hopping rhythm. *Thesm.* 352–4 (not to be emended) twice combines bacchiac syncopation with resolution:[1]

ξυνευχόμεθα τέλεα μὲν	∪ –⌒ | ∪⌒ ∪ –
πόλει τέλεα δὲ δήμῳ	∪ – ∪⌒ | ∪ – –
τάδ' εὔγματα γενέσθαι,	∪ –⌒ | ∪ – –

cf. a similar trimeter *Ach.* 1196

Δικαιόπολις εἴ μ' ἴδοι τετρωμένον.	∪ –⌒ | ∪ – ∪ – | ∪ – ∪ –

The use of iambics in polymetric mixture in comedy is less common than in tragedy (the end of the *Acharnians*, 1190ff., is a rollicking parody of such mixture in a θρῆνος), and calls for no special comment, except for a curious combination of iambic with short choriambic cola of the form × – ∪ ∪ – ∪ – (telesillean), or, more commonly, the catalectic form of this × – ∪ ∪ – –, called 'reizianum' after Hermann's teacher Reiz who discovered this colon in Latin verse. The final song of the Mystic procession, *Ran.* 449–59, has strophe and antistrophe each of two periods:

χωρῶμεν ἐς πολυρρόδους	i. dim.
λειμῶνας ἀνθεμώδεις, ||	i. dim. cat.
τὸν ἡμέτερον τρόπον	tel.
τὸν καλλιχορώτατον	tel.
παίζοντες, ὃν ὄλβιοι	tel.
Μοῖραι ξυνάγουσιν.	reiz.

Here the association of the two factors is external, as it were, but the reizianum is sometimes found attached as a pendant close to a blunt length of iambic: so *Ach.* 836ff.

εὐδαιμονεῖ γ' ἄνθρωπος. οὐκ	i. dim.
ἤκουσας οἷ προβαίνει ||	i. dim. cat.
τὸ πρᾶγμα τοῦ βουλεύματος;	i. dim.
καρπώσεται γὰρ ἀνήρ ||	i. dim. cat.
ἐν τἀγορᾷ καθήμενος·	i. dim.

[1] Cf. pp. 73–4.

κἂν εἰσίη τις Κτησίας   i. dim.
ἢ συκοφάντης ἄλλος, οἱ-   i. dim.
-μώζων καθεδεῖται.   reiz.

The final period here, three dims.+reiz., is obviously analogous to the tel.-reiz. period of the stanza quoted above, but the clausula actually forms a synartete dicolon with the last dimeter. This dicolon is called *versus reizianus*, since it was Reiz who noticed its frequent appearance in Plautus. It is again a final clausula *Pax* 954, and a similar dicolon is formed of trimeter+reiz., *Nub.* 1303–4

οἷον τὸ πραγμάτων ἐρᾶν φλαύρων· ὁ γὰρ
γέρων ὅδ' ἐρασθείς,

and thrice repeated 1345–50. The formation is more characteristic of comedy than of tragedy, but Soph. *Aj.* 408 is a *versus reizianus*:

πᾶς δὲ στρατὸς δίπαλτος ἂν
με χειρὶ φονεύοι.

From the catchy, sometimes vulgar, rhythms of comedy to the iambics of tragedy is indeed a long step, yet the greatest master of iambic measure, Aeschylus, builds up his grave stanzas on metrically simple lines, with a technique at its most characteristic in the *Agamemnon*. They often have no, or very little, admixture of other metres, and the preponderance of the light *anceps* is striking; there are many stanzas which keep the short form throughout; others contain merely an occasional lengthening of the initial syllable of a colon. Syncopation is very frequent, and usually so distributed as to avoid too obvious a pattern; dimeters and trimeters are unevenly interspaced and grouped unevenly (by word-overlap, rhetorical pause and the like) into larger periods. Within the cola, word-end is carefully studied so as to produce new syllable-groups cutting across the metra:

ἐπεὶ δ' ἀνάγκας ⋮ ἔδυ λέπαδνον.

The close correspondence of word-end from strophe to antistrophe often underlines these inner groupings: so *Ag.* 220ff.

∪ – ∪   ⌒∪ –   ∪ –
ἄναγνον   ἀνίερον   τόθεν
ἔθεντο   φιλόμαχοι βραβῆς.

6

⏑ – ⏑ – –   ⏑ –   ⏑ – –
τὸ παντότολμον φρονεῖν μετέγνω.
φράσεν δ' ἀόзοις πατὴρ μετ' εὐχὰν

⏑ –   ⏑ – – –   ⏑ –   ⏑ – –
βροτοὺς θρασύνει γὰρ αἰσχρόμητις
δίκαν χιμαίρας ὕπερθε βωμοῦ

⏑ – ⏑   ⏖ ⏑ –   – ⏑ – –
τάλαινα παρακοπὰ πρωτοπήμων
πέπλοισι περιπετῆ παντὶ θυμῷ

Resolution[1] is on the whole sparingly used, mostly in exact responsion, and where a larger patch occurs the correspondence of word-groups is particularly noticeable, as in *Supp.* 112–13 ~ 123–4:

⏑ – ⏑   ⏖ ⏑   ⏖ ⏑   ⏖ ⏑ – ⏑ –
τοιαῦτα πάθεα μέλεα θρεομένα λέγω
θεοῖς δ' ἐναγέα τέλεα πελομένων καλῶς

⏑ ⏖   ⏑ ⏖   ⏑   ⏖ ⏑ –
λιγέα βαρέα δακρυοπετῆ
ἐπίδρομ' ὁπόθι θάνατος ἐπῇ.

The cola used are exclusively dimeters and trimeters, and where word-overlap occurs there is often little to choose between various possible groupings on the printed page. The extraordinary flexibility of this metre in Aeschylus's hands, its stateliness and variety are nowhere better seen than in the great κομμός of the *Choephoroe*. Consider, for instance, 423 ff.:

ἔκοψα κομμὸν ⋮ Ἄριον ἔν τε Κισσίας
νόμοις ἰηλεμιστρίας.
ἀπρικτόπληκτα ⋮ πολυπάλακτα δ' ἦν ἰδεῖν
ἐπασσυτεροτριβῆ ⋮ τὰ χερὸς ὀρέγματα,
ἄνωθεν ἀνέκαθεν, ⋮ κτύπῳ δ' ἐπερρόθει
κροτητὸν ἀμὸν ⋮ καὶ πανάθλιον κάρα.

Here, with the one dimeter, are simply five unsyncopated acatalectic trimeters, probably each an independent minor period. Shape is given to the stanza by the pairing 423 = 425, 426 = 427 (a wholly

---

[1] *Pers.* 256 appears to contain a proceleusmatic ἄνι' ἄνια κακά ⏖ ⏖ ⏑ ⏖ ~ ἢ μακροβίοτος ⏓ ⏖ ⏑ ⏖. This is unparalleled in lyric iambics.

unstichic rhythm), and a return in the clausula to the normal stichic
type. 434 ff.

τὸ πᾶν ἀτίμως ἔλεξας, οἴμοι.	∪ – ∪ – | – ∪ – | ∪ – –
πατρὸς δ᾽ ἀτίμωσιν ἄρα τείσει	∪ – ∪ – | – ∪ – | ∪ – –
ἕκατι μὲν δαιμόνων	∪ – ∪ – | – ∪ –
ἕκατι δ᾽ ἁμᾶν χερῶν.	∪ – ∪ – | – ∪ –
ἔπειτ᾽ ἐγὼ νοσφίσας ὀλοίμαν	∪ – ∪ – | – ∪ – | ∪ – –

gives a straightforward pattern *aabba* (like a limerick), with syncopation at the same place in each line. Aeschylus at the height of
tragedy ventures nearer the simplicity of popular song measure than
either of his successors. The function of the pattern here in under-
lining the sense is clear enough, in the echoes ἀτίμως-ἀτίμωσιν and
the repeated ἕκατι, and the rhetorical separation of the last line.

Iambic rhythm supplies its own clausulae in the catalectic dimeter
(or the ithyphallic) and trimeter, variously syncopated, e.g.

φάσμα δόξει δόμων ἀνάσσειν.

Aeschylus prefers sometimes, however, to emphasize a close by
choriambic anaclasis: in place of ∪ – ∪ – ∪ – – he turns round the
first metron – ∪ ∪ – ∪ – –, giving the choriambic colon often
called 'aristophanean'. So *Ag.* 380 εὖ πραπίδων λαχόντι at the end
of a long iambic passage, forming a transition to the four-lined
choriambic ephymnion which follows. 447 similarly uses the
choriambic enneasyllable:

ἀλλοτρίας διαὶ γυναικός.   – ∪ ∪ – ∪ – ∪ – –

He has one clausular practice which is notably at variance with the
younger poets' technique: frequent use of the lekythion as a final
colon. Blunt clausulae in general are much less common than
pendant in Greek lyric (our own sense of rhythm accepts this pre-
ference), and elsewhere the lekythion is chiefly so used where the
prevailing rhythm is trochaic, i.e. it appears as a simple catalectic
close: so Eur. *Phoen.* 638 ff., and many comic choruses. But in
Sept. 832 ff., though the stanza opens trochaic, it continues in blunt
iambic and ends

νεκροὺς κλύουσα δυσμόρως
θανόντας· ἦ δύσορνις ἄ-
-δε ξυναυλία δορός.

More often, however, a penultimate phrase in some other metre (e.g. dactylic, *Ag.* 165 dact. pent., *Cho.* 30 the same contracted) intervenes and gives the final lekythion a greater contrast.

In Sophocles' lyrics the iambic plays a much smaller part. The only instance of a uniformly iambic stanza is the epode *Tr.* 132–40 (5 dim.+3 trim.); the rest of his iambics form periods, or enter into mixed compounds, in polymetric odes. The lyrics of *Ant.* show, on the whole, most resemblance to the Aeschylean technique, cf. 357–64 (especially the responsion 360 ~ 370

παντόπορος· ἄπορος ἐπ' οὐδὲν ἔρχεται   – ∪ ⌣⌣ | ∪ ⌣⌣ ∪ – ∪ – ∪ –
ὑψίπολις· ἄπολις ὅτῳ τὸ μὴ καλόν),

586–92, 847–56 with its four-line ephymnion. In these the light *anceps* is almost carried through, but more frequently Sophocles' iambics have a heavier movement like that of epitrites:[1]

εἰ μὴ τὸ κέρδος κερδανεῖ δικαίως
καὶ τῶν ἀσέπτων ἔρξεται,
ἢ τῶν ἀθίκτων ἕξεται ματάζων. (*O.T.* 889ff.)

His fondness for letting iambics follow dactylic cola ending – ∪ ∪ has already been noticed,[2] and in such contexts an initial metron ⊽ ⌣⌣ ∪ – in the iambic cola sometimes plays on this curiously twisted rhythm, cf. *El.* 207–12:

αἳ τὸν ἐμὸν εἷλον βίον   ⊼ ⌣⌣ ∪ – | – ∪ –
πρόδοτον, αἵ μ' ἀπώλεσαν.   ⌣⌣ ∪ – | ∪ – ∪ –
οἷς θεὸς ὁ μέγας 'Ολύμπιος   ⊼ ⌣⌣ ∪ ⌣⌣ | ∪ – ∪ –
ποίνιμα πάθεα παθεῖν πόροι,   ⊼ ⌣⌣ ∪ ⌣⌣ | ∪ – ∪ –
μηδέ ποτ' ἀγλαΐας ἀποναίατο   – ∪ ∪ – ∪ ∪ – ∪ ∪ – ∪ ∪
τοιάδ' ἀνύσαντες ἔργα.   ⊼ ⌣⌣ ∪ – | ∪ – –

The dimeter with spondaic contraction ⊻ – ∪ – | – – ὑπεστί μοι θάρσος, rather rare in Aeschylus (*Supp.* 139, *Eum.* 383, 387) and

---

[1] See below, p. 184. The context of such passages (e.g. *O.T.* 863–910) often shows an admixture of aeolo-choriambic or dactylic cola, i.e. something nearly related to dactylo-epitrite movement.
[2] See above, p. 37.

Euripides (*Supp.* 781), is a favourite with Sophocles.[1] The long protraction (or some similar device of delivery) of this spondaic metron appears to be a recognized vehicle of dramatic emphasis, to judge from Σεμναί (*Eum.* 383), Ξέρξης (*Pers.* 552), εὐοῖ and Παιάν (*Tr.* 219, 221), τλάμων (*O.T.* 1332), Φωκεύς (*Or.* 1447).

Euripides returns to the predominantly light *anceps*; in the *Supplices*, for instance, the most iambic of his plays, there are scarcely any exceptions. This has also several clausulae with choriambic anaclasis, but of trimeter, not dimeter, length: so 1131

εὐδοκίμων δήποτ' ἐν Μυκήναις. — ⏑ ⏑ — — — ⏑ — ⏑ — —

On the whole, however, his lyrics have less syncopation and more resolution than Aeschylus's. *Supp.* 1153–8 is typical:

ἔτ' εἰσορᾶν σε, πάτερ, ἐπ' ὀμμάτων δοκῶ.	⏑ — ⏑ — | ⏑ ⏒ ⏑ — | ⏑ — ⏑ —
—φίλον φίλημα παρὰ γένυν τιθέντα σόν.	⏑ — ⏑ — | ⏑ ⏒ ⏑ — | ⏑ — ⏑ —
—λόγων δὲ παρακέλευσμα σῶν	⏑ — ⏑ ⏒ | ⏑ — ⏑ —
ἀέρι φερόμενον οἴχεται.	⏑ ⏒ ⏑ ⏒ | ⏑ — ⏑ —
—δυοῖν δ' ἄχη, ματρί τ' ἔλιπεν,	⏑ — ⏑ — | x̱ ⏒ ⏑ —
σέ τ' οὔποτ' ἄλγη πατρῷα λείψει.	⏑ — ⏑ — | — ⏑ — | ⏑ — —

In *Tro.* 1310 ff. the resolutions multiply as the κομμός rises to a wild keening:

ἀγόμεθα φερόμεθ'· — ἄλγος ἄλγος βοᾷς.
⏑ ⏒ ⏑ ⏒ \| ⏑ — ⏑ — \| — ⏑ —

— δούλειον ὑπὸ μέλαθρον. — ἐκ πάτρας γ' ἐμᾶς·
x̱ — ⏑ ⏒ \| ⏑ — ⏑ — \| ⏑ — ⏑ —

— ἰώ.
Πρίαμε Πρίαμε σὺ μὲν ὀλόμενος ἄταφος ἄφιλος
⏑ ⏒ ⏑ ⏒ \| ⏑ ⏒ ⏑ ⏒ \| ⏑ ⏒ ⏑ ⏒

ἄτας ἐμᾶς ἄιστος εἶ.
x̱ — ⏑ — \| ⏑ — ⏑ —

— μέλας γὰρ ὄσσε κατεκάλυ-
⏑ — ⏑ — \| ⏑ ⏒ ⏑ —

-ψε θάνατος ὅσιος ἀνοσίαις σφαγαῖσιν.
⏑ ⏒ ⏑ ⏒ \| ⏑ ⏒ ⏑ — \| ⏑ — —

Characteristic is his fondness for long πνίγη of dimeters, unsyncopated and with light *anceps*, as *Tro.* 551 ff.

[1] Cf. *Aj.* 193, 198, 221; *El.* 479; *O.C.* 1076; *O.T.* 1332. For *El.* 512, see below, p. 103.

ἐγὼ δὲ τὰν ὀρεστέραν
τότ' ἀμφὶ μέλαθρα παρθένον
Διὸς κόραν ἐμελπόμαν
χοροῖσι· φοινία δ' ἀνὰ
    πτόλιν βοὰ κατεῖχε Περ-
    -γάμων ἕδρας· βρέφη δὲ φίλι-
    -α περὶ πέπλους ἔβαλλε μα-
    -τρὶ χεῖρας ἐπτοημένας,

and even more breathlessly *Or.* 1444ff.

The occurrence of acatalectic trimeters in lyrics gives rise to un-answered speculation about their delivery.[1] These are specially frequent in κομμοί, mixed with dochmiacs. It is sometimes clear that one character is speaking while the other sings, as, for instance, the Coryphaeus *O.T.* 1312, 1319–20 in his responses to the lyrically lamenting Oedipus. But among Oedipus's lines are also some (1317–18, 1335 and the corresponding ones) which have a rhythm no less indistinguishable from that of dialogue, and the phenomenon is a common one in Sophocles (cf. *Ant.* 1261ff., *El.* 1232ff.) and Euripides (*Hcld.* 75ff., *Hipp.* 817ff.). In Aeschylus it is rare: *Sept.* 100 and 104 lift themselves clearly from the context as spoken inter-jections of one member of the chorus; but *P.V.* 116, 118–19 present the same ambiguity, particularly puzzling when, as so often, the lines occur in the middle of a sentence which is completed by lyrical phrases which could obviously only be sung. It is most natural to suppose a form of chanted delivery which could make these transitions without absurdity; but this must not be taken to admit a blurring of the distinction between spoken and sung metres. The rigidity with which certain characters (presumably those whose actors were not credited with a singing voice) are excluded from the use of lyric metres makes this quite clear.[2]

---

[1] See further on this subject ch. XIII, pp. 207 ff.

[2] The Byzantine emendation συλλαβών at Ar. *Nub.* 1169, giving Socrates a dochmiac, should on these grounds be rejected. Socrates does not sing, and a dochmiac cannot be spoken. The whole exchange must be ana-paestic, with variants $- \cup \cup - \cup \cup \mid \cup \cup - \cup \cup -$. Possibly ἄπιθι σὺ λαβών may be kept as a 'syllabic' anapaest of the type discussed above, p. 65.

TROCHAIC

The trochaic, like the iambic, is found in its most unadulterated form in comedy, and with even more reason, since it was clearly capable of being taken at a tempo which lent itself to vigorous dancing. The form of the metron, with its take-off from the long syllable, and its series of pendants, which cannot run to a pause except by catalexis,[1] give an effect of precipitation where the metre is continued over several cola (cf. the spanking pace which the Frogs set Dionysus in their πνῖγος 241–9). Moreover, unlike iambics, the overwhelming majority of cola are dimeters or compounds of dimeters (the trimeter is comparatively rare, though there are three consecutive *Ran.* 229–31), and comic dancing expresses itself most naturally in paired rhythms.

As in iambics, the simplest form of lyric proceeds like the tetrameter of dialogue but with a period which can expand to any number of full dimeters before the catalectic closing one. Thus *Ran.* 533–41 contains four periods, of 3, 3, 3, 2 dimeters, each pause being marked by catalexis. Within the period word-overlap is frequent, even in the extreme form πάλιν/πει-|-ράσεται, which reduces to a minimum the separateness of the colon within the period, and is an effect confined to comedy. *Av.* 1470 ff. introduces consecutive catalectic dimeters:[2]

> πολλὰ δὴ καὶ καινὰ καὶ θαυ-
> ⎰ -μάστ' ἐπεπτόμεσθα καὶ
> ⎱ δεινὰ πράγματ' εἴδομεν.
> ἔστι γὰρ δένδρον πεφυκὸς
> ἔκτοπόν τι Καρδίας ἀ-
> -πωτέρω Κλεώνυμος,
> ⎰ χρήσιμον μὲν οὐδὲν ἀλ-
> ⎱ -λως δὲ δειλὸν καὶ μέγα, κτλ.

Clearly no pause is possible at καὶ and ἀλ-, and it is probable that

---

[1] *Eccl.* 899 exceptionally gives an acatalectic dimeter clausula. Perhaps this indicates that the Girl interrupts the Hag quickly, as if no period closed there.

[2] Autocrates' Τυμπανισταί has a series κατὰ στίχον (fr. 1 K.).

protraction took its place here. The ithyphallic is sometimes used as an alternative form of clausula.

In the comic trochaic, as in the comic iambic, the long *anceps* is no less common than the short. Even the catalectic dimeter often has the form $- \cup - \underline{\times} - \cup -$, which in tragedy is very rare in iambic and trochaic contexts, though common in epitrites. So striking, in fact, is this difference that we ought perhaps to make a distinction between the lekythion proper $- \cup - \cup - \cup -$ and the catalectic trochaic dimeter, identical with the double epitrite, $- \cup - \underline{\cup} - \cup -$. When the preceding long is resolved this *anceps* is usually short, and a line such as

και κεροβάτας Πὰν ὁ καλαμόφθογγα παίζων,

where the less common $- \cup \frown \underline{\times}$ is twice repeated, has a curiously rough effect and a syllabic sequence identical with one form of iambic. In general, resolution of the first long $\frown \cup - \times$ is far commoner, leaving pendant $- \times$ intact and the metron consequently more self-supporting; similarly, in a whole dimeter the opening long is a favourite resolution:

χαλεπὸν οὖν ἔργον διαιρεῖν,
ὅταν ὁ μὲν τείνῃ βιαίως,
ὁ δ' ἐπαναστρέφειν δύνηται κτλ.

Resolutions may occur out of responsion here and there, so long as the whole impression of strophe and antistrophe is not very different; where discrepancies do occur they are often balanced in the same strophe: thus *Ran.* 1099 ∼ 1109

        ∪ ∪   ∪ ∪
μέγα τὸ πρᾶγμα, πολὺ τὸ νεῖκος, ἀδρὸς ὁ πόλεμος ἔρχεται

and
        ̄
εἰ δὲ τοῦτο καταφοβεῖσθον, μὴ τις ἀμαθία προσῇ.

Syncopation in comedy is mostly confined to suppression of the first *anceps*:

πολυκολύμβοισι μέλεσιν,　$\frown \cup - | - \cup \frown \cup$

and the palimbacchius $- - \cup$ scarcely seems to occur. Initial spondee (double syncopation) is occasionally found: *Lys.* 659–60

ταῦτ' οὖν | οὐχ ὕβρις τὰ πράγματ' ἐστὶ
πολλή ; | κἀπιδώσειν μοι δοκεῖ τὸ χρῆμα μᾶλλον.

A special problem of syncopation is created by the many contexts where cretic-paeonic measure appears in trochaic company, as it is often impossible to be sure whether a cretic has the value of five χρόνοι (and can therefore be resolved into a paeon – ◡ ⌒) or of six, as a syncopated trochaic metron, and whether any such distinction was in fact always clearly made. The relation of the two metres was clearly a very close one in comedy. *Lys.* 659 ff. after a trochaic opening has three paeonic dimeters, then a trochaic line, and finally

πᾶν τὸ σῶμα κἀποσείσασθαι τὸ γῆρας τόδε.

The double cretic close may seem here an obvious trochaic syncopation, but the curious thing is that mixed trochaic-paeonic cola occur. *Lys.* 1014 ff. has a series of tetrameters κατὰ στίχον

– ◡ – ◡̲ – ◡ – ◡̲ | – ◡ ◡ ◡ – ◡ –:

ἐξὸν ὧ πόνηρέ σοι βέβαιον ἔμ' ἔχειν φίλην.

More remarkably *Ach.* 280–3 (preceding a strophe in which Dicaeopolis speaks—or sings—trochaic tetrameters and the Chorus reply in cretic-paeonic):

οὗτος αὐτός ἐστιν, οὗτος.
βάλλε βάλλε βάλλε βάλλε
παῖε παῖε τὸν μιαρόν.   – ◡ – ◡ | – ◡ ◡ ◡
οὐ βαλεῖς; οὐ βαλεῖς;

The explanation of a 'resolved palimbacchius' – ⌒◡ ◡ is not convincing, since there appear to be cases where a mixed trochaic-paeonic colon actually corresponds with an orthodox trochaic: *Vesp.* 1062 ~ 1093

– ◡ ◡ ◡
καὶ κατ' αὐτὸ τοῦτο μόνον ἄνδρες ἀλκιμώτατοι

and

– ◡ – ◡
τοὺς ἐναντίους πλέων ἐκεῖσε ταῖς τριήρεσιν,

cf. 1064 ~ 1095, *Lys.* 781 ff. (see below, p. 97). It seems clear therefore that this is another instance[1] where syllable-counting takes the place of quantitative accuracy in responsion, the four-syllable groups – ◡ – ◡ and – ◡ ◡ ◡ being accepted as equivalent just as, inversely,

[1] See above, pp. 65 ff.

– ∪ ∪ ∪ and ∪ ∪ ∪ ∪ in comic anapaests. It is hard to resist the inference that the relation of – to ∪ in the comic trochee and paeon was far from being the rigid 2 : 1 that might appear from the mathematical precision of the ancient musicians' formulas. Attention to syllable-groups of a similar kind, but in threes instead of fours, brings order and intelligibility into the festive dance-measure at the end of *Lys.* (1279ff.):

πρόσαγε χορόν, ἔπαγε Χάριτας,	⌒ ∪⌒ ⌒ ∪⌒ ∪
ἐπὶ δὲ κάλεσον Ἄρτεμιν,	⌒ ∪⌒ ∪ – ∪ ‿
ἐπὶ δὲ δίδυμον ἀγέχορον Ἰ-	⌒ ∪⌒ ∪ – ∪⌒ ∪
-ήιον εὔφρον', ἐπὶ δὲ Νύσιον,	– ∪ ∪ – ∪ ⌒∪ – ∪ ∪
1284 ὃς μετὰ μαινάσι Βάκχιος ὄμμασι δαίεται,	– ∪∪ – ∪∪ – ∪∪ – ∪∪ – ∪ –
Δία τε πυρὶ φλεγόμενον, ἐπί τε	⌒ ∪⌒ ∪ ⌒ ∪⌒ ∪
πότνιαν ἄλοχον ὀλβίαν ·	⌒ ∪⌒ ∪ – ∪ –
εἶτα δὲ δαίμονας, οἷς ἐπιμάρτυσι	– ∪ ∪ – ∪ ∪ – ∪ ∪ – ∪ ∪
χρησόμεθ' οὐκ ἐπιλήσμοσιν	– ∪ ∪ – ∪ ∪ – ∪ ‿
Ἡσυχίας πέρι τῆς ἀγανόφρονος	– ∪ ∪ – ∪ ∪ – ∪ ∪ – ∪ ∪
1290 ἣν ἐποίησε θεὰ Κύπρις.	– ∪ ∪ – ∪ ∪ – ∪ –.

We may label 1284 'aeolic dactyl', 1288 and 1290 'ibycean', and the rest dactylic tetrameters, lekythia, and the like; but the result would serve only to obscure the real homogeneity of the rhythm. It is clear that this is a dance to a skipping three-time measure in which the first step is given double the time of the second (as in 'Sir Roger de Coverley'). For this purpose ⌣ ∪ and – ∪ ∪ are alternative equivalents, the long of the dactyl being doubtless lingered on slightly more than the first syllable of the tribrach. This would explain the mongrel colon 1283, where the two proper names, as so often (for instance in tragic iambic trimeters), assume a special licence for irrational lengthening.[1] Enger's ⟨δέ⟩ is usually inserted to regularize the first line, but the sense and natural rhythm of the words strongly suggest that the text is right here and that a pause (of one χρόνος) divided this colon into two little colaria. Recognition of the special empirical conditions of delivery of such verses to lively

---

[1] Conversely, in Alcman's *Parthenion*, 1, 51 in place of the regular enoplian of the other stanzas ⌣ – ∪ ∪ – ∪ – – the proper name Ἐνετικός produces a variant ∪ ∪ ∪ ∪ – ∪ – –. But this may be simply a question of orthography.

dance-accompaniment should not be confused with a wholesale acceptance of theories of 'cyclic dactyls' and the like; it is the facts of the text itself which force us to realize that we cannot in every respect measure tragic and comic metres by the same rule.

This song constitutes only a wider and more formalized application of the licence to lengthen a short syllable in a resolved trochaic – ∪ – ∪ ∪ or – ∪ ∪ – ∪ or even – ∪ ∪ – ∪ ∪ which is sporadically, though rarely, employed in comedy, and is analogous to the 'anapaestic' iambic. Such exceptions appear *Equ.* 406 πῖνε πῖν' ἐπὶ συμφοραῖς (~ 332 – ∪ – ∪), *Thesm.* 436 οὐδὲ δεινότερον λεγούσης – ∪ – ∪ ∪ (~ 522 – ∪ – ∪), *Thesm.* 462 οἷα κατεστωμύλατο – ∪ ∪ – –, and 437 πάντα δ' ἐβάστασε(ν) – ∪ ∪ – ∪ ∪ (~ 525 ∪ ∪ ∪ ∪ ∪ ∪). So too the apparently regular aeolic cola *Thesm.* 955 and 957, which occur in a ring dance, were probably assimilated to trochaic time, i.e. 957 βαῖνε καρπαλίμοιν ποδοῖν was equated to 954 κοῦφα ποσὶν ἄγ' ἐς κύκλον, being really an irrationally lengthened trochaic dimeter – ∪ – ∪ ∪ | – ∪ –. This special case naturally does not imply that a glyconic was normally given four equidistant stresses as we tend to speak it: tumí te tumí te-te tumí te tumí.

It is conceivable that the same licence, applied conversely, would account for the odd ionic, so hard to emend, in the πνῖγος *Pax* 339 ff. This ends

> ἐς πανηγύρεις θεωρεῖν,
> ἐστιᾶσθαι κοτταβίζειν,
> συβαρίζειν,   ∪ ∪ – –
> ἰοῦ ἰοῦ κεκραγέναι.

Possibly a pause equivalent to ∪ here intervened before συβαρίζειν. It is at least clear that, in comedy especially, metrical irregularities traceably similar in type, where the text is otherwise irreproachable, occur so often that emendation of all to conformity with a rigid metrical scheme is mistaken purism. But some of these cases admittedly remain only on the verge of the possible.

In tragedy the full trochaic is among the least common metres, a great part of what is normally reckoned to its credit being of the types here called iambo-trochaic or cretic-paeonic. This is not a mere arbitrary detail of classification; the boundaries fluctuate, but there is a real distinction of rhythmical species between trochaics whose normal, non-clausular cola end pendant and those which end blunt and thread in and out of iambics or cretics. In Aeschylus the only continuous trochaic passage is *P.V.* 415–17 ∼ 420–2, three dimeters preceding an aeolic dicolon of the type known as priapean:[1]

> Κολχίδος τε γᾶς ἔνοικοι
> παρθένοι μάχας ἄτρεστοι
> καὶ Σκύθης ὅμιλος, οἳ γᾶς
> ἔσχατον τόπον ἀμφὶ Μαι-
> -ῶτιν ἔχουσι λίμναν.

The middle *anceps* is short each time. Soph. *El.* 1281 ff. ends an epode with trochaics noteworthy for the use of trimeters and syncopation:

ὦ φίλ', ἔκλυον ἃν ἐγὼ οὐδ' ἂν ἤλπισ' αὐδάν.	trim.
ἔσχον ὀργὰν ἄναυδον	$- \cup - \mid - \cup - \cup$
οὐδὲ σὺν βοᾷ κλύουσ' ἁ τάλαινα.	$- \cup - \cup \mid - \cup - \mid - \cup - \cup$
νῦν δ' ἔχω σε· προυφάνης δὲ	dim.
φιλτάταν ἔχων πρόσοψιν,	dim.
ἃς ἐγὼ οὐδ' ἂν ἐν κακοῖς λαθοίμαν.	$- \cup - \cup \ - \cup - \cup - -$

The last line (which could of course be scanned iambically) is a trimeter version of the ithyphallic, found in a more resolved form as a twin clausula, Eur. *Phoen.* 1756–7.[2] Elsewhere the clearest trochaic passages in Sophocles occur in *O.C.*, perhaps under Euripidean influence. Continuous trochaics are almost entirely lacking in Euripides' early and middle plays, but appear in *Hel.*, *Phoen.*, *Or.* and *I.A.* These are mostly of the same type, of which the earlier choruses of the *Helena* give the most interesting examples. They are usually combined with iambics and lekythia, and the almost exclusive use of the short *anceps* makes the effect very different from that of comic trochaics, and much further removed from stichic rhythm. Total resolution is common, the syllable groups tending to coincide with the metra, sometimes in four tribrachic words: πάθεσι

---

[1] See below, p. 134.
[2] Elmsley's ἀχάριτον is essential, since otherwise the second colon would be i. trim. cat. and violate the law against *anceps iuxta anceps*, above p. 75.

πάθεα μέλεσι μέλεα. There are experiments with syncopation, entailing free use of the palimbacchiac: so *Hel.* 173 ff.:

μουσεῖα θρηνήμασι ξυνῳδὰ	– – ⏑ | – – ⏑ | – ⏑ – ⏑
πέμψειε Φερσέφασσα	– – ⏑ | – ⏑ – ⏑
φόνια χάριτας ἵν᾽ ἐπὶ δάκρυσι	⌢ ⏑⌢ ⏑ | ⌢ ⏑⌢ ⏑
παρ᾽ ἐμέθεν ὑπὸ μέλαθρα νύχια	⌢ ⏑⌢ ⏑ | ⌢ ⏑⌢ ⏑
παιᾶνα νέκυσιν ὀλομένοις λάβῃ.	– – ⏑ | ⌢ ⏑⌢ ⏑ | – ⏑ –

The catalectic colon – – ⏑ | – ⏑ – (a sort of inverted ithyphallic) is also found, and even – – ⏑ | – – ⏑ ὦ μᾶτερ ὦ μᾶτερ (*I.A.* 1313). Double syncopation gives the forms – – | – ⏑ – ⏑ Εὐρώταν θανόντος, – ⏑ – | – – ᾽Ιλίῳ πεύκαν, and an apparent ithyphallic with protraction instead of catalexis and pause, as in the second and penultimate cola of the following (*Hel.* 200 ff.):

Λήδα δ᾽ ἐν ἀγχόναις	– – ⏑ | – ⏑ –
θάνατον ἔλαβεν αἰσχύ-	⌢ ⏑⌢ ⏑ | – –
-νας ἐμᾶς ὑπ᾽ ἀλγέων.	– ⏑ – ⏑ | – ⏑ –
ὁ δ᾽ ἐμὸς ἐν ἁλὶ πολυπλανὴς	⌢ ⏑⌢ ⏑ | ⌢ ⏑ –
πόσις ὀλόμενος οἴχεται,	⌢ ⏑⌢ ⏑ | – ⏑ –
Κάστορός τε συγγόνου τε	– ⏑ – ⏑ | – ⏑ – ⏑
διδυμογενὲς ἄγαλμα πατρίδος	⌢ ⏑⌢ ⏑ | – ⏑⌢ ⏑
ἀφανὲς ἀφανὲς ἱππόκροτα λέ-	⌢ ⏑⌢ ⏑ | – ⏑ ⌢ ⏑
-λοιπε δάπεδα γυμνάσιά τε	– ⏑⌢ ⏑ | – ⏑⌢ ⏑
δονακόεντος Εὐρώ-	⌢ ⏑ – ⏑ | – –
-τα νεανιᾶν πόνον.	– ⏑ – ⏑ | – ⏑ –

It is a type of lyric which could easily degenerate into a somewhat empty *coloratura* performance of the δάκρυα δάκρυα type ridiculed by Aristophanes.

IAMBO-TROCHAIC

The ins and outs of iambic and trochaic metre rarely give rise to any ambiguity in comedy. Philocleon's drunken little kick-up *Vesp.* 1335 ff.

> ἰὴ ἰεῦ, καλούμενοι.
> ἀρχαῖά γ᾽ ὑμῶν· ἀρά γ᾽ ἴσθ᾽
> ὡς οὐδ᾽ ἀκούων ἀνέχομαι
> δικῶν; ἰαιβοῖ αἰβοῖ.
> τάδε μ᾽ ἀρέσκει· βάλλε κημούς.
> οὐκ ἄπεισι — ποῦ ᾽στιν; —
> ἡλιαστὴς ἐκποδών;

could be shown as iambic throughout by dividing κη-|-μούς with overlap, but the incidence of word-end makes the distinction into four iambic+three trochaic cola the most natural and obvious. Tragedy on the other hand presents many lyrics where the two are so closely interwoven that there can be no question of any difference in tempo, and occasionally there is nothing to choose between alternative schemes of colometry. Word-end is usually a guide, though it must be remembered that in a πνῖγος word-overlap is often deliberately sought; rhetorical pause is safer still; further, the rule that *anceps* at the end of a colon must not precede initial *anceps* except where an intervening pause is possible holds absolutely.[1] *O.C.* 1683 ff. can thus be sorted out:

τάλαινα, νῷν δ' ὀλεθρία	iamb.
νὺξ ἐπ' ὄμμασιν βέβακε·	troch.
πῶς γὰρ ἢ τιν' ἀπίαν	lek.
γᾶν ἢ πόντιον	$--\mid-\cup-$
κλύδων' ἀλώμεναι βίου	iamb.
δύσοιστον ἕξομεν τροφόν;	iamb.

and there is no possibility of division ἀπίαν γᾶν | ἢ πόντιον κτλ. 1724 ff. again begins iambic and changes 1730 to trochaic; the final three lines run:

αἰαῖ δυστάλαινα,	$--\mid-\cup-\cup$
ποῦ δῆτ' αὖθις ὧδ' ἔρημος ἄπορος	$--\mid-\cup-\cup\mid-\cup\!\smile\!\cup$
αἰῶνα τλάμον' ἕξω;	$--\cup\mid-\cup--$

The last line cannot be an iambic dimeter catalectic, since there is no pause possible after ἄπορος and the syllable αἰ- must therefore be long and not *anceps*. This line is therefore one of the strongest indications of the reality of the palimbacchiac as an analytical unit and of a difference in enunciation—probably through some form of protraction—between this colon as an iambic and as a trochaic line. Taken as the latter it would *qua* clausula stand to trochaics as the lekythion $-\cup-\mid\cup-\cup-$ to iambics, i.e. it would be shorter than the full dimeter but strictly speaking syncopated, not catalectic.

[1] Soph. *Tr.* 823 is an epitrite, and in dactylo-epitrite metre $-\cup-\underset{\times}{}$ $-\cup-\underset{\times}{}$ is a clausula.

Apart from the many choruses which shuttle backwards and forwards between iambic and trochaic, there are those whose movement is dominated by cola which are actually themselves ambiguous. The commonest colon of this class is the lekythion, which in Aeschylus often gives the key-movement of a stanza—a falling start with blunt end, with occasional variations of trimeter length or interludes of cretic (– ∪ – or ⌒∪ ∪ –), the cretic being the shortest unit of such movement. *Eum.* 916ff. is typical:

δέξομαι Παλλάδος ξυνοικίαν	– ∪ – | – ∪ – ∪ – ∪ –
οὐδ' ἀτιμάσω πόλιν·	lek.
τὰν καὶ Ζεὺς ὁ παγκρατὴς Ἄρης τε	– – | – ∪ – ∪ | – ∪ – ∪
φρούριον θεῶν νέμει,	lek.
ῥυσίβωμον Ἑλλά-	– ∪ – ∪ – –
-νων ἄγαλμα δαιμόνων·	lek.
ᾷτ' ἐγὼ κατεύχομαι	lek.
θεσπίσασα πρευμενῶς	lek.
ἐπισσύτους βίου τύχας ὀνησίμους	iam. trim.
γαίας ἐξαμβρῦσαι	– ∸ – ∸ – –
φαιδρὸν ἁλίου σέλας.	lek.

(The penultimate, here taken as contracted dactylic, might be analysed in various ways; it is in any case a penultimate strip of different movement, after the manner of Aeschylus.) The lekythia turn first to trochaic, in the third colon, then lead into iambics towards the close. Euripides builds similar stanzas in *Phoen.* and *I.A.* (cf., for instance, *Phoen.* 239–49 which at the end tilts over into trochaic).

The ithyphallic has often been mentioned as a neutral clausula, and the little colarion – ∪ – –, in form like a trochaic monometer or epitrite, which is used as a clausula to iambo-trochaics *Ant.* 364 ξυμπέφρασται and Eur. *Supp.* 368, 372, is in effect a sort of abbreviated ithyphallic. Rarer species of iambo-trochaic cola are (besides the pentasyllable and 'alcaic enneasyllable' referred to, pp. 70f.) *Pers.* 575 βοᾶτιν τάλαιναν αὐδάν ∪ – – ∪ – ∪ – – and its resolved form *Or.* 1012 δόμων πολυπόνοις ἀνάγκαις ∪ – ⌒∪ ∪ – ∪ – –. This starts with a kind of anaclasis (the initial syllable is true short, not *anceps*), so that if we try to analyse it as a dimeter there appears in place of an orthodox metron what Hephaestion called an 'antispast' ∪ — — ∪ and regarded (mistakenly) as a common and recognizable unit of movement.[1]

[1] Much has been written in denial or defence of the antispast's existence. The facts are that this sequence of syllables occasionally appears as the first half of a colon of dimeter length (i.e. octosyllabic when not resolved) of which the second half forms a recognized metron, as here — ∪ — —, or the choriamb in ∪ — — ∪ | — ∪ ∪ —. The collocation, however, is hardly common enough to be worth a special name; at least it is misleading if the name is taken to imply that the antispast is a 'metron', i.e. the unit of a typical movement. It is merely on the same footing as, for instance, ∪ — — —, — — — ∪, or — — — — in a similar position. Hephaestion arrives at the concept through his habit of starting at the beginning of a colon and numbering off in fours: thus one form of glyconic would be ◡ — — ∪ | ∪ — ∪ — = antispast+iambic. It need hardly be said that such an analysis, with its inorganic division of a double-short, is false and misleading, while his grouping of 'lengths' (starting from the dochmiac as an 'antispastic penthemimer' ∪ — — ∪ —) is even more fantastic.

VI

CRETIC-PAEONIC

Ambiguity with syncopated iambic and trochaic—Pure cretic-paeonic mostly in comedy—Comparative rarity and ambiguity in tragedy—Bacchiac and molossus.

The existence of a group of metres in five-time, comprising the cretic – ∪ – with paeonic forms – ∪ ∪ ∪ and ∪ ∪ ∪ –,[1] the bacchiac ∪ – – and palimbacchiac – – ∪, was recognized by ancient metricians. It has been seen in the two previous chapters how these classes overlap with iambics and trochaics and to a less extent with anapaests. The overlap is of two kinds, of which the first is common to tragedy and comedy, the second found in comedy alone. On the one hand these metra may be syncopated forms of iambic and trochaic, the most natural hypothesis being an extra prolongation of one of the long quantities; on the other they may proceed by syllable-equation, – ∪ – being assimilated to ∪ ∪ –, – ∪ ∪ ∪ to ∪ ∪ ∪ ∪ or – ∪ – ∪. (The bacchiac and palimbacchiac are not susceptible of this treatment.) The second class is much the rarer, being rather an occasional licence than an accredited variation, but is, nevertheless, a characteristic licence in comic metre, especially in patter-rhythms.

In spite of these infringements from two sides, a certain sphere of independence remains to the group. This is clearest in comedy. Aristophanes (most in his early plays), Cratinus, Eupolis, Theopompus, Eubulus, all compose odes running wholly or predominantly in cretics and paeons. *Ach.* 210ff. (after four trochaic tetrameters) proceeds:

ἐκπέφευγ᾽, οἴχεται	2 cr.
φροῦδος· οἴμοι τάλας	2 cr.
τῶν ἐτῶν τῶν ἐμῶν. ||	2 cr.

[1] These are sometimes called first and fourth paeons respectively, since some of the ancient metricians recognized a second ∪ – ∪ ∪ and third ∪ ∪ – ∪. These latter are, however, a piece of schematic invention.

οὐκ ἂν ἐπ' ἐμῆς γε νεότητος ὅτ' ἐγὼ φέρων   3 p.+cr.
ἀνθράκων φορτίον ‖   2 cr.
ἠκολούθουν Φαύλλῳ τρέχων, ὧδε φαύλως ἂν ὁ   5 cr.
σπονδοφόρος οὗτος ὑπ' ἐμοῦ τότε διωκόμενος   4 p.
ἐξέφυγεν οὐδ' ἂν ἐλαφρῶς ἂν ἀπεπλίξατο.   3 p.+cr.

There are probably three periods; at least it is clear that the last
three cola form a πνῖγος. Neither cretic nor paeon can claim to be
primary;[1] the relation of the contracted to the resolved form is much
the same as in comic anapaests, and just as – – can resolve into
∪ ∪ – or – ∪ ∪, so ∪ ∪ ∪ – is an alternative (comparatively rare in
comedy) to – ∪ ∪ ∪:

ἐν ἀγορᾷ δ' αὖ πλάτανον εὖ διαφυτεύσομεν. (Fr. 111 K.)

A period, of course, must always end in a long (in practice always
in a cretic). Responsion is usually exact. Colon-lengths vary
greatly, and often run into long πνίγη, but specially common is the
tetrameter of three paeons+cretic; *Ach.* 976–83 shows a series of
eight, the line being in effect used κατὰ στίχον. The dimeter
– ∪ ∪ ∪ | – ∪ – is also characteristic, cf. *Ach.* 973

ὧν τὰ μὲν ἐν οἰκίᾳ
χρήσιμα, τὰ δ' αὖ πρέπει
χλιαρὰ κατεσθίειν.

Occasionally a syncopated cretic – – is found in this company.
Lys. 781 ff. shows a series of such syncopations in a cretic-paeonic
passage adulterated with trochaics:

μῦθον βούλομαι λέξαι τιν' ὑμῖν ὅν ποτ' ἤκουσ'   – – | – ∪ – – | – ∪ – – | – ∪ – –
    αὐτὸς ἔτι παῖς ὤν.   – ∪ ∪ ∪ | – –
οὕτως ἦν νεανίσκος Μελανίων τις   – – | – ∪ – – | – ∪ ∪ ∪ | – –
ὃς φεύγων γάμον ἀφίκετ' ἐς ἐρημίαν καὶ   – – | – ∪ ∪ ∪ | – ∪ ∪ ∪ | – ∪ – –
    τοῖς ὄρεσιν ᾤκει·   – ∪ ∪ ∪ | – –
κᾆτ' ἐλαγοθήρει   – ∪ ∪ ∪ | – –
πλεξάμενος ἄρκυς,   – ∪ ∪ ∪ | – –
καὶ κύνα τιν' εἶχεν,   – ∪ ∪ ∪ | – –
κοὐκέτι κατῆλθε πάλιν οἴκαδ' ὑπὸ μίσους.   – ∪ ∪ ∪ | – ∪ ∪ ∪ | – ∪ ∪ ∪ | – –
οὕτω τὰς γυναῖκας ἐβδελύχθη   – – | – ∪ – ∪ | – ∪ – –
'κεῖνος ἡμεῖς τ' οὐδὲν ἧττον   – ∪ – – | – ∪ – –
τοῦ Μελανίωνος οἱ σώφρονες.   – ∪ ∪ ∪ | – ∪ – | – ∪ –

---

[1] In comic usage, that is; in basic theory the cretic is primary, since more
than two consecutive shorts always implies resolution.

This metre is not much favoured in tragedy. Aeschylus used it for one chorus of his *Supplices* (418ff.) in precisely the Aristophanic manner:

φρόντισον καὶ γενοῦ	
πανδίκως εὐσεβὴς πρόξενος.	5 cr.
τὰν φυγάδα μὴ προδῷς	p.+cr.
τὰν ἔκαθεν ἐκβολαῖς	p.+cr.
δυσθέοις ὁρμέναν.	2 cr.

The antistrophe has one rising paeon ◡◡◡‒ corresponding to πανδίκως. The next pair of stanzas begin with a cretic-paeonic trimeter and then pass into dochmiacs. Euripides (*Or.* 1418ff.) allows the Phrygian Slave one cretic-paeonic patch in his slightly preposterous aria:

προσεῖπε δ' ἄλλος ἄλλον ἐν φόβῳ πεσὼν	iamb. trim.
μή τις εἴη δόλος.	2 cr.
κἀδόκει τοῖς μὲν οὔ,	2 cr.
τοῖς δ' ἐς ἀρκυστάταν	2 cr.
μηχανὰν ἐμπλέκειν.	2 cr.
παῖδα τὰν Τυνδαρίδ' ὁ	cr.+p.
μητροφόντας δράκων.	2 cr.

Hec. 1100, in an agitated astrophic passage, has one paeonic tetrameter passing into irregular dochmiacs:

ἀμπτάμενος οὐράνιον ὑψιπετὲς ἐς μέλαθρον.

Soph. *El.* 1249 similarly has a paeonic trimeter among dochmiacs. There is no other instance of cretic-paeonic so composed that it cannot be interpreted as syncopated iambic: none, that is to say, containing falling paeons.[1] The preference of tragedy for e.g. ‒◡‒ | ◡◡◡‒ over ‒◡◡◡ | ‒◡‒ is analogous to its preference for iambics over trochaics.

The question then arises whether we should always reckon these other passages, containing cola such as ‒◡‒ | ◡◡◡‒, to the credit of iambo-trochaics, or whether a separate classification is justified. We can never hope to answer this in terms of χρόνοι; what does emerge, however, is the special rhythmical effect of these shorter metra when they appear in a series of appreciable length, an

[1] See above, p. 73.

effect so unlike that of normal iambic and trochaic that there are grounds for grouping them with the trisyllabics rather than the tetrasyllabics.

The Binding Song of the Eumenides (321 ff.) is full of such runs, especially of rising paeons:

ἐπὶ δὲ τῷ τεθυμένῳ	∪ ∪ ∪ – | ∪ ∪ ∪ –
τόδε μέλος παρακοπά	∪ ∪ ∪ – | ∪ ∪ ∪ –
παραφορὰ φρενοδαλής.	∽ ∪ – ∪ ∪ – – (pher.)

This pherecratean is echoed in a later ephymnion (372ff.):

μάλα γὰρ οὖν ἁλομένα	∪ ∪ ∪ – | ∪ ∪ ∪ –
ἀνέκαθεν βαρυπεσῆ	∪ ∪ ∪ – | ∪ ∪ ∪ –
καταφέρω ποδὸς ἀκμάν·	∽ ∪ – ∪ ∪ – – pher.[1]
σφαλερὰ ⟨γὰρ⟩ τανυδρόμοις	∪ ∪ ∪ – | ∪ ∪ ∪ –
κῶλα, δύσφορον ἄταν.	– ∪ – ∪ ∪ – – pher.

Eur. *Phoen.* 1524–5 has a cretic pentameter

τίν' ἐπὶ πρῶτον ἀπὸ χαίτας σπαραγμοῖς ἀπαρχὰς βάλω;

But in general long cretic runs are left to comedy (cf. *Av.* 410ff., a little diluted with iambo-trochaics) and satyr-plays (there are long cretic πνίγη with bacchiac closes in the *Ichneutae*). Tragedy usually melts cretics into iambo-trochaics so that they can only be taken as syncopated metra: so *Pers.* 126ff.

πᾶς γὰρ ἱππηλάτας	2 cr.
καὶ πεδοστιβὴς λεὼς	lek.
σμῆνος ὡς ἐκλέλοιπεν μελισ-	3 cr.
-σᾶν σὺν ὀρχάμῳ στρατοῦ	lek.
τὸν ἀμφίζευκτον ἐξαμείψας	∪ – – | – ∪ – | ∪ – –
ἀμφοτέρας ἄλιον	dact. hemiep.
πρῶνα κοινὸν αἴας.	– ∪ – | ∪ – – ithyph.

---

[1] Pherecratean, I think, rather than a double paeon; cf. 354–9 where I would scan 355 as pher. with Ἄρης – –. (358–9 are corrupt; I suspect the latter should be lek., but have nothing to suggest.) Thus I believe that at *P.V.* 567 Wilam.'s ingenious emendation ἀλεῦμαι for ἃ δᾶ· φοβοῦμαι, giving three cat. trims., should be rejected. (I should be reluctant to add yet another technical reason for doubting Aeschylean authorship!)

These, unlike the paeons of the Eumenides quoted above, are not emphasized by diaeresis, and the general practice of the tragedians is to avoid doing so. A series of cretics comprising single words, especially with a suggestion of rhyme, inevitably suggests the comic manner, like the Farmers' ἥδομαί γ' ἥδομαι or the Satyrs' τυφέτω καιέτω, or at best the army challenge of *Rhes.* 682

τίς ὁ λόχος; πόθεν ἔβας; ποδαπὸς εἶ;

In the stanza from the *Persae* quoted above, the syncopated trimeter and dimeter (ithyphallic) also use only trisyllabic metra. The bacchiac, like the cretic, is common enough in iambic and trochaic, and in sporadic appearances is most naturally taken either as $\cup - \wedge -$ or as an ordinary pendant close. But a series of bacchiacs, especially with diaereses, has a most striking effect: Wilamowitz speaks of the emotion with which he first read *P.V.* 115

τίς ἀχώ, τίς ὀδμὰ προσέπτα μ' ἀφεγγής;

Such lines are found here and there in the tragedians,[1] the longest occurring in the Phrygian's baroque ἄστροφα (*Or.* 1437)

προσεῖπεν δ' 'Ορέστας
Λάκαιναν κόραν· 'ω
Διὸς παῖ θὲς ἴχνος
πέδῳ δεῦρ' ἀποστᾶσα κλισμοῦ.

Further, the molossus $- - -$, to judge by the contexts in which it occurs, should also be recognized as a variant of these trisyllabic metra. Soph. *Tr.* 524–5 gives two dimeters:

ἁ δ' εὐῶπις ἁβρὰ $\overline{\times} - - \mid \cup - -$
τηλαυγεῖ παρ' ὄχθῳ, $\overline{\times} - - \mid \cup - -$

where the initial long syllable is substituted for the short of a bacchiac. This is like the initial *anceps* of an iambic metron, and it is not surprising to find it even in responsion: *Ion* 190 ~ 201

ἰδοὺ τάνδ', ἄθρησον $\cup - - \mid \cup - -$

and

καὶ μὰν τόνδ' ἄθρησον, $\overline{\times} - - \mid \cup - -$

---

[1] E.g. *Cho.* 350; *P.V.* 579; Soph. *Phil.* 396; Eur. *H.F.* 906; *Phoen.* 295, 1536; *Bacch.* 994; *Ion* 1446; *Hel.* 642–3; *Rhes.* 706–8.

but this long *anceps* can occur only at the opening of a colon. The molossus is also found in responsion with a cretic.[1] *Ion* 676 ~ 695

<blockquote>
ὁρῶ δάκρυα καὶ πενθίμους   ∪ – ∪ ∪ – | – ∪ –
</blockquote>

and

<blockquote>
φίλαι, πότερ' ἐμᾷ δεσποίνᾳ,   ∪ – ∪ ∪ – | – ×̄ –
</blockquote>

Or. 168 ~ 189

<blockquote>
θωΰξασ' ἔβαλες ἐξ ὕπνου   – ×̄ – | ∪ ∪ ∪ – ∪ –
</blockquote>

and

<blockquote>
οὐδὲ γὰρ πόθον ἔχει βορᾶς.   – ∪ – | ∪ ∪ ∪ – ∪ –
</blockquote>

It is significant that in each of these cases the colon is a compound of dochmiac+trisyllable: it will be seen in the next chapter how often single cretics are found among dochmiacs, and the variant – – – shows the same 'drag' as in dochmiacs themselves, where, for instance, ∪ – – ∪ – can respond to ∪ – – – –.

Soph. *Tr.* 653 ~ 661 has in iambic context a double molossus νῦν δ' Ἄρης οἰστρηθεὶς ~ τᾶς πειθοῦς παγχρίστῳ. More puzzling to analyse is a short colon, a favourite of Sophocles, which can lay claim to the most diverse connections. In *El.* 160–1 it appears from the context to be an iambic dimeter with double syncopation, a variant of ὕπεστί μοι θάρσος (see above, p. 84):

ὄλβιος ὃν ἁ κλεινὰ	– ∪ ∪ ∪ –	– –
γᾶ ποτε Μυκηναίων	– ∪ ∪ ∪ –	– –
δέξεται εὐπατρίδαν, Διὸς εὔφρονι	dact. tetram.
βήματι μολόντα τάνδε γᾶν 'Ορέσταν.	×̄ ⌢ ∪ –	∪ – ∪ –	∪ – –

Here it is natural to take it in the same sense as the final iambic trimeter. In *Tr.* 827–8 it has the same form and there is again an iambic trimeter in the context (825) with the same opening. It is followed, however, by a resolved dochmiac; and in the next pair of stanzas (846 ~ 857) ἦ που ὀλοὰ στένει corresponds to ἃ τότε θοὰν νύμφαν, – ∪ ∪ ∪ – ∪ – to – ∪ ∪ ∪ – – –, reminiscent again of the dochmiac dragged close. Here, where iambic analysis is excluded, it would be possible to interpret – ∪ ∪ ∪ | – ⌣̄ –, showing a kinship

---

[1] For this phenomenon in Soph. see ch. VII, Additional note, p. 118.

with the cretic-paeonic of this chapter. But there is a unique epode, *El.* 504ff.:

ὦ Πέλοπος ἁ πρόσθεν	– ∪ ∪ ∪ – – –
πολύπονος ἱππεία	∪ ∪ ∪ ∪ – – –
ὡς ἔμολες αἰανὴς τᾷδε γᾷ.	– ∪ ∪ ∪ – – – – ∪ –
εὖτε γὰρ ὁ ποντισθεὶς	– ∪ ∪ ∪ – – –
Μυρτίλος ἐκοιμάθη	– ∪ ∪ ∪ – – –
παγχρύσων δίφρων	– – – ∪̆ –
δυστάνοις αἰκείαις	– – – – – –
πρόρριζος ἐκριφθείς, οὔ τί πω	– – ∪ – – – – – ∪ –
ἔλιπεν ἐκ τοῦδ' οἴκου	∪ ∪ ∪ – – – –
πολύπονος αἰκεία.	∪ ∪ ∪ ∪ – – –

The second and the final cola are actually identical with Euripides' 'anapaestic dochmiacs' νοτερὸν ὕδωρ βάλλων (see above, pp. 59ff.), and the cretic insertions τᾷδε γᾷ and οὔ τί πω are also in the dochmiac manner. παγχρύσων δίφρων might be a dochmiac. It is best to recognize an independent form of colarion showing various affinities and therefore capable of diverse association, in the manner of its variation reminiscent of the dochmiac but slightly longer, roughly the equivalent of a hexasyllable instead of a pentasyllable.

VII

DOCHMIAC

A colarion of great diversity, with various affinities—Iambo-dochmiacs and admixture of cretic-paeonic—Emotional connotation and admixture of trimeters—Use in ἀπολελυμένα—Analyses—Responsion—In comedy mostly for parody—Note on rare forms of dochmiac—Analysis of S. *Phil.* 827ff.

The δοχμιακόν is a metre which 'runs askew', an apt name for this curious, irregular, checking movement. As an independent rhythmical type dominating a lyric stanza, it was worked out with full consequence in drama alone; Pindar's 'dochmiacs' are mostly segments of compounds in syncopated single-short which cannot be fitted into a scheme κατὰ μέτρον (this kind is found in drama too, described in this chapter as 'iambo-dochmiacs'). Possibly Aeschylus himself was the creator of dochmiac lyric. The dochmiac is not a metron, an analytic unit of recurring movement in a colon; it is a self-sufficient colarion of remarkably diverse form, able to stand singly, and frequently doing so, for instance, as a clausula. But it is the grouping of dochmiacs in a series that enables the ear to grasp the typical movement; and the method of pairing, which is of all rhythmical devices the one to which the ear responds most readily, is here too the most common. Such dochmiac pairs, or 'dimeters' as they are sometimes loosely called, may be welded together by overlap, but much more often there is diaeresis between the two and the pairing is emphasized by identity of form *aa*:

κατακονὰ μὲν οὖν | ἀβίοτος βίου ⏑⏕ – ⏑ – *bis*

or

νέφος ἐμὸν ἀπότροπον | ἐπιπλόμενον ἄφατον, ⏑⏕⏕ ⏑⏕ *bis*

by a slight but responsive divergence *aa'*:

βαρύποτμον, γύναι, | προσαυδῶν τύχω ⏑⏕ – ⏑ – | ⏑ – – ⏑ –

or

ὤμοι ἐμῶν κακῶν· | ἔπαθον, ὦ πόλις, –⏕ – ⏑ – | ⏑⏕ – ⏑ –

[104]

or by anaphora:

Ἀπόλλων τάδ' ἦν, | Ἀπόλλων, φίλοι.

The *aaa′* group is also common:

τίνι μόρῳ θνῄσκεις, | τίνι πότμῳ κεῖσαι ◡⌣ – × – *bis*
πρὸς τίνος ἀνθρώπων; – ⌣ – × –

The Protean diversity of form shown by this colarion (thirty-two species have been counted, though textual uncertainties and lack of agreement as to what should or should not be reckoned under this head makes all enumerations somewhat arbitrary) is accounted for by the extent to which it avails itself of two principles of equation, quantity and syllable-counting. If the commonest ◡ – – ◡ –[1] be taken as the norm, any or all of its three longs can be resolved (commonest are ◡⌣ – ◡ –, ◡ – ⌣ ◡ – and ◡⌣⌣◡⌣). The first syllable may become *anceps* as in an iambic metron, giving such forms as ⊽ – – ◡ –, ⊽⌣ – ◡ –, ⊽⌣⌣◡ –, ⊽⌣⌣◡⌣. The dragged close – × – can be substituted for the cretic, giving ⊽ – – × –, ⊽⌣ – × –; and various freak forms arise now and again from irrational resolution of an *anceps*, ⌣̂× – ⌣ ◡ – or ◡⌣ – ⌣̂× –, or ⌣̂× – – × –. It is little more than a question of terminology whether the 'hypodochmius' – ◡ – ◡ – be reckoned as a species of dochmiac by anaclasis or as a kindred colarion; it is at least often found among dochmiacs, and appears to have a resolved form – ◡⌣◡ –.

It is natural that a colon of such diverse form should have affinities branching off in the most varied directions. Euripides' assimilation of dragged dochmiacs × – – × – or – ◡◡ – × – to anapaests has already been noticed, as also the transition from resolved anapaests ◡◡◡◡◡◡ – to dochmiacs of the same form or – ◡◡◡◡◡ –.[2] In *Eum.* 956ff. a complex relationship emerges:

[1] *Sic*, rather than × – – × –; apart from relative frequency, a pentasyll. containing three true longs must fill up with two shorts in its basic form if it is to be intelligibly expressed. The treatment of each short as *anceps* is a secondary development, quite unlike × – ◡ – as the basic iambic.

[2] See above, pp. 53ff., 59.

ἀνδροκμῆτας δ' ἀώ-	2 cr.
-ρους ἀπεννέπω τύχας,	lek.
νεανίδων τ' ἐπηράτων	i. dim.
ἀνδροτυχεῖς βιότους δότε κύρι' ἔχοντες,	dact. pentam.
θεαί τ' ὦ Μοῖραι	∪ − − − −
ματροκασιγνῆται,	− ∪ ∪ − − −
δαίμονες ὀρθονόμοι,	− ∪ ∪ − ∪ ∪ − (hemiep.)
παντὶ δόμῳ μετάκοινοι,	hemiep. pendant
παντὶ χρόνῳ δ' ἐπιβριθεῖς,	hemiep. pendant
ἐνδίκαις ὁμιλίαις	lek.
πάντᾳ τιμιώταται θεῶν.	− − | − ∪ − ∪ − ∪ −

Here is a mixture of iambo-trochaic and dactylic, and in the middle
two cola which are identical with two forms of dochmiac but might
equally well here be syncopated iambic ∪ − − \| − − (cf. the final
clausula) and contracted blunt hemiepes − ∪ ∪ − ⁀ − respectively.[1]
The form − ∪ ∪ − ∪ − is identical[2] with an aeolo-choriambic
colarion, and in such contexts where there is no dochmiac
support it is not appropriately labelled 'dochmiac', cf. Aesch.
Cho. 345:

εἰ γὰρ ὑπ' Ἰλίῳ	− ∪ ∪ − ∪ −
πρός τινος Λυκίων, πάτερ	− ∪ − ∪ ∪ − ∪ − glyc.,

but the common form makes a transition to aeolics easy, as when
Aeschylus more than once joins up an 'aristophanean' clausula to
dochmiacs by word-overlap: *Supp.* 402ff.

ἀμφοτέροις ὁμαίμων τόδ' ἐπισκοπεῖ	− ∪ ∪ − ∪ − | − ∪ ∪ − ∪ −
Ζεὺς ἑτερορρεπής, νέμων εἰκότως	− ∪ ∪ − ∪ − | ∪ − − ∪ −
ἄδικα μὲν κακοῖς, ὅσια δ' ἐννόμοις.	∪⌢ − ∪ − | ∪⌢ − ∪ −
τί τῶνδ' ἐξ ἴσου ῥεπομένων μεταλ-	∪ − − ∪ − | ∪⌢ − ∪ −
-γὲς τὸ δίκαιον ἔρξαι;	− ∪ ∪ − ∪ − −

---

[1] See above, p. 43. Cf. also p. 32 for − ⁀ − ⁀ − as a contracted hemiepes.

[2] This transition is so frequent that probably any distinction between −
and ⲝ had here worn off; the opening sequence − ∪ ∪ − must of itself
have exerted a pull towards choriambic enunciation. Cf. E. *Hel.* 664
ἀπέπτυσα μὲν λόγον οἶον   οἶον ἐσοίσομαι, paroem.+doch. ∪ − ∪ ∪ −
∪ ∪ − ∪   − ∪ ∪ − ∪ − where the second οἶον must begin with true
long, since *anceps iuxta anceps* is impossible.

He also introduces longer aeolic cola, as in *Sept.* 206, two cret.+chor. dim. after six dochmiacs:

ἱππικοί τ' ἄπυον   – ⏑ – | – ⏑ –
πηδαλίων διὰ στόμια,   – ⏑ ⏑ – ⏑ – ⏑◠

and in 481 a trimeter

ἐπεύχομαι δή σε μὲν εὐτυχεῖν, ἰὼ   ⏑ – ⏑ – – ⏑ ⏑ – ⏑ – ⏑ –
πρόμαχ' ἐμῶν δόμων, | τοῖσι δὲ δυστυχεῖν.   2 doch.

Supp. 630–97 gives an admirably clear example of the interweaving of dochmiac and aeolo-choriambic by means of this link – ⏑ ⏑ – ⏑ –. It is a peculiarly Aeschylean blend.

Beneath all this diversity of form certain characteristics of the movement emerge: the shortness of the phrase, and the blunt ends emphasized by frequent diaeresis but blurred from time to time by resolution (even of such curious form as ⏑ – – $\underset{\times}{-}$ ◠) or by the *rallentando* close – $\underset{\times}{-}$ –. The likeness of some of its forms to syncopated iambic is clear, and there are a great many passages where dochmiacs are mixed with iambic trimeters or dimeters. But besides mere juxtaposition the two metres sometimes coalesce in a single colon: *Sept.* 888

δι' εὐωνύμων τετυμμένοι   ⏑ – – ⏑ – | ⏑ – ⏑ –

or (Aesch. *Supp.* 347)

Παλαίχθονος τέκος, κλῦθί μου   ⏑ – ⏑ – | ⏑ – – ⏑ –
πρόφρονι καρδίᾳ, Πελασγῶν ἄναξ,   2 doch.

and dimeters or lekythia may similarly be joined to a dochmiac:

πατρίδα δεκέτεσιν σποραῖσιν ἐλθόντ' ἐμάν[1]   (Eur. *El.* 1152).

Such insertions, however, are less commonly full iambic metra than the shorter, bacchiac and cretic (or paeonic). The appropriateness of these as supplements to a metre with basic form ⏑ – – ⏑ – need not be laboured. The bacchiac usually has its 'leading-in', not its tail, position, since the characteristic dochmiac movement ends blunt,

---

[1] This could be analysed alternatively ◠ ⏑◠ ⏑ – ⏑ – | ⏑ – – ⏑ – lek.+doch., or ⏑◠◠ ⏑ – | ⏑ – ⏑ – | – ⏑ –, doch.+sync. iamb. dim. Such ambiguities are inevitable, and have no answer.

not pendant. For this reason, in the many cases where analytical division appears ambiguous (is ἰὼ γᾶ τε καὶ παμφαής ∪ – – |
∪ – – ∪ – or ∪ – – ∪ – | – ∪ –?) the cretic alternative is theoretically preferable; so too the double cretic in

κλύεις φθέγμα τᾶς | βούκερω | παρθένου;[1]

Bacch. 1018 has bacch.+paeon+doch.

δράκων ἢ πυριφλέγων ὁρᾶσθαι λέων.   ∪ – – | ∪ ∪ ∪ – | ∪ – – ∪ –

It is obvious how similar in such mixed cola the whole impression of the movement is to syncopated iambic; often the only difference is that the cola will not analyse into regular metra. It is in such contexts that the segments – ∪ – ∪ – and even ⏔ – ∪ – ⏔, the iambo-trochaic pentasyllable, emerge and force us to consider whether these too must not be included, by a kind of anaclasis, under the variants of dochmiac: *O.T.* 1339 (in iambic and dochmiac context)

ἔτ' ἔστ' ἀκούειν ἁδονᾷ, φίλοι.[2]   ∪ – ∪ – ⏓ | – ∪ – ∪ –

This iambo-dochmiac metre can of course pass easily into true iambic and true dochmiac, and in such mixed passages analysis, and even colometry, often leave many uncertainties. *P.V.* 574 is typical:

ὑπὸ δὲ κηρόπλαστος ὀτοβεῖ δόναξ
∪ ∪ ∪ – ∪ – | ∪ ∪ ∪ – ∪ –

ἀχέτας ὑπνοδόταν νόμον·
– ∪ – | ∪ ∪ ∪ – ∪ –

ἰὼ ἰὼ πόποι, ποῖ μ' ἄγουσι τηλέπλαγκτοι πλάναι;
∪ ∪ ∪ – ∪ – | – ∪ – ∪ – | ∪ – – ∪ –

τί ποτέ μ', ὦ Κρόνιε παῖ, τί ποτε ταῖσδ'
∪ ∪ ∪ – | ∪ ∪ ∪ – | ∪ ∪ ∪ –

ἐνέζευξας εὑρὼν ἁμαρτοῦσαν ἐν πημοναῖσιν, ἒ ἔ,[3]
4 bacch.+ ∪ – ∪ – –

οἰστρηλάτῳ δὲ δείματι δειλαίαν
⏓ – ∪ – ∪ | – ∪ ∪ – ∪ –

παράκοπον ὧδε τείρεις;
∪⏖ ∪ – | ∪ – –

[1] Cf. *Ag.* 1118 κατολολυξάτω | θύματος | λευσίμου.
[2] Cf. *Phil.* 1173.   [3] ἒ ἔ in Aesch. has full spondaic value, like αἰαῖ.

πυρί με φλέξον ἢ χθονὶ κάλυψον ἢ ποντίοις

∪ ∪ ∪ − ∪ − | ∪ ∪ ∪ − ∪ − | − ∪ −

δάκεσι δὸς βοράν.

∪ ∪ ∪ − ∪ −

μηδέ μοι φθονήσῃς εὐγμάτων, ἄναξ.

− ∪ − | ∪ − − | − ∪ − ∪ −

ᾄδην με πολύπλανοι πλάναι

∪ − ∪◠ | ∪ − ∪ −   iamb. dim.

γεγυμνάκασιν οὐδ' ἔχω μαθεῖν ὅπᾳ
iamb. trim.

πημονὰς ἀλύξω.

− ∪ − | ∪ − −

κλύεις φθέγμα τᾶς βούκερω παρθένου;

∪ − − ∪ − | − ∪ − | − ∪ −

Here, except for an iambic dimeter and trimeter shortly before the
end, the elements are either dochmiac or bacchiac-cretic-paeonic or
the 'associated' pentasylls. But perhaps they are better regarded as
'associated', simply, the one as a prolongation of bacchiac, the
other of cretic. To the question where, if anywhere, protraction
occurs in these there is no answer. But it is significant that there
are dochmiac passages where resolved cretics ∪ ∪ ∪ ∪ ∪ occur as
insertions: *Ag.* 1140

φρενομανής τις εἶ θεοφόρητος, ἀμ-   ∪ ∪ ∪ − ∪ − | ∪ ∪ ∪ − ∪ −
-φὶ δ' αὐτᾶς θροεῖς | νόμον ἄνομον.   ∪ − − ∪ − | ◠ ∪◠

So *Ion* 776

τόδ' ἐπὶ τῷδε κακὸν | ἄκρον ἔλακες   ∪◠ − ∪◠ | ◠ ∪◠
ἄχος ἐμοὶ στένειν,   ∪ ∪ ∪ − ∪ −

and *I.T.* 897

πόρον ἄπορον | ἐξανύσας δυοῖν,   ◠ ∪◠ | − ∪ ∪ − ∪ −

and it is probable that *I.T.* 832[1] should be taken as

κατὰ δὲ δάκρυ | κατὰ δὲ γόος | ἅμα χαρᾷ
◠ ∪◠ | ◠ ∪◠ | ∪ ∪ ∪ −

[1] This line should in any case be given to Iphigeneia in our texts. Orestes'
is not a singing part.

(cf. τόδ' ἔτι βρέφος 834), since this points the anaphora of κατὰ δέ, as in *El.* 592 ἄνεχε χέρας | ἄνεχε λόγον, and recalls the triple paeon of Soph. *El.* 1249 in similar context:

ἀνέφελον ἐνέβαλες | οὔ ποτε καταλύσιμον

∪⌒⌒ ∪⌒ | ⪥ ⌒⌒ ∪⌒

οὐδέ ποτε | λησόμενον | ἁμέτερον

− ∪ ∪ ∪ | − ∪ ∪ ∪ | − ∪ ∪ ∪

οἷον ἔφυ κακόν.

− ∪ ∪ − ∪ −

These passages then give a strong indication that − ∪ −, − ∪ ⌒, ⌒ ∪ ⌒ are in such contexts not syncopated iambic metra but 'true' cretics, behaving in resolution exactly like the dochmiac itself, being in fact shorter units of the same type. Only on this supposition, too, is the responsion of molossus to cretic in such units intelligible (see above, p. 102).

Dochmiac and iambo-dochmiac metre is exceedingly common in tragedy, and to a much greater extent than any other metrical type appears to have a definite emotional connotation. All three tragedians use it freely to express strong feeling, grief, fear, despair, horror, excitement, occasionally triumph or joy. There are a few exceptions, and in particular Aeschylus in his earlier plays sometimes uses it like any other metre for appeal or reflection (nearly the whole of the lyric of the *Septem* is dochmiac or iambo-dochmiac). But its characteristic use is for the panic of the Theban women under siege, the half-articulate prophecies of Cassandra, Theseus' lament for Phaedra, the ravings of Agave, the howls of the blinded Polymestor, the extravagant joy of the female in a scene of ἀναγνώρισις. In ἀμοιβαῖα or 'responses' the impassioned dochmiacs of the one party may beat against the other's calmer spoken trimeters, as in the Recognition of Iphigeneia and Orestes or the scene between Hecuba and the herald Talthybius; but curiously enough several of the most passionate or exalted solo-lyrics are just those in which dochmiacs and trimeters are mixed, as in the Cassandra-scene, *Ag.* 1072–1177, and the anguish of the newly blinded Oedipus, *O.T.* 1307–66. The great majority of these trimeters have the ordinary dialogue-rhythm, though now and again one breaks quite away from it, as *Or.* 1414

περὶ δὲ γόνυ χέρας ἱκεσίους ἔβαλον ἔβαλον.

Aeschylus's dochmiacs are not difficult to read at sight, even if theoretical analysis of his iambo-dochmiacs is sometimes ambiguous. Diaeresis usually underlines the phrasing, and where there is a πνῖγος the forms are so regular that the rhythm is unmistakable, as in *Sept.* 698 ff.:

ἀλλὰ σὺ μὴ 'ποτρύ-|-νου, κακὸς οὐ κεκλή-
-ση βίον εὖ κυρή-|-σας, μελάναιγις οὐκ
εἶσι δόμων 'Ερι-|-νύς, ὅταν ἐκ χερῶν
θεοὶ θυσίαν δέχωνται.

The long iambo-dochmiac ἄστροφα, *Sept.* 78 ff., are lucidity itself (metrically speaking) compared with similar passages of Euripides —for instance, *H.F.* 1016–85. Euripides, probably following the new musical tendencies of his day, developed a wholly different technique of metrical construction in such ἀπολελυμένα, in which the dochmiac with its freedom of form played a great part. He also introduced here a great variety of longer phrases (analysed in this book under the head 'prosodiac-enoplian', see ch. x) which had the same freedom of blunt or dragged close as the dochmiac, as for instance $- \cup \cup - \cup \cup - \underset{\smile}{\cup} -$.[1] But even in unbroken series of dochmiacs his variety of forms is greater and the rhythm more difficult to seize in reading deprived of music, especially in ἀπολελυμένα. Some of his interlocked pairs are not easily sorted: *Tro.* 244

τίν' ἄρα τίς ἔλαχε; τί-|-να πότμος εὐτυχής.

He is fond of the ending ⌒, even apart from eight-syllabled forms. It is noteworthy how freely the heptasyllabic dochmiac plays with longs and shorts, so long as the count of syllables remains seven: *I.A.* 1288 $\cup \cup \cup - \cup \cup \cup$ θανατόεντι Πάριν; *Or.* 1302 $\cup - ⌒ \underset{\times}{\times} ⌒$ φονεύετε καίνετε; *I.A.* 1485 $- \cup \cup - \cup ⌒$ αἵμασι θύμασί τε, cf. 1489, 1493; Aeschylus, *Sept.* 935, $\cup ⌒ - \underset{\times}{⌒} -$ ἔριδι μαινομένα (cf. *Eum.*

---

[1] Cf. also Aesch. *Sept.* 222 ∼ 229.

837 ἐμὲ παθεῖν τάδε, φεῦ). Aristophanes once (*Av.* 427–30) forms a group on this principle:

πότερα μαινόμενος;	⏑ ⏑ ⏑ – ⏑ ⏑ ⏑
— ἄφατον ὡς φρόνιμος.	⏑ ⏑ ⏑ – ⏑ ⏑ ⏑
— ἔνι σοφόν τι φρενί;	⏑ ⏑ ⏑ – ⏑ ⏑ ⏑
— πυκνότατον κίναδος,	⏑ ⏑ ⏑ – ⏑ ⏑ –
σόφισμα κύρμα τρῖμμα παιπάλημ᾽ ὅλον,	i. trim.

and in *H.F.* 759 even $\underset{x}{\text{—}}$ ⏑ ⏑ – $\widehat{⏑⏑}$ – οὐρανίων μακάρων appears to correspond to ⏑ ⏑ ⏑ – ⏑ ⏑ ⏑ 745 ἃ πάρος οὔποτε δι-|-ὰ φρενὸς ἤλπισ᾽ ἄν.[1]

For Sophocles, the Ode to Sleep, *Phil.* 827ff. is a good illustration of his metrical inventiveness in the use of cola which defy strict codification while showing a clear rhythmical interrelation. Unfortunately the metrical style has been in part distorted by ancient 'corrections'. I have attempted a reconstruction, with some discussion, in Additional note, p. 117.

Dochmiac response is usually very close, but occasional divergences in Sophocles and still more in Euripides show how in all its diversity the dochmiac is a single type with variants: Soph. *Phil.* 395 ~ 510

σὲ κἀκεῖ μᾶτερ πότνι᾽ ἐπηυδώμαν   ⏑ – – $\underset{x}{\text{—}}$ – | ⏑ $\widehat{⏑⏑}$ – $\underset{x}{\text{—}}$ –

and

εἰ δὲ πικρούς, ἄναξ, ἔχθεις ᾽Ατρείδας. $\underset{x}{\text{—}}$ ⏑ ⏑ – ⏑ – | $\underset{x}{\text{—}}$ – – $\underset{x}{\text{—}}$ –

Or. 140ff. ~ 153ff. illustrates both imperfect and typically close responsion:

σῖγα σῖγα λεπτὸν ἴχνος ἀρβύλης	– ⏑ – ⏑ –	⏑ ⏑ ⏑ – ⏑ –
πῶς ἔχει; λόγου μετάδος, ὦ φίλα·	
τίθετε, μὴ ψοφεῖτε μηδ᾽ ἔστω κτύπος.[2]	⏑ ⏑ ⏑ – ⏑ –	⏑ – – – ⏑ –?
τίνα τύχαν εἴπω; τίνα δὲ συμφοράν;	⏑ ⏑ ⏑ – $\underset{x}{\text{—}}$ –	⏑ ⏑ ⏑ – ⏑ –

[1] The notation in this paragraph indicates how the syllabic sequences *could* be made to conform to dochmiac measure, but the context in *Av.* 427–30 shows that here at least the determining factor was, in Ar.'s manner, more probably syllable-counting.

[2] The text of this line is quite uncertain.

— ἀποπρὸ βᾶτ᾽ ἐκεῖσ᾽ ἀποπρό μοι κοίτας.   ᴗ ᴗ ᴗ − ᴗ − | ᴗ ᴗ ᴗ − x̲ −

— ἔτι μὲν ἐμπνέει, βραχὺ δ᾽ ἀναστένει·   ᴗ ᴗ ᴗ − ᴗ − | ᴗ ᴗ ᴗ − ᴗ −

— ἰδοὺ πείθομαι.   ᴗ − − ᴗ −

— τί φής; ὦ τάλας.

— ἆ ἆ σύριγγος ὅπως πνοὰ   x̲ − − | x̲ ᴗ ᴗ − ᴗ −

— ὀλεῖς εἰ βλέφαρα κινήσεις   ᴗ − − | ᴗ ᴗ ᴗ − x̲ −

λεπτοῦ δόνακος, ὦ φίλα, φώνει μοι.   x̲ − ᴗ ᴗ ᴗ − | ᴗ − − x̲ −

ὕπνου γλυκυτάταν φερομένῳ χάριν.   ᴗ − ᴗ ᴗ ᴗ − | ᴗ⌣ − ᴗ −

— ἴδ᾽ ἀτρεμαῖον ὡς ὑπόροφον φέρω   ᴗ ᴗ ᴗ − ᴗ − | ᴗ ᴗ ᴗ − ᴗ −

— μέλεος ἐχθίστων θεόθεν ἐργμάτων,   ᴗ ᴗ ᴗ − x̲ − | ᴗ ᴗ ᴗ − ᴗ −

βοάν·   — ναί, οὕτως.   ᴗ − − − −

τάλας.   — φεῦ μόχθων.

κάταγε κάταγε πρόσιθ᾽ ἀτρέμας ἀτρέμας ἴθι·

ἄδικος ἄδικα τότ᾽ ἄρ᾽ ἔλακεν ἔλακεν, ἀπό-

ᴗ ᴗ ᴗ ᴗ ᴗ ᴗ ᴗ ᴗ | ᴗ ᴗ ᴗ ᴗ ᴗ ᴗ ᴗ ᴗ

λόγον ἀπόδος ἐφ᾽ ὅ τι χρέος ἐμόλετέ ποτε.

-φονον ὅτ᾽ ἐπὶ τρίποδι Θέμιδος ἄρ᾽ ἐδίκασε

ᴗ ᴗ ᴗ ᴗ ᴗ ᴗ ᴗ ᴗ | ᴗ ᴗ ᴗ ᴗ ᴗ ᴗ ᴗ ᴗ

χρόνια γὰρ πεσὼν ὅδ᾽ εὐνάζεται.

φόνον ὁ Λοξίας ἐμᾶς ματέρος.

ᴗ ᴗ ᴗ − ᴗ − | ᴗ − − ᴗ −

Such verse, especially the last closely responding period, was never meant to be read in cold blood; it is operatic, and only designed for effect in such production. The ἀντιλαβή, or change of speakers in the middle of a metrical phrase, has a close parallel in iambo-dochmiacs, *O.C.* 836 ~ 879.

The dochmiac is peculiarly a tragic metre, and its use in comedy is rare. Such passages as *Nub.* 1163–4, − ᴗ ᴗ − ᴗ − | − ᴗ ᴗ − ᴗ −, twice repeated in a strain of cheerful jollity, are not in the context to be taken as dochmiac but as the aeolo-choriambic cola found as ingredients in σκόλια.[1] Most of the genuinely dochmiac passages appear to use the metre in one of two ways: (1) in παρατραγῳδία, (2) for deliberately and unsuitably prosaic sentiments. In *Ach.* 1219, 1221 Lamachus, as the Scholiast says, θρηνῶν παρατραγῳδεῖ. Euripides' Cousin in the guise of Helen (*Thesm.* 912) has a beautiful

---

[1] See below, pp. 133 and 139.

parody of an impassioned ἀναγνωρισμός with Euripides-Menelaus:

> ὦ χρόνιος ἐλθὼν σῆς δάμαρτος ἐσχάρας,
> i. trim.
>
> λαβέ με λαβέ με πόσι, περίβαλε δὲ χέρας.
> ∪◠◠ ∪◠ | ∪◠◠ ∪ −
>
> φέρε σὲ κύσω. ἄπαγέ μ' ἄπαγ' ἄπαγ' ἄπαγέ με.
> ∪◠◠ ∪◠ | ∪◠◠ ∪◠

Ach. 385 ff. however (the Chorus's ungracious consent to Dicaeopolis's request for time to collect rags for pleading in) is parody not
of the words of tragedy but of the use of a metre normally only
heard as the vehicle of tragic emotion:

> τί ταῦτα στρέφει τεχνάζεις τε καὶ πορίζεις τριβάς;
> λαβὲ δ' ἐμοῦ γ' ἕνεκα παρ' Ἱερωνύμου
> σκοτοδασυπυκνότριχά τιν' Ἄιδος κυνῆν

(*appassionato*) 'Take it for a-all I ca-are'—and the ludicrous compound gives a complete resolved dochmiac in a single word.

NOTE ON SOME RARE FORMS OF DOCHMIAC

The 'hypodochmius' − ∪ − ∪ − appears several times as a segment
of a colon formed of two dochmiacs, as in *Or.* 140 quoted above and
Ion 799 οἷον οἷον ἄλγος ἔπαθον, φίλαι, where the context is pure
dochmiac, so that the phrase is either a real dochmiac variant or
(cf. pp. 108, 109) a close associate. *Ion* 1490 σπάργαν' ἀμφίβολα
− ∪ − ∪ ◠ in a similar position looks like a resolved form, and
I.T. 870 δείν' ἔτλαν ὤμοι like the same with dragged close − ∪ − x̄ −.
− ∪ ◠ ∪ − must be assigned to the same group: cf. Eur. *Hec.* 1089

> αἰαῖ, ἰὼ Θρήκης λογχοφόρον ἐνο-   − ∪ ∪ − x̄ − | − ∪◠ ∪ −
> -πλον εὔιππον Ἄρει κάτοχον γένος,   ∪ − − ∪ − | − ∪ ∪ − ∪ −

Hec. 1105 ἢ τὸν ἐς Ἀΐδα, and Ar. *Ach.* 570

> τειχομάχος ἀνήρ.   − ∪◠ ∪ −

The colarion − ∪ − ∪ − is a peculiar one, however, in that there are
several passages where it occurs twice or three times consecutively
(*Alc.* 213, *Or.* 992, *Phoen.* 1023, *O.T.* 1208) in iambo-trochaics

without further dochmiacs in the context, and sometimes in the middle of these series with *brevis in longo* at the close (notice the responsion of *Aj.* 401–2 with 417–18), suggesting that in these passages it stands by itself as a little colon-period. In Soph. *Aj.* 401 ff.

ἀλλά μ' ἁ Διὸς	– ∪ – ∪ ◡
ἀλκίμα θεὸς	– ∪ – ∪ ◡
ὀλέθριον αἰκίƺει.	⌒ ∪ ∪ – – –
ποῖ τις οὖν φύγῃ;	– ∪ – ∪ –
ποῖ μολὼν μένω;	– ∪ – ∪ –

the stanza has begun with iambo-dochmiacs, and the phrase is associated with the colarion discussed on p. 103 (in the antistrophe εὔφρονες 'Αργείοις – ∪ ∪ – – –) and identical with the 'anapaestic dochmiacs' of Eur. *Ion* 149 Κασταλίας δῖναι, | νοτερὸν ὕδωρ βάλλων.[1]

There are some instances of colaria both slightly longer and slightly shorter than the normal dochmiac, which are, nevertheless, so involved in dochmiac contexts that it seems most practical to class them as variants. The longer might be grouped together as the hexasyllable ∪ – ∪ – ∪ – with its equivalents (resolved and dragged).[2] Soph. *Ant.* 1275 ∼ 1299

οἴμοι λακπάτητον ἀντρέπων χαράν, x̄ – ⏑̱ ∪ – | ∪ – ∪ – ∪ –

and

τάλας, τὸν δ' ἔναντα προσβλέπω νεκρόν ∪ – – ∪ – | ∪ – ∪ – ∪ –

in iambo-dochmiac context *might* conceivably be explained as syncopated trimeters ◡ – – | ∪ – ∪ – | ∪ – ∪ –, but there are other cola which cannot be so analysed, such as *Hec.* 1084

τέκνων ἐμῶν φύλαξ ὀλέθριον κοίταν, ∪ – ∪ – ∪ – | ∪⌒ – x̄ –

Hipp. 593

τὰ κρυπτὰ γὰρ πέφηνε, διὰ δ' ὄλλυσαι ∪ – ∪ – ∪ – | ∪⌒ – ∪ –

or *Phoen.* 331, where ἀνῆξε μὲν ξίφους is clearly isolated as a single colon. Resolved forms include *Eum.* 158 ὑπὸ φρένας, ὑπὸ λοβόν

---

[1] See above, pp. 59 ff.   [2] Cf. also p. 103.

(cf. *H.F.* 1057 ἀδύνατ' ἀδύνατά μοι, *Sept.* 789 διὰ χερί ποτε λαχεῖν) ∪ ∪ ∪ ∪ ∪ ∪ ∪ –, Aesch. *Supp.* 120

πολλάκι δ' ἐμπίτνω ξὺν λακίδι λινοσινεῖ   – ∪ ∪ – ∪ – │ – ⌒ ∪ ⌒ ∪ –

(where Weil's improbable transposition is, nevertheless, widely accepted), *O.C.* 1725 ἵμερος ἔχει μέ τις, *Bacch.* 983 ἢ σκόλοπος ὄψεται ⊼ ⌒ ∪ – ∪ – and *Tro.* 311 μακάριος ὁ γαμέτας ∪ ⌒ ∪ ⌒ ∪ – ~ 328 τύχαις· ὁ χορὸς ὅσιος ∪ – ∪ ⌒ ∪ ⌒. But in the nature of things this kind of metre is beset with ambiguities, and even a small degree of textual corruption, or a small modification in colometry, can upset a tentative analysis. It is probable, for instance, that S. *El.* 1239 ~ 1260 should with Seidler be reduced to orthodox dochmiacs, discarding ἀλλ':

οὐ τὰν Ἄρτεμιν   τὰν ἀεὶ ἀδμήταν
~ τίς οὖν ἀξίαν   σοῦ γε πεφηνότος

and similarly the intrusion of δὲ twice has bedevilled S. *Phil.* 834 (p. 117).

Among shorter cola, the use of – – – – as a transition phrase between anapaestics and dochmiacs has already been mentioned.[1] The same ambiguity affects the resolved forms ∪ ∪ – ∪ ∪ – *O.C.* 1562 ξένον ἐξανύσαι,[2] ∪ ∪ – – – *H.F.* 1085 ἀναβακχεύσει │ Καδμείων πόλιν, and – – ∪ ∪ – *Eum.* 843 πλευρὰς ὀδύνα, cf. *Aj.* 399, ch. ix Additional note, p. 154.

The many variations of the heptasyllable (see above, p. 111) should make us chary of emending away some of the rarer ones. Thus *Hipp.* 1276 σκυλάκων πελαγίων ∪ ∪ – ∪ ∪ ∪ – is unexceptionable in itself and supported by the same form in Aristophanes' parody *Ran.* 1343 τὸν ἀλεκτρυόνα μου. So too the octosyllable *H.F.* 888 γένος ἄγονον αὐτίκα ∪ ∪ ∪ ∪ ∪ – ∪ ∪ has its counterpart *Ran.* 1337 μελανονεκυείμονα. Aristophanes is parodying the metrical habits as well as the diction of his victim.

---

[1] See above, pp. 54 ff., and cf. Soph. *Phil.* 837 γνώμαν ἴσχων (p. 118).

[2] This form + rising paeon θρέομαι φοβερὰ μεγάλ' ἄχη ∪ ∪ – ∪ ∪ – ⌒ ∪ – *Sept.* 78 (as MP) seems to me more probable than the 'fearful great woes', with the strange spondee θρεῦμαι, canonized in our texts.

Additional note

Ode to Sleep: *Phil.* 827–38 ∼ 843–54 str. ant., 855–64 ep.
The subtle and exquisite metrical art of this ode has bewitched
all who have ears to hear it. It emerges spontaneously from the
sense of the first part of the strophe, and continues in serene
detachment from the anxious ditherings of the sentiments that
follow. The main difficulties of interpretation lie in the opening
phrase and in 834 ∼ 850 (859 is surely an intrusion, too silly even
for this Chorus). Is 827 dact. tetram. ending ἀλγέων – – in abnormal
responsion to 843 ὄψεται – ◡ ◡ (in synaphea with the following),
or have we here a line of so-called 'aeolic dactyls', ending – ◡ – ||
with 'final *anceps*' in Hephaestion's sense (see p. 157, n. 2) though
without the 'aeolic base' to start it off (cf. E. *Med.* 135–6, on which
see the article quoted p. 25, n. 1)—or should one then rather call
the line 'prosodiac' (see ch. x)? Such a line, under whatever name,
would be totally uncharacteristic of Soph., whereas the tetram. is a
favourite of his. Wilam. (*G.V.* p. 347), unable to take the anomalous responsion at colon-end, continues through εὐαὲς ἡμῖν to make
hexam., deleting μ' in 844 to give Pause. But even in a hexam. the
responsion ◡◡ at bucolic diaeresis with rhetorical pause is hardly
less conspicuous. I think the justification for accepting the abnormal
responsion at tetram.-end may be found in the fainter echo in
860–1, two B-tetrams. (p. 36) of which the first ends in the unusual
– –, the second in – ◡ ◡, in synaphea with the following ia. dim.
The dominant rhythm in str. ant. is the long *rallentando* of the
closes, the three long sylls., whether part of a dragged doch. or
isolable as a molossus (= dragged cretic, in either form a legitimate
inset among dochs.) or 'spondee' (= sync. ia.? see p. 102) with
preceding long. In the fifth and the last colon there is a cretic
variation. The earlier part of most lines is either choriambic or
iambic with resolved first long, – ◡ ◡ – or ◡̲ ◠ ◡ –. It always
disturbed my ear to have 834 suddenly swinging with banal effect
into ordinary epitrites – ◡ – x̲ – ◡ – x̲ – –, leaving an antistrophe difficult to pull out to the required length. But the tendency of vigorous asyndeta to get tidied away by an inserted δὲ is

notorious, and here surely the Chorus warn urgently in a triple question ὅρα ποῦ στάσῃ, | ποῖ βάσῃ, πῶς μοι τἀντεῦθεν | φροντίδος. 850 is then short of only one syllable: κεῖνό μοι, κεῖνο ⟨δὴ⟩ λάθρᾳ, and the cretic stands twice (easier than once) in responsion to molossus, see above p. 102, and cf. *O.C.* 117 ~ 149 ποῦ ναίει ~ ὀμμάτων, 1559 ~ 1571

> Αἰδωνεῦ Αἰδωνεῦ λίσσομαι   − − − − − − − ⌣ −
> ~ εὐνᾶσθαι κνυζεῖσθαί τ' ἐξ ἄντρων.

Conceivably there is a slight anticipation of this in the fourth phrase if LA are right in ἀντέχοις.

I would then suggest:

str. ⌜	Ὕπν' ὀδύνας ἀδαής, Ὕπνε δ' ἀλγέων,	dact. tetram. − ⌣͡⌣
ant. ⌊	ἀλλὰ τέκνον τάδε μὲν θεὸς ὄψεται.	
	⌜ εὐαὲς ἡμῖν ἔλθοις,	− ⌣ ⌣ − − − −
	⌊ ὧν δ' ἂν ἀμείβῃ μ' αὖθις	
	εὐαίων εὐαίων, ὦναξ.	− − − − − − −
	βαιάν μοι, βαιὰν ὦ τέκνον	
	ὄμμασι δ' ἀντίσχοις τάνδ' αἴγλαν	− ⌣ ⌣ − ⌣̣? − − − −
	πέμπε λόγων φάμαν· ὡς πάντων	
	ἃ τέταται τανῦν.	− ⌣ ⌣ − ⌣ − doch. ⁻⌣⁻
	ἐν νόσῳ εὐδρακής	
	ἴθι ἴθι μοι παιών.	⌣͡⌣ ⌣ − − − ‖
	ὕπνος ἄυπνος λεύσσειν.	
	ὦ τέκνον ὅρα ποῦ στάσῃ,	− ⌣͡⌣ ⌣ − − − −
	ἀλλ' ὅ τι δύνᾳ μάκιστον,	
	ποῖ βάσῃ, πῶς μοι τἀντεῦθεν	− ⌣̣ − − ⌣̣ − − − ‖
	κεῖνό μοι, κεῖνο ⟨δὴ⟩ λάθρᾳ	
	φροντίδος. ὁρᾷς; εὕδει.	− ⌣ ⌣ ⌣ − − −
	ἐξιδοῦ ὅπως πράξεις.	
	πρὸς τί μένομεν πράσσειν;	− ⌣ ⌣ ⌣ − − −
	οἶσθα γὰρ ὃν αὐδῶμαι,	
	καιρός τοι πάντων γνώμαν ἴσχων	− − − − − − − −
	εἰ ταύτᾳ τούτῳ γνώμαν ἴσχεις,	
	⟨πολύ τι⟩ πολὺ παρὰ πόδα κράτος ἄρνυται.	2 doch. ⁻⌣⁻
	μάλα τοι ἄπορα πυκινά τ' ἐνιδεῖν πάθη.	

I owe the modification in 854 to Miss L. P. E. Parker; where the two doch. are so closely and similarly interlaced the long *anceps* in response to short in the middle of resolutions is unlikely; the sense is at least as good. Otherwise we must give up Hermann's simple supplement πολύ τι and mark a lacuna ⟨◡◡ ⤬⟩ after πόδα:

ep. οὖρός τοι τέκνον οὖρος· ἀ-	glyc.
‑νὴρ δ' ἀνόμματος, οὐδ' ἔχων ἀρωγάν,	‖ + phal.
⎰ἐκτέταται νύχιος	– ◡ ◡ – ◡◡ dodrans
⎱οὐ χερός, οὐ ποδός, οὔ τινος ἄρχων,	dact. tetr. ‾‾
⎰ἀλλά τις ὡς 'Αίδα πάρα κείμενος.	dact. tetr. ‾◡◡
⎨ὅρα, βλέπ' εἰ καίρια	ia. dim.
⎱φθέγγῃ· τὸ δ' ἁλώσιμον ‖	teles. ◡
⎰ἐμᾷ φροντίδι, παῖ, πόνος	pher. ◡◡
⎱ὁ μὴ φοβῶν κράτιστος.	ia. dim. cat.

VIII

IONIC

Ionic though κατὰ μέτρον much interwoven with 'ametric' aeolics—
Variants of the metron—Theory of 'major' and 'minor' ionics—
Analyses—Ethical significance in Greek theory—Anacreontics—Ionics in
the *Bacchae*—Aeolo-ionics.

Of all the metres which run κατὰ μέτρον the ionic is the most difficult of analysis in such terms. The characteristic ionic movement is
the alternation of double-short and double-long, ... ∪ ∪ – – ∪ ∪
– – ∪ ∪ – – ∪ ∪ ... (in ἐπιπλοκή[1] therefore with pure choriambic), and its regular metron is reckoned ∪ ∪ – –, with typical
dimeter ἴτε βάκχαι, ἴτε βάκχαι. In certain circumstances, however, it
seems to produce ∪ ∪ – ∪ or – ∪ – –. But neither of these two
variants can repeat consecutively, and their normal use is together
in the 'anaclastic' dimeter ∪ ∪ – ∪ | – ∪ – – discussed below; the
second, that is, appears as a kind of reaction to the first, so that the
division into two separate tetrasyllabic metra is not fully appropriate
here.

The ionic in drama is a purely lyric metre, and there are many
passages where it is so interwoven with aeolic of various forms that
its cola are there best taken as unified wholes without metra, like
the irreducible aeolics. Some cola which are often taken as ionic I
have preferred to treat as aeolic; the dividing line is often difficult
to draw.[2] But tragedy and comedy contain a considerable volume of
unequivocally ionic passages, and the metre is one which more than
any other except the dochmiac impressed its contemporary hearers
and users as possessing marked ethical characteristics of its own;
its prominence in the *Persae* and the *Bacchae* is a reflection of this
significance. These purely or predominantly ionic passages have a
varying degree of regularity in their construction κατὰ μέτρον, and

[1] See above, p. 41 and cf. E. *Bacch.* 398–401 analysed in the next
chapter, p. 145.
[2] See below, pp. 143–4.

in the Lesbian poets and Anacreon there are regular ionics κατὰ στίχον which must have been in the same line of tradition and can therefore be conveniently taken as a norm by which to measure irregularities and variants.

As with the other tetrasyllabic metra in lyric the commonest colon length is the dimeter, but the ionic tends often to continue in long runs or πνίγη. Irregularities are also analogous: metra may be catalectic ∪ ∪ − (even in the middle of a colon, though much less often than in the parallel forms of syncopated iambo-trochaics); either of the longs may be resolved ∪ ∪ ⌢ − or ∪ ∪ − ⌢, though this is relatively rare; the two shorts may coalesce into a single long ≍ − −; this molossus may have *anceps* in the outside position, i.e. an initial metron may appear as ∪ − −, or it may be acephalous ∧ − − at the beginning or catalectic − − ∧ at the end of a colon. The final syllable of a metron takes the short form before a molossus ∪ ∪ − ∪ | − − − or a catalectic molossus as in the clausula ∪ ∪ − ∪ | − −. It is usually short when the succeeding metron begins long, and the dimeter ∪ ∪ − ∪ | − ∪ − −, the 'anaclastic' ionic used κατὰ στίχον by Anacreon and possibly invented by him, is common in tragedy, both sporadically among other ionics and in series. Conversely, the final syllable of a metron is never shortened unless the succeeding metron begins long. It was this fact that led some ancient metricians to represent the ionic ἀνακλώμενον as a dimeter in which the two middle syllables had changed places by what we now call 'anaclasis', but the not uncommon ∪ ∪ − x̲ | − ∪ − −[1] makes the formula less than perfectly applicable.

The most usual account given of ionics is that they are of two kinds, *a maiore* when they take off from longs − − ∪ ∪ and *a minore* when they take off from shorts ∪ ∪ − −. It is true that this gives a neater superficial parallel with the pairs dactyl-anapaest, iambic-

---

[1] Probably first used by Aeschylus, since it is by no means certain that the Anacreon fragment P. Oxy. 2321, 4 (Page, *P.M.G.* 346) is in ionic metre. It would seem that when there are three apparent consecutive longs the middle one becomes long *anceps*: thus ∪ ∪ − x̲ − ∪ − − can correspond to ∪ ∪ − − ∪ ∪ − − (*P.V.* 399 ∼ 408) as well as to the anacreontic ∪ ∪ − ∪ − ∪ − −, cf. below, p. 125 on Ar. *Ran.* 323–36.

trochaic, but there are difficulties in the theory. Metra of the form
– – ◡ ◡ with their double-short cannot of course run to a pause any
more than the dactylic – ◡ ◡, and just as the dactylic period must
end in the disyllabic – $\underset{\times}{\times}$ or the catalectic –, so the ionic would
have to end in a molossus – – – or catalectic – –. The former is
comparatively rare in drama; one of the clearest instances is the
pentameter *Trach.* 850. I believe these from their contexts and
affinities to be better classed as aeolic; the subject is discussed in the
next chapter.[1] The catalectic, for instance in the form – – ◡ ◡ – –,
can equally well be taken as headless 'minor'; there is the same
ambiguity as in iambo-trochaics or dactylo-anapaests, with the
difference that there both 'polar' species have a flourishing existence
of their own whereas major ionics have but a shadowy claim to
self-sufficiency.

A further development of the 'major ionic' theory which has died
hard since the time of Hephaestion is that there are cola which begin
with the metron – – ◡ ◡ and end with a trochaic – ◡ – –. But this
will not do. It is inconsistent with all the practice of tetrasyllabic
metra to vary their *inside* syllables. The trochaic-seeming – ◡ – –,
as we have seen, follows naturally in the 'minor' ionic sequence
◡ ◡ – ◡̣ | – ◡ – –, where the second metron is heard as a kind of
variant of the first; it is the long third syllable of each which is
cardinal. But in a 'major ionic' sequence the cardinal long is the
second syllable, and a 'trochaic' metron cannot keep the continuity
of this movement.[2] In fact, in such a colon as – – ◡ ◡ – ◡ – – the

---

[1] I have omitted as irrelevant to the drama all discussion of forms found
only in lyric poets or late Hellenistic varieties such as the sotadean and
galliambic which were only intended for recitation.

[2] The only way to account for such a colon as – – ◡ ◡ | – ◡ – – in
tetrasyllabic terms would be to assume a metron ◡ ◡ – – changed to
– – – by contraction and then to – – ◡ ◡ by resolution, by the same
process as anapaests which assume dactylic form. I have sometimes
wondered whether Sophocles did not in fact avail himself of this device
in some of his clausulae, e.g. *El.* 1069 after two anacreontics has ἀχό-
ρευτα φέρουσ' ὀνείδη ◡ ◡ – ◡ ◡ | – ◡ – –, and so with a further
development 833–6 after – – – – ◡ ◡ – – might be a long ionic of seven
metra – – ◡ ◡ ending in the unresolved molossus – – –. It is worth

division into two tetrasyllabic metra is a piece of pencil and paper scansion, the legacy of Hephaestion (or his predecessors) with his propensity to start from the beginning and number off in fours. The colon, together with analogous longer versions, is in fact a common aeolic type.

An example of ionics at their simplest is Aesch. *Supp.* 1052–6 = 1057–61, stanzas consisting of five dimeters with no special clausula. 1034–42 = 1043–51 of the same play are pure ionics with a single anacreontic clausula. The preceding pair of stanzas is nearly as simple, dividing into two periods:

ἴτε μὰν ἀστυάνακτας	∪ ∪ – – ∣ ∪ ∪ – –
μάκαρας θεοὺς γανάοντες	∪ ∪ – – ∣ ∪ ∪ – –
πολιούχους τε καὶ οἳ χεῦμ' 'Ερασίνου	∪ ∪ – – ∣ ∪ ∪ – – ∣ ∪ ∪ – –
περιναίουσιν παλαιόν.	∪ ∪ – x̱ ∣ – ∪ – – ∥
ὑποδέξασθε δ' ὀπαδοὶ	∪ ∪ – – ∣ ∪ ∪ – –
μέλος· αἶνος δὲ πόλιν τάνδε Πελασγῶν	∪ ∪ – – ∣ ∪ ∪ – – ∣ ∪ ∪ – –
ἐχέτω μηδ' ἔτι Νείλου	∪ ∪ – – ∣ ∪ ∪ – –
προχοὰς σέβωμεν ὕμνοις.	∪ ∪ – ∪ ∣ – ∪ – –

The clausula of the first period is a modified, of the second a regular, anacreontic dimeter.

The first two stanzas of Eur. *Supp.* are also homogeneous:

48 ἐσιδοῦσ' οἰκτρὰ μὲν ὄσσων	
δάκρυ' ἀμφὶ βλεφάροις, ῥυ-	
-σὰ δὲ σαρκῶν πολιᾶν	hexam. cat.
καταδρύμματα χειρῶν·	∪ ∪ – ∣ ∪ ∪ – –
τί γάρ; ἃ φθιμένους παῖ-	∪ ∪ – ∣ ∪ ∪ – –
-δας ἐμοὺς οὔτε δόμοις	∪ ∪ – – ∣ ∪ ∪ –
προθέμαν οὔτε τάφων χώματα γαίας ἐσορῶ.	tetram. cat.

noting in this connection that the Hellenistic 'galliambic' (adapted by Catullus for his *Attis*) quoted by Hephaestion has the lines

Γαλλαὶ μητρὸς ὀρείης φιλόθυρσοι δρομάδες
– – – ∣ ∪ ∪ – – ∣ ∪ ∪ – – ∣ ∪ ∪ ◡

αἷς ἔντεα παταγεῖται καὶ χάλκεα κρόταλα
– – ∪ ∪ ∣ ∪ ∪ – – ∣ – – ∪ ∪ ∣ ∪ ∪ ◡

where in the second line there is a kind of anaclasis recalling the ana-paestic effect – ∪ ∪ ∪ ∪ – ∣ – ∪ ∪ ∪ ∪ –. But it is rather more likely that in the drama these ambiguous lines are aeolic, cf. below, pp. 143–4. Certainly – – ∪ ∪ – ∪ – – is a common aeolic colon.

ἔτεκες καὶ σύ ποτ', ὦ πότνια, κοῦρον
φίλα ποιησαμένα λέκτρα πόσει σῷ· μέτα νυν   heptam. cat.
δὸς ἐμοὶ σᾶς διανοίας, μετάδος δ' ὅσ-
-σον ἐπαλγῶ μελέα ⟨'γὼ⟩ φθιμένων οὓς ἔτεκον·   heptam. cat.
παράπεισον δὲ σόν, ὦ, λισσόμεθ', ἐλθεῖν   trim.
τέκνον Ἰσμηνὸν ἐμάν τ' ἐς χέρα θεῖναι   trim.
νεκύων θαλερᾷ σώματ' ἀλαίνοντ' ἄταφα.

∪ ∪ – | ∪ ∪ – – | ∪ ∪ – – | ∪ ∪ ⌣

The long runs are characteristic of this metre. The clausular rhythms
are throughout catalectic, and there are three cases of catalexis in
initial metra.

There is nothing in the context of the odes so far quoted to
suggest any particular ethical significance in the choice of this metre,
associated as it was with the worship of Cybele and Asiatic religious
influences, and in anacreontic form perhaps fancifully held to
contain some suggestion of effeminacy and even lasciviousness. The
preponderance of ionic in the earlier songs of the Persian statesmen,
however, is probably meant like the Oriental robes to reinforce the
impression of an un-Greek culture and code of behaviour. The
stanzas are metrically simple: in the first pair ten straight metra are
followed by two dimeters of the form ∪ ∪ – ∪ ∪ – – and the
clausula is a trimeter of the same character ∪ ∪ – ∪ ∪ – – ∪ ∪ – –.
The second pair are plain ionics with anacreontic clausula. The third
pair show repeatedly that cola ending in the 'catalectic' metron
∪ ∪ – may be in synaphea with the following (i.e. in such places it
marks a 'hold', not Pause), and there is a fairly strong probability
that the last syllable here, like the first long in the reverse Ἀθαμαν-
τίδος Ἑλλάς, should be given in ionic context the value of two longs.

109   ἔμαθον δ' εὐρυπόροι-   ∪ ∪ – – | ∪ ∪ –
      -ο θαλάσσας πολιαι-   ∪ ∪ – – | ∪ ∪ –
      -νομένας πνεύματι λάβρῳ   ∪ ∪ – – | ∪ ∪ – –   ‖
      ἐσορᾶν πόντιον ἄλσος   ∪ ∪ – – | ∪ ∪ – –
      πίσυνοι λεπτοδόμοις πείσμασι λα-   ∪ ∪ – – | ∪ ∪ – – | ∪ ∪ –
      -οπόροις τε μηχαναῖς.   ∪ ∪ – ∪ | – ∪ –

The clausular anacreontic is here catalectic. A more remarkable
clausula is found at 696 = 702 of the same play, where a little stanza
of two ionic dimeters is given a paroemiac close:

Ionic 125

σέβομαι μὲν προσιδέσθαι   ∪∪−− | ∪∪−−
σέβομαι δ᾽ ἀντία λέξαι   ∪∪−− | ∪∪−−
σέθεν ἀρχαίῳ περὶ τάρβει.   ∪∪ − ∸ − ∪∪ − −

Here the opening and closing rhythms of the last phrase pick up the ionics, and the extra syllable which so often distinguishes a clausula from its context is sandwiched in the middle.

Iacchus, called forth to lead the mystic procession in *Ran.* 323–36 = 340–53, is appropriately addressed in ionic metre (...ἐγκατα-κρούων ποδὶ τὰν ἀκόλαστον φιλοπαίγμονα τιμάν). The stanzas give repeated examples of all the varieties of free responsion normal in ionics: ∪∪−−∼ −∪−−, ∪∪−∪∼ ∪∪−−, and by a combination of these two[1] a regular dimeter ∪∪−− | ∪∪−−∼ anacreontic ∪∪−∪ | −∪−−. Three varieties of initial metron are ∪∪−, −∪−, and ∪−−, and the ritual cry Ἴακχ᾽ ὦ Ἴακχε is fitted into the ionic scheme as ∪− | −∪−⌣ (period-end and hiatus). This is formally in order as a variant of −− | ∪∪−− but is in effect simply a detachable colarion which can be fitted to various metrical contexts. One form of it occurs again with ionics, *Phil.* 1180 ἴωμεν ἴωμεν, but it is equally at home among aeolic or mixed metres, as in Eur. *Alc.* 906 and 908 = 929 and 931.

The anacreontic has hitherto appeared as an occasional variant, often clausular, among regular ionics. But it had become familiar to Athenians κατὰ στίχον in the lyrics of its eponymous master, and is so used in *P.V.* 402–6 = 410–14,[2] and Eur. *Cyc.* 495–502 = 503–10 = 511–18, where the two semi-choruses of satyrs sing the first and last verses and the drunken Cyclops the middle one. The scene is a κῶμος and reads like a bibulous parody of songs perhaps sung at feasts after the model of φέρ᾽ ὕδωρ, φέρ᾽ οἶνον, ὦ παῖ.

503   παπαπᾶ· πλέως μὲν οἴνου   ∪∪−∪−∪−−
      γάνυμαι δὲ δαιτὸς ἥβῃ   ∪∪−∪−∪−−

[1] It should be noted that the free responsion of *Vesp.* 276 εἶτ᾽ ἐφλέγμηνεν αὐτοῦ ∼ 284 διὰ τοῦτ᾽ ὀδυνηθείς is quite in order: −∪− | −∪−−∼ ∪∪− | ∪∪−−. There are other ionic phrases in the dactylo-epitrite context and there is no reason whatever for emending the antistrophe. For the admixture of dactylo-epitrites and ionics, see below, pp. 190 ff.
[2] See below, p. 129.

σκάφος ὁλκὰς ὡς γεμισθείς   ∪ ∪ – ∪ – ∪ – –
ποτὶ σέλμα γαστρὸς ἄκρας.   ∪ ∪ – ∪ – ∪ – – ‖
ὑπάγει μ' ὁ χόρτος εὔφρων   ∪ ∪ – ∪ – ∪ – –
ἐπὶ κῶμον ἦρος ὥραις   ∪ ∪ – ∪ – ∪ – –
ἐπὶ Κυκλῶπας ἀδελφούς.   ∪ ∪ – – ∪ ∪ – – ‖
φέρε μοι ξεῖνε φέρ' ἀσκὸν ἔνδος μοι.   ∪ ∪ – – ∪ ∪ – ∪ – – –

The pure ionic dimeter as the penultimate phrase in anacreontics is characteristic of Anacreon himself, cf. Page, *P.M.G.* 395. The final clausula ends in a molossus instead of the normal 'trochaic' metron.

No choric fragments survive of the Aeschylean tetralogy *Lycurgeia*, so that we do not know whether Euripides in the *Bacchae* was following the older master in this as in certain other points of the tradition when he composed all the earlier choruses with a predominance of ionic measure. This rhythm, reminiscent of orgiastic Eastern cults with their ecstasies and cruelties, predominates strongly up to l. 575 and as it were sets the tone of the drama; in the middle part the aeolic which has already appeared among the earlier ionic takes over the lead, while the last part with its frenzy and revulsion is predominantly dochmiac.

The irregularities of Euripides' ionics are of the types already noted, though he makes rather more use of resolution (sometimes out of strict responsion) and of the molossus. But the main difficulties are caused by the admixture of aeolic cola, with the effect that colometry becomes uncertain and it is often impossible to decide where there is a real change of rhythm and where the question of nomenclature is merely academic. In particular the pherecratean of the form – – – ∪ ∪ – – is identical on paper with one form of ionic dimeter. The strange medley of metres in the rushing epode 135–69 is so complicated by difficulties of text and interpretation that I have not attempted its analysis here.

The προοίμιον 64–71 is simple, starting with the double 'hold' Ἀσίας ἀπὸ γᾶς ∪ ∪ – | ∪ ∪ – and running in two major periods of which the first ends catalectic εὐαζομένα and the second with a molossus Διόνυσον ὑμνήσω ∪ ∪ – ∪ | – – –. This closing rhythm is picked up and echoed all through the first major period of the next pair of stanzas, which open with a phrase (l. 72) impossible to define, since we cannot tell whether the penultimate syllable is dragged (with long *anceps*) or the crucial true long of ionic. There follow two ionic dimeters of the form Διόνυσον ὑμνήσω. Here probably (at ἁγιστεύει) there is period close and the same three phrases are repeated. The rest is pure ionic, with a clausula which adds a catalectic metron ∪ ∪ – to the Διόνυσον ὑμνήσω rhythm.[1]

72 ὦ μάκαρ ὅστις εὐδαίμων   – ∪ ∪ – ∪ – – –
    τελετὰς θεῶν εἰδὼς   ∪ ∪ – ∪ – – –
    βιοτὰν ἁγιστεύει   ∪ ∪ – ∪ – – – |
    καὶ θιασεύεται ψυχὰν   – ∪ ∪ – ∪ – – –
    ἐν ὄρεσσι βακχεύων   ∪ ∪ – ∪ – – –
    ὁσίοις καθαρμοῖσιν.   ∪ ∪ – ∪ – – – ||
    τά τε ματρὸς μεγάλας ὄρ-   ∪ ∪ – – ∪ ∪ – –
    -για Κυβέλας θεμιτεύων   ∪ ∪◠ – ∪ ∪ – – |
    ἀνὰ θύρσον τε τινάσσων   ∪ ∪ – ∪ – – –
    κισσῷ τε στεφανωθεὶς   ≃ – – ∪ ∪ – –
    Διόνυσον θεραπεύει.   ∪ ∪ – – ∪ ∪ – – ||
    ἴτε βάκχαι ἴτε βάκχαι   ∪ ∪ – – ∪ ∪ – –
    Βρόμιον παῖδα θεὸν θεοῦ   ∪ ∪ – – ∪ ∪ – –
    Διόνυσον κατάγουσαι   ∪ ∪ – – ∪ ∪ – –
    Φρυγίων ἐξ ὀρέων Ἑλλάδος εἰς εὐ- ∪ ∪ – – ∪ ∪ – – ∪ ∪ – –
    -ρυχόρους ἀγυιὰς τὸν Βρόμιον.   ∪ ∪ – ∪ – – – ∪ ∪ –

The next pair repeat once more the opening phrase – ∪ ∪ – ∪ – – – with a colarion added ∪ ∪ – ∪ – – which is a catalectic version of Διόνυσον ὑμνήσω. Whether this colarion should be reckoned as ionic or aeolic, and whether it matters which, are questions as difficult to answer as the further one—are ll. 113–14 ionic or aeolic? Strophe and antistrophe have in any case exactly responsive phrasing:

ὦ Σεμέλας τροφοὶ Θῆβαι,   στεφανοῦσθε κισσῷ.
ὦ θαλάμευμα Κουρήτων   ζάθεοί τε Κρήτας.

[1] I think this colometry more probable than either one which cuts off the first syllable (even if ὦ were in some sense *extra metrum* there is no reason why ὅν should be in the antistrophe) or one in which aeolic dims. of the form – ∪ ∪ – ∪ – – are in continual synapheia with the following line, making the cut – | ∪ ∪ – ∪ – –. It is true that the 'aristophanean' is occasionally not catalectic, but the repeated caesura after a pendant close is improbable, and still leaves the ending of 74 and 77 problematic.

Some of these ambiguous rhythms are further discussed in the next two chapters.

The next stasimon contains two stanzas in straightforward ionic, with a probable switch over to aeolic clausula,[1] and two in aeolic. The next (519–75) has again a first pair ionic (οἶαν οἶαν ὀργάν should probably be deleted in ant. 537), with some anaclastic cola (one of them in responsion with an ordinary dimeter) and an anaclastic clausula catalectic ἔτι τοι τοῦ Βρομίου μελήσει ∪ ∪ – – | ∪ ∪ – ∪ | – –;[2] the epode is ionic passing over into iambo-aeolic in the last two periods.

The sporadic use of ionic is a subject fraught with difficulty because of the ambiguity already indicated between ionic and aeolic rhythm and sometimes also between ionic and the wide group of metres which for convenience I have classified under the general head of 'dactylo-epitrite'. The whole question can better be discussed after the main types of aeolic and dactylo-epitrite have been elucidated. One point may be mentioned here: the claim of Hephaestion that ionic cola may have an alien base, as in what he calls the 'epionic' trimeter of Alcman Ἰνὼ σαλασσομέδοισ' ἂν ἀπὸ μάσδων x̱ – ∪ – ∪ ∪ – – ∪ ∪ – – with iambic base. But this mixture of single and double short is typically aeolic, though it is liable to mix with cola that are embarrassingly ambiguous. Such a line occurs in fact, *Rhes.* 363 = 373, in a stanza of three major periods, the first iambo-choriambic, the second aeolo-ionic and the third aeolic:

ἄρά ποτ' αὖθις ἁ παλαιὰ Τροία	– ∪ ∪ – ∪ – ∪ – – ∪ ∪ –
τοὺς προπότας παναμερεύ-	– ∪ ∪ – ∪ – ∪ –
-σει θιάσους ἐρώτων	– ∪ ∪ – ∪ – – ‖
363 ψαλμοῖσι καὶ κυλίκων οἰνοπλανήτοις	– – ∪ – ∪ ∪ – – ∪ ∪ – –
ὑποδεξίαις ἁμίλλαις	∪ ∪ – ∪ – ∪ – –

---

[1] See below, p. 145.

[2] I am aware that this description of a clausula already found in Corinna may be over-elaborate. The full ionic colon, like the full dactylic, already has a pendant close ... ∪ ∪ – –; then, rather than end up blunt, the *final* clausula in either metre (see below, p. 161) can be distinguished by inserting as it were an extra change of step: instead of ... ∪ ∪ – – it is drawn out to ... ∪ ∪ – ∪ – –.

κατὰ πόντον Ἀτρειδᾶν   ⏑ ⏑ – ⏑ ⏑ – –
Σπάρταν οἰχομένων Ἰλιάδος παρ’ ἀκτᾶς;   – – – ⏑⏑ – – ⏑⏑ – ⏑ – – ‖
ὢ φίλος εἴθε μοι   – ⏑ ⏑ – ⏑ –
σᾷ χερὶ καὶ σῷ δορὶ πρά-   – ⏑ ⏑ – – ⏑ ⏑ –
-ξας τάδ’ ἐς οἶκον ἔλθοις.   – ⏑ ⏑ – ⏑ – –

Perhaps more deserving of the term 'epionic' are the curious compound cola, confined to Aeschylus, which begin with an iambic penthemimer ⏑ – ⏑ – – and continue in ionic or anacreontic. *P.V.* 128 = 144 and 399 = 407 are by themselves analysable as aeolo-choriambic cola (see the next chapter) like Soph. *Ant.* 839 = 857, but the ionic-anacreontic contexts give them the effect of anacreontics with a five-syllabled base, ⏑ – ⏑ – – instead of the ionic opening ⏑ ⏑ – –:

399   στένω σε τᾶς οὐλομένας τύχας, Προμηθεῦ,   ⏑–⏑– – | ⏑⏑ – ⏑ – ⏑ – –
     δακρυσίστακτον δ’ ἀπ’ ὄσσων   ⏑ ⏑ – – ⏑̲ ⏑ – –
     ῥαδινὰν λειβομένα ῥέος παρειὰν   ⏑⏑ – – ⏑⏑ – ⏑ – ⏑ – –
     νοτίοις ἔτεγξα παγαῖς.   ⏑ ⏑ – ⏑ – ⏑ – –
     ἀμέγαρτα γὰρ τάδε Ζεὺς   ⏑ ⏑ – ⏑ – ⏑ – –
     ἰδίοις νόμοις κρατύνων   ⏑ ⏑ – ⏑ – ⏑ – –
     ὑπερήφανον θεοῖς τοῖς   ⏑ ⏑ – ⏑ – ⏑ – …
       πάρος ἐνδείκνυσιν αἰχμάν.   ⏑ ⏑ – ⏓ – ⏑ – –

In *P.V.* 131 μόγις παρειποῦσα φρένας has the effect less of an iambo-choriambic dimeter than of a catalectic ionic colon ⏑ – ⏑ – – | ⏑⏑ –. The acatalectic version is found in *Sept.* 720 = 727, in just the same kind of context:

     πέφρικα τὰν ὠλεσίοικον   ⏑ – ⏑ – – | ⏑ ⏑ – –
     θεὸν οὐ θεοῖς ὁμοίαν   ⏑ ⏑ – ⏑ – ⏑ – –
     παναληθῆ κακόμαντιν   ⏑ ⏑ – – ⏑ ⏑ – –
     πατρὸς εὐκταίαν Ἐρινὺν   ⏑ ⏑ – ⏑̲ – ⏑ – –
     τελέσαι τὰς περιθύμους   ⏑ ⏑ – – ⏑ ⏑ – –
     κατάρας Οἰδιπόδα βλαψίφρονος·   ⏑ ⏑ – – ⏑ ⏑ – – ⏑ ⏑ –
     παιδολέτωρ δ’ ἔρις ἅδ’ ὀτρύνει.   – ⏑ ⏑ – ⏑ ⏑ – ⏑ – –

The clausula, an 'alcaic decasyllable', again recalls *P.V.* 131-2

       μόγις παρειποῦσα φρένας·
       κραιπνοφόροι δέ μ’ ἔπεμψαν αὖραι.

Soph. *Phil.* 1181 gives among ionics a dimeter with a choriambic base – ⏑ ⏑ – | – ⏑ – –. The colon might in itself perhaps be classed as an unusual variety of 'choriambic dimeter', but in its strongly ionic context it gives the effect of an anacreontic with a curious anaclasis:

1173 Ch. τί τοῦτ' ἔλεξας; Ph. εἰ σὺ τὰν[1]   ∪ – ∪ – | ∪ – ∪ –
         στυγερὰν Τρῳάδα γᾶν μ' ἤλπισας ἄξειν.   ∪∪ – – | ∪∪ – – | ∪∪ – –
     Ch. τόδε γὰρ νοῶ κράτιστον.   ∪ ∪ – ∪ | – ∪ – –
     Ph. ἀπὸ νύν με λείπετ' ἤδη.   ∪ ∪ – ∪ | – ∪ – –
     Ch. φίλα μοι φίλα ταῦτα παρήγγει-   ∪∪ – | ∪∪ – | ∪∪ – –
         -λας ἑκόντι τε πράσσειν.   ∪ ∪ – | ∪ ∪ – –
         ἴωμεν ἴωμεν   ∪ – ∪ ∪ – – –[2]
1181   ναὸς ἵν' ἡμῖν τέτακται.   – ∪ ∪ – | – ∪ – –

An apparent trimeter with choriambic base appears as the first line of Eur. *Hipp.* 732–41 = 742–51, which opens in what might be ionic rhythm:

ἠλιβάτοις ὑπὸ κευθμῶσι γενοίμαν   – ∪ ∪ – | ∪ ∪ – – | ∪ ∪ – –
ἵνα με πτεροῦσσαν ὄρνιν κτλ.   ∪ ∪ – ∪ | – ∪ – –

Finally, in *Ag.* 689 the curious introduction of a choriamb in the second metron appears to be the result of the deliberate play upon the name of Helen. The metre switches from aeolic to ionic and back to aeolic, but the choriamb is firmly embedded in an ionic tetrameter:

       τὰν δορίγαμβρον ἀμφινει-   – ∪ ∪ – ∪ – ∪ –
       -κῆ θ' Ἑλέναν; ἐπεὶ πρεπόντως   – ∪ ∪ – ∪ – ∪ – – ||
689 Ἑλέναυς ἕλανδρος ἑλέ-   ∪ ∪ – ∪ | – ∪ ∪ –
       -πτολις ἐκ τῶν ἁβροπήνων   ∪ ∪ – – | ∪ ∪ – –
       προκαλυμμάτων ἔπλευσεν   ∪ ∪ – ∪ | – ∪ – –
       Ζεφύρου γίγαντος αὔρᾳ   ∪ ∪ – ∪ | – ∪ – –
       κατ' ἴχνος πλατᾶν ἄφαντον   ∪ ∪ – ∪ | – ∪ – – ||
       κελσάντων Σιμόεντος ἀκ-   – – – ∪ ∪ – ∪ –
       -τὰς ἐπ' ἀεξιφύλλους   – ∪ ∪ – ∪ – – |
       δι' ἔριν αἱματόεσσαν.   ∪ ∪ ∪ – ∪ ∪ – –

The effect is again one of anaclasis, and this at least is probably a genuine case of a freak ionic.

---

[1] Text uncertain, see p. 108.
[2] See above, p. 125.

IX

AEOLIC: (1) AEOLO-CHORIAMBIC

Origin in Lesbian lyric with modifications introduced by the dramatic poets—Iambo-choriambic—Aeolic blunt octosyllables with catalectic heptasyllables: glyconic, pherecratean, aeolic dimeters A and B, aristophanean: free responsion—Classification according to number of syllables in prototypes; blunt and pendant in each length—Choriambic enoplian A and B—Telesillean, reizianum, blunt heptasyllable B—Blunt hexasyllables A and B, or 'dodrans'—Adonean—Longer cola: enneasyllables, decasyllables, hendecasyllables, dodecasyllables, other lengths—Ambiguity with ionic—Characteristic aeolic usage in each of the three tragedians and in comedy—General scheme of aeolo-choriambic scansion.

The extant poems and fragments of Sappho and Alcaeus include many of a metrical type not based on a recurrent metron but containing as a nucleus the choriamb − ∪ ∪ − with accretions of various lengths variously disposed about it. This book does not profess to study the historical development of the lyric metres of drama from their earlier antecedents, but the very large and widely used class of metres here grouped as aeolic or (in this chapter) aeolo-choriambic owe many of their peculiarities to the older solo-lyric of Lesbos, though the dramatists introduced modifications of their own and the influence of other dramatic metres was in itself a powerful modifying factor.

΄ Though most Lesbian cola do not move κατὰ μέτρον—are in this sense 'ametric'—the choriamb itself is one of the tetrasyllabic metra, and before passing on to aeolic proper we may disengage a relatively small class of pure choriambic or (more commonly) iambo-choriambic cola which in most of their forms are still analysable into metra although they shade off into the ametric aeolics. These are more common in comedy and in Aeschylus and earlier Sophocles than in later fifth-century tragedy. Pure choriambics are confined to single cola—dimeters, trimeters, tetrameters or even longer[1]—or at

---

[1] Euripides has a πνῖγος of nine metra at *Phoen.* 1519.

most to single periods as at the end of the stanza Aesch. *Supp.*
538-46,

> φῦλα, διχῇ δ' ἀντίπορον
> γαῖαν ἐν αἴσᾳ διατέμνοντα πόρον κυματίαν ὁρίζει.

The detachable dimeter is followed by a pentameter catalectic,
ending, as catalectic choriambics always do,[1] in the bacchiac ⌣ – –.
It has been noted how often iambics end in the clausula – ⌣ ⌣ –
⌣ – –, the 'aristophanean' which is in form a choriambic dimeter
catalectic, the choriamb giving an effect of iambic anaclasis. In the
same way cola of various lengths, blunt and pendant, are built up
of mixed choriambic and iambic metra, and whole stanzas can be
put together of this mixture interspersed with pure iambic or pure
choriambic; the whole is more flexible and varied than the simple
choriambic series. Ar. *Nub.* 949-58 = 1024-33 is a straightforward
example:

νῦν δείξετον τὼ πισύνω	x̱ – ⌣ – – ⌣ ⌣ –
τοῖς περιδεξίοισι	– ⌣ ⌣ – ⌣ – –
λόγοισι καὶ φροντίσι καὶ	⌣ – ⌣ – – ⌣ ⌣ –
γνωμοτύποις μερίμναις,	– ⌣ ⌣ – ⌣ – –
ὁπότερος αὐτοῖν λέγων	⌣◠ ⌣ – – ⌣ –
ἀμείνων φανήσεται.	⌣ – – ⌣ – ⌣ –
νῦν γὰρ ἅπας ἐνθάδε κίν-	– ⌣ ⌣ – – ⌣ ⌣ –
-δυνος ἀνεῖται σοφίας,	– ⌣ ⌣ – – ⌣ ⌣ –
ἧς πέρι τοῖς ἐμοῖς φίλοις	– ⌣ ⌣ – ⌣ – ⌣ –
ἐστὶν ἀγὼν μέγιστος.	– ⌣ ⌣ – ⌣ – –

In iambo-choriambic the light form of iambic ⌣ – ⌣ – is preferred
to the heavier x̱ – ⌣ –, particularly in dimeters with the first metron
a choriamb, perhaps because – ⌣ ⌣ – ⌣ – ⌣ – is a more integrated
colon than – ⌣ ⌣ – x̱ – ⌣ –.

Just as the tragedians, especially Aeschylus, composed iambo-
dochmiacs where though the type of movement was continuous the
extra length of the dochmiac broke the scheme κατὰ μέτρον,[2] so in

---

[1] Except in the eupolidean, see below, p. 147. It seems however to be
a general principle that the closing rhythm of a catalectic colon is the
opposite of the acatalectic; thus as the choriambic ends blunt its
catalexis has the pendant form.

[2] See above, pp. 107 ff.

iambo-choriambic the colarion – ∪ – ∪ ∪ – or – ∪ ∪ – ∪ – is used as an ingredient among iambic and choriambic dimeters, trimeters, etc. These colaria, as we shall see, are common aeolic hexasyllables, but here they form a link between iambic and choriambic, as for instance in Aesch. *Supp.* 57–62:

εἰ δὲ κυρεῖ τις πέλας οἰωνοπόλων	chor. trim.
ἔγγαιος οἶκτον ἀΐων,	iamb. dim.
δοξάσει μὲν ἀκού-	– ∪ – ∪ ∪ –
-ειν ὄπα τᾶς Τηρείας Μήτιδος οἰκτρᾶς ἀλόχου,	+ chor. tetram.
κιρκηλάτας ἀηδόνος.	iamb. dim.

Passing further into the domain of pure aeolic we find a group of cola which in drama are the commonest of all of this type. The name 'choriambic dimeter' given to some of them by Wilamowitz indicates that they are not yet wholly emancipated from the metron, but the chief applicability of the term 'dimeter' is to the total length of each colon—they are obviously treated as the equivalent of iambic or trochaic dimeters—rather than to its internal structure; they run as it were κατὰ δίμετρον. They are in fact aeolic blunt octosyllables (disregarding resolution for the moment) with seven-syllabled catalectic forms. The choriamb which they all contain may occupy the first four, the middle four or the last four syllables, and in the two latter cases the syllables which precede the choriamb are variable, forming what was called by Hermann the 'aeolic base', since Sappho and Alcaeus make much use of this variable opening.

Taking tragedy and comedy as a whole the commonest aeolic dimeter is the glyconic, which has its choriamb in the middle, with its catalectic form the pherecratean. Nothing is known of the eponymous Glycon; Pherecrates is the comic poet who wrote pherecrateans of the form – – – ∪ ∪ – – κατὰ στίχον and called them συμπτύκτοις ἀναπαίστοις.[1] The first two syllables may be – –, – ∪ or (rather less often) ∪ –; the ∪ ∪ which was also permissible in the syllable-counting Lesbian poets was not used by the dramatists because unlike the Lesbians they allowed resolution in the base, so that the double-short would have made the line not a glyconic but

[1] See above, p. 61 with n. 1.

a resolved blunt heptasyllable of the type called telesillean.¹ ∪ ∪ ∪
was allowed as a resolution of – ∪ or ∪ –, x̄ – is occasionally
resolved into x̄ ᴖ,² and Euripides has two or three instances of
ᴖ x̄, mocked by Aristophanes in the *Frogs*; ᴖ ᴖ is not found.
The last two syllables are usually ∪ –, but the dragged x̄ – is not
uncommon.³ The dicolon formed by glyconic+pherecratean,
sometimes called 'priapean', is exceedingly common as a clausula
or period-close; very often it has word-division, usually with one
syllable overlapping into the pherecratean:

> ὡς ὑμᾶς ἴσα καὶ τὸ μη-   – x̄ – ∪ ∪ – ∪ –
> -δὲν ζώσας ἐναριθμῶ.   – x̄ – ∪ ∪ – –

It is evident that the rhythm of a priapean has analogies with that
of the iambo-choriambic clausula quoted above

> ἧς πέρι τοῖς ἐμοῖς φίλοις   – ∪ ∪ – ∪ – ∪ –
> ἐστὶν ἀγὼν μέγιστος,   – ∪ ∪ – ∪ – –

and indeed the relation between all three forms of aeolic dimeter
– ∪ ∪ – ∪ – ∪ – (aeolic dimeter A), – × – ∪ ∪ – ∪ –⁴ (glyconic)
and – × – × – ∪ ∪ – (aeolic dimeter B) and between the catalectic
forms – × – ∪ ∪ – – (pherecratean) and – ∪ ∪ – ∪ – – (aristophanean) is very close. Sophocles makes a dicolon of dim. A+glyc.

> πολλὰ τὰ δεινὰ κοὐδὲν ἀν-   – ∪ ∪ – ∪ – ∪ –
> -θρώπου δεινότερον πέλει,   – x̄ – ∪ ∪ – ∪ –

and the pherecratean and aristophanean are used indifferently as
catalectic cola following any of the three forms of dimeter:

> εὔιππον χώραν ὕδασιν   – x̄ – x̄ – ∪ ∪ –   dim. B
> καλλίστοισι λιπαίνειν.   – x̄ – ∪ ∪ – –   pher.

---

¹ This point has often been ignored, by Wilamowitz and many others.
Cf., unmistakably, E. *Hyps.* 1 ii 23 ~ iii 26: ἱερὸν δέρος ὃ περὶ δρυὸς
ᴖ – ∪ ∪ᴖ ∪ᴖ ~ τρισσοῖς ἔλιπεν κράτος – – ∪ ∪ – ∪ –, so possibly
Hel. 1342 = 1358, though there resolution in both str. and ant. makes
it less certain, since ∪ ∪ – ∪ ∪ – ∪ – (–) may also be enoplians of the
type described in the next chapter, p. 167.

² As E. *I.T.* 1092 εὐξύνετον ~ 1109 ὀλομένων, cf. 1129 = 1144.

³ As *I.T.* 1123, 1126, 1127. In responsion to ∪ – *Phil.* 1128 = 1151.

⁴ In these general formulae for types with aeolic base initial – × must
always be taken to include the inversion × –.

More significant, the glyconic is several times used in free responsion to dim. B. In Eur. *El.* 167–89 = 190–212 there are no fewer than five instances, e.g. 184–5 = 207–8

184 σκέψαι μου πιναρὰν κόμαν   − ⏓ − ⏑ ⏑ − ⏑ −
      καὶ τρύχη τάδ᾽ ἐμῶν πέπλων   − ⏓ − ⏑ ⏑ − ⏑ −
207 αὐτὰ δ᾽ ἐν χερνῆσι δόμοις   − ⏓ − ⏓ − ⏑ ⏑ −
      ναίω ψυχὰν τακομένα.   − ⏓ − ⏓ − ⏑ ⏑ −

Responsion of dim. A to glyconic is much rarer, but there is no need to doubt the text of Ar. *Vesp.* 529 = 634

μὴ κατὰ τὸν νεανίαν   − ⏑ ⏑ − ⏑ − ⏑ −
ὡς δὲ πάντ᾽ ἐπελήλυθεν.   − ⏑ − ⏑ ⏑ − ⏑ −

In general, however, the closest connection is that between dim. B and glyconic. 'A'-dimeters are, as we have seen, an ingredient in iambo-choriambic, and in aeolic proper are much less common than the more characteristic dim. B. But occasionally dim. A is modified by dragged close,[1] as in Soph. *Tr.* 949 δύσκριτ᾽ ἔμοιγε δυστάνῳ (a clausula), and in Eur. *Hipp.* 70 the pendant aristophanean is dragged:

χαῖρέ μοι ὦ καλλίστα.   − ⏑ ⏑ − ⏓ − −

The distinction between iambo-choriambic and aeolic κατὰ δίμετρον is in fact tenuous and the one passes into the other very easily. In the first stanza of the κλητικὸς ὕμνος, *Nub.* 563–74, Zeus and Poseidon are summoned in iambo-choriambic, Aether in dactylic and Helios in chor. dims. and priapean:

ὑψιμέδοντα μὲν θεῶν   − ⏑ − − ⏑ − ⏑ −
Ζῆνα τύραννον ἐς χορὸν   − ⏑ − − ⏑ − ⏑ −
πρῶτα μέγαν κικλήσκω.   − ⏑ ⏑ − ⏑ − − ‖
τόν τε μεγασθενῆ τριαίνης ταμίαν   − ⏑ ⏑ − ⏑ − ⏑ − − ⏑ ⏑ −
γῆς τε καὶ ἁλμυρᾶς θαλάσ-   − ⏑ ⏑ − ⏑ − ⏑ −
-σης ἄγριον μοχλευτήν ·   − ⏑ ⏑ − ⏑ − − ‖
καὶ μεγαλώνυμον ἡμέτερον πατέρ᾽   − ⏑ ⏑ − ⏑ ⏑ − ⏑ ⏑ − ⏑ ⏑
Αἰθέρα σεμνότατον βιοθρέμμονα πάντων·   − ⏑ ⏑ − ⏑ ⏑ − ⏑ ⏑ − ⏑ ⏑ − − ‖
τόν θ᾽ ἱππονώμαν, ὃς ὑπερ-   ⏓ − ⏑ − − ⏑ ⏑ −
-λάμπροις ἀκτῖσιν κατέχει   − ⏓ − ⏓ − ⏑ ⏑ −
γῆς πέδον, μέγας ἐν θεοῖς   − ⏑ − ⏑ ⏑ − ⏑ −
ἐν θνητοῖσί τε δαίμων.   − ⏓ − ⏑ ⏑ − −

[1] See below, Additional note, p. 155.

The change in the character of the rhythm from the first two periods to the fourth is slight but unmistakable. The colon most responsible for the difference is the 'B'-dimeter. Where this takes an iambic opening form ◡ – ◡ – – ◡ ◡ – it of course falls easily into iambo-choriambic rhythm, and even the 'antispastic' ◡ – – ◡ – ◡ ◡ – may merely have an effect of anaclasis; but its more characteristic forms are the heavy – x̱ – ᴗ – ◡ ◡ – or the resolved ⌒ ◡ – x̱ – ◡ ◡ – or even the curious x̱ ⌒ – x̱ – ◡ ◡ –.[1] These are breaking away from the dimeter construction.

The aeolic κατὰ δίμετρον is in fact not strictly a separate type of aeolic rhythm, but a simple form of aeolic octosyllables with seven-syllabled catalectics such as has been most nearly assimilated to the common dimetric metres. Like their Lesbian prototypes the aeolics of drama are for the most part hardly to be classified except as lengths of so many syllables,[2] each length having both blunt and pendant types.

The blunt octosyllables, which are the equivalent of dimeters, have been described. In pendant octosyllables the choriamb shifts to syllables 2–5 × – ◡ ◡ – ◡ – – or 4–7 with a variable base × – × – ◡ ◡ – –. As these two cola are variants of the enoplian to be considered in the next chapter they can be called choriambic enoplian A and B respectively.[3] Like the different forms of blunt octosyllable they can be used in free responsion, as in Soph. *O.C.* 512 ὅμως δ' ἔραμαι πυθέσθαι ◡ – ◡ ◡ – ◡ – – ~ 523 τούτων δ' αὐθαί-ρετον οὐδέν x̱ – x̱ – ◡ ◡ – –, cf. *Trach.* 960 = 969.

The heptasyllables so far discussed, the pherecratean and aristo-phanean, have been pendant cola used as the equivalent of catalectic

[1] S. *Aj.* 702 Ἰκαρίων δ' ὑπὲρ πελαγέων x̱⌒ – ◡ – ◡ ◡ – ~ 715. It should be noted that Ἰκαρίων must on no account be taken as a chori-amb, since the line is too short for a compound, and no uncompounded colon can move from double to single short and then back to double. The maximum of resolution allowed is ⌒ ◡⌒ ◡ – ◡ ◡ –, as E. *Hipp.* 61 πότνια πότνια σεμνοτάτα.

[2] The labels apply less strictly in dramatic cola than in Lesbian lyric because of resolution; ⌒ counts as one syllable.

[3] Choriambic enoplian A is one of Hephaestion's 'ionics *a maiore*', see above, p. 122.

dimeters. But both of them are used extensively in contexts where there is no particular effect of catalexis. Pherecrateans especially are often used in series; Aesch. *Sept.* 287–303 has six sandwiched between two iambic periods, and consecutive groups of two or three are very common. There is no well-authenticated instance of free response between pherecratean and aristophanean;[1] this phenomenon appears in fact to be almost confined to octosyllables.[2]

Blunt heptasyllables are again of two types according to the shift of the choriamb, and both are very common. The A-type ⏕ – ⏑ ⏑ – ⏑ –, or with dragged close ⏕ – ⏑ ⏑ – ⏓̣ –, was a favourite of the poetess Telesilla and has been named after her. Its commonest use is in company with its pendant catalectic the

---

[1] Perhaps *Hyps.* parodos 4–5 with ant., but the text is incomplete. The example sometimes quoted, Eur. *El.* 168 = 191, rests on incorrect colometry. It is usually given in the form

	Ἀγαμέμνονος ὦ κόρα,	⏑⏑ – ⏑⏑ – ⏑ – ‖
	ἤλυθον, Ἠλέκτρα, ποτὶ	– ⏑⏑ – – – ⏑⏑
168	σὰν ἀγρότειραν αὐλάν.	– ⏑⏑ – ⏑ – –
	μεγάλα θεός· ἀλλ' ἴθι	⏑⏑ – ⏑⏑ – ⏑ ◡ ‖
	καὶ παρ' ἐμοῦ χρῆσαι πολύ-	– ⏑⏑ – – – ⏑⏑
191	-πηνα φάρεα δῦναι.	– ⏑ – ⏑ ⏑ – –

But in this arrangement the middle lines defy rational analysis. A chor. dim. of this form where the last syllable cannot be *brevis in longo* is a solecism. In the aeolics of drama any double-short except that inside a choriamb is a resolution. And needless to say a dragged aristophanean with the last syllable resolved, καὶ ταῦτα in synaphea with pherecratean, would be a grotesquerie. The first colon is a long enoplian (see next chapter) ending at Ἠλέκτρα and χρῆσαι, and is followed by another enoplian of octosyllabic type but with resolved first syllable, echoing the opening of the preceding line:

Ἀγαμέμνονος ὦ κόρα, ἤλυθον, Ἠλέκτρα, ⏑⏑ – ⏑⏑ – ⏑⏑ – ⏑⏑ – ⏓̣ –
ποτὶ σὰν ἀγρότειραν αὐλάν. ◠ – ⏑⏑ – ⏑ – –

In the antistrophe the second line gives ◠ – ⏑ – ⏑⏑ – –, i.e. enoplian A is in free response to enoplian B, which is quite in order.

[2] Eur. *Phaethon* frag. 773 N.[2] appears to show a telesillean, l. 25 ὀρθρευομένα γόοις – – ⏑ – – ⏑ – corresponding to l. 33 παγαῖς τ' ἐπ' Ὠκεανοῦ – – ⏑ – ⏑ ⏑ –.

reizianum¹ × − ∪ ∪ − −, but it is often found sporadically among the longer aeolics. The B-type, ending in a choriamb, has a multi-variable base,² the commonest form being × − × − ∪ ∪ −, with occasional resolution of the first or second syllable. Euripides also uses a cretic base *Hel.* 1340–1, as an acephalous form of the preceding iambo-choriambics 1338–9:

ματρὸς ὀργὰς ἐνέπει   − ∪ − − ∪ ∪ −
Βᾶτε σεμναὶ Χάριτες.   − ∪ − − ∪ ∪ −

The effect of this heptasyllable among choriambic dimeters is analogous to that of the lekythion with iambic dimeters:

παῖ γενναίων μὲν πατέρων,   − x̄ − x̄ − ∪ ∪ −
γενναίων δ' ἐκ τοκάδων,   x̄ − x̄ − ∪ ∪ −

the shorter line being in both cases acephalous in relation to the longer line. Sophocles in *O.C.* 242 and 249 twice uses what might be a third form of blunt heptasyllable − ∪ ∪ − − ∪ −, in each case to close a dactylic series: a curious colon,³ possibly a kind of equivalent, by double anaclasis, of iamb. dim. cat. ∪ − ∪ − ∪ − −.

¹ Wilamowitz was, I think, responsible for a strange heresy about the reizianum, echoed after him by many scholars. He believed it to be a 'popular' colarion with freedom of 'Doppelsenkung', i.e. ∪͜∪ − ∪͜∪ − −. The whole notion of such popular free rhythms is far too loosely applied (the special case of the iambics of comedy is properly a different kind of phenomenon, see above, p. 77); in any case, such a licence is wholly irrelevant to tragic lyric, and × − ∪ ∪ − − is no more a variant of × − ∪ − − than, for instance, − ∪ − ∪ ∪ − − (pherecratean) is of − ∪ − ∪ − − (ithyphallic).

² Forms with two consecutive shorts in the base are of course excluded; such cola are either resolved hexasyllables or belong to quite different categories such as the hemiepes − ∪ ∪ − ∪ ∪ −.

³ It looks like a short form of the curious rhythm four times repeated *O.C.* 216, 218, 220 and 222 ὤμοι ἐγὼ τί πάθω, τέκνον ἐμόν; − ∪ ∪ − ∪ ∪ −⌢ ∪ − sometimes described as 'meiuric' or stub-tailed dactyls, i.e. with the final − ∪̆ twisted round to the blunt ∪ −. It is quite uncertain whether this explanation has any objective validity, or whether they should be called blunt hemiepes + resolved cretic (paeon). Meiuric dactyls are known otherwise only from hexameters dating from the stress-accent period. The context in *O.C.* is ἀπολελυμένα including iambic, aeolic, ionic, enoplian and dactylic rhythms.

The phrase is a familiar one in Pindar, but in drama heptasyllables which start with the choriamb are elsewhere always pendant.

Of hexasyllables, the pendant form or reizianum has already been noted; it is a common clausula in both aeolic and mixed contexts. Blunt hexasyllables (called by Schroeder 'dodrans') A and B, – ⏑ ⏑ – × – and – × – ⏑ ⏑ –, have appeared already as a form of dochmiac, and in their light forms as colaria in iambo-choriambic. B, like the glyconic, may always have initial inversion × –. They are common ingredients in all forms of aeolic compound; for instance Ar. *Eccl.* 941 οὐ γὰρ ἀνασχετὸν τοῦτό γ' ἐλευθέρῳ – ⏑ ⏑ – ⏑ – – ⏑ ⏑ – ⏑ –, which is the last line of an Attic skolion quatrain,[1] is dodrans A twice repeated, – ⏑ ⏑ – ⏑ – ⏑ – – ⏑ ⏑ – (*Nub.* 566) could be described as dim. A+chor. or as dodrans A+B, while – × – ⏑ ⏑ – – ⏑ ⏑ – ⏑̄ –, the 'asclepiad' which Horace adopted from Alcaeus, could be B+A. Metricians, in their search for accepted terminology, sometimes call dodrans B 'Maecenas atavis' and dodrans A 'edite regibus' from the Horatian asclepiad. But the division into two hexasyllables is not the only possible way of splitting the asclepiad itself; it can, for instance, be represented in a series of this type:

– × – ⏑ ⏑ – ⏑̄ –	glyc. (8 syll.)
– × – ⏑ ⏑ – – ⏑ ⏑ – ⏑̄ –	asclep. (12 syll.)[2]
– × – ⏑ ⏑ – – ⏑ ⏑ – – ⏑ ⏑ – ⏑̄ –	'greater asclep.' (16 syll.)

In any case, this kind of ambiguity amounts for us to little more than an ἀπορία of classification. As a clearly separate colon dodrans A is more frequent than B, occurring for instance in the clausula Eur. *Hec.* 637, Ἅλιος αὐγάζει – ⏑ ⏑ – ⏓ –. Eupolis frag. 163K. uses – ⏑ ⏑ – ⏑ – as a catalectic clausula to three aristophaneans in a neat little piece of scurrility.

[1] Aristophanes is in this context (*Eccl.* 938–41) giving a skolion in the metre of the famous Harmodios and Aristogeiton song.

[2] A striking instance of the presence in the mind of the poet of this relation between glyc. and asclep. is Soph. frag. 223 N.[2]

ῥηγνὺς χρυσόδετον κέρας,
ῥηγνὺς ἁρμονίαν χορδοτόνου λύρας.

The pendant adonean $- \cup \cup - -$, which we met as a dactylic colarion, is occasionally found as an aeolic closing rhythm, as in *O.C.* 1058 τούσδ' ἀνὰ χώρους. It is of course descended (in aeolic context) from the close of the 'sapphic' stanza. This is the shortest aeolic length; the blunt pentasyllable does not appear.

Cola longer than the dimeter fall into two main types: those with only one choriamb, all accretions apart from the 'base' being in single-short (or dragged), and those which repeat the choriamb once or more. In the dimeter itself the pure choriambic $- \cup \cup - - \cup \cup -$ might be added to the blunt octosyllables, though its regularity and construction κατὰ μέτρον place it half outside aeolic proper. The following table gives shortly the chief forms to be found in drama.

Enneasyllables.

Most commonly pendant. With single choriamb:

$- \cup \cup - \cup - \cup - -$ τῶν ξένε πάμμορ' εὖ φύλαξαι.   *O.C.* 161.

$- \times - \cup \cup - \cup - -$ ξανθὰν Ἁρμονίαν φυτεῦσαι.   *Med.* 832.

(This, the 'hipponactean', is the commonest of the enneasyllables.)

$\underset{\cup}{} - \cup - - \cup \cup - -$ τελεῖ τελεῖ Ζεύς τι κατ' ἆμαρ.   *O.C.* 1079.

With double choriamb (as it were interior anaclasis of *O.C.* 161 above):

$- \cup \cup - - \cup \cup - -$ τὰν ὁ μέγας μῦθος ἀέξει.   *Aj.* 226.

Blunt with single choriamb:

$\overline{\times} - \cup \cup - \cup - \underset{\cup}{} -$ οὔθ' ἀμερίων ἔτ' ἄξιος.   *Aj.* 399.

$\overline{\times} - \cup \cup - \cup - \overline{\times} -$ κεῖνος γὰρ ἔπερσεν ἀνθρώπους.   *Aj.* 1198.

$\overline{\times} - \overline{\times} - \cup \cup - \cup -$ καὶ γνώμας λειπομένα σοφᾶς.   Soph. *El.* 474.

The double choriamb is not found in this length.[1]

Decasyllables.

Blunt with single choriamb:

$\overset{\frown}{\underset{-\times}{\cup \cup}} \cup - \cup \cup - \cup - \overline{\times} -$ ὅτι πόσιν κελαδεῖς ἀεὶ μολπαῖς.   *I.T.* 1093.

$- \overline{\times} - \cup - \cup \cup - \overline{\times} -$ πέμπουσαι χορούς μετὰ Νηρῄδων.   Eur. *El.* 434.

---

[1] For *Aj.* 702 see above, p. 136, n. 1.

With double choriamb:

$-\underset{\times}{-}-\cup\cup--\cup\cup-$ εἰ μὴ 'γὼ παράφρων μάντις ἔφυν. Soph. *El.* 473.

Pendant:

$\underset{\times}{-}-\cup\cup-\cup-\cup--$ μηδ' ἐξετάσῃς πέρα ματεύων.   *O.C.* 211.

$\overline{\cup}-\underset{\times}{-}-\cup\cup-\cup--$ κακᾷ μ' εὐνᾷ πόλις οὐδὲν ἴδριν.   *O.C.* 525.

Hendecasyllables.

Pendant with single choriamb:

$-\underset{\times}{-}-\cup\cup-\cup-\cup--$ δοῦποι καὶ πολιᾶς ἄμυγμα χαίτας.   *Aj.* 634.

(The 'phalaecean', a bacchiac prolongation of glyc.)
  Or with dragged close (very rare):

$-\cup-\cup\cup-\cup-\underset{\times}{-}--$ λεύσιμοι δὲ καταφθοραὶ δεσποίνᾳ.   *Ion* 1237.

$\cup--\cup-\cup\cup-\cup--$ ὑπὲρ κλιτὺν ἢ στονόεντα πορθμόν.   *Ant.* 1145.

(A bacchiac prolongation of chor. dim. B; in the form $-\cup-\times$
$-\cup\cup-\cup--$ the first line of the 'sapphic' stanza.[1])
  With double choriamb (like phal. with interior anaclasis):

$-\underset{\times}{-}-\cup\cup--\cup\cup--$ οὐδ' οἰκτρᾶς γόον ὄρνιθος ἀηδοῦς.   *Aj.* 629.

Blunt:

$\underset{\times}{-}-\cup-\underset{\times}{-}-\cup\cup-\cup-$ λεύσσων δ' ὅπου γνοίη στατὸν εἰς ὕδωρ.

(The first line of the 'alcaic' stanza.[1])   *Phil.* 716.

$\underset{\times}{-}-\underset{\times}{-}-\cup\cup-\cup-\underset{\times}{-}-^2$ ματρὸς κοινᾶς ἀπέβλαστον ὠδῖνος.   *O.C.* 533.

Dodecasyllables.[3]

Blunt with single choriamb:

$-\cup\cup-\cup-\cup-\underset{\times}{-}-\cup-$ ἀλλ' ἀμενηνὸν ἄνδρα μὴ λεύσσειν ὅπου.
        Aj. 890.

---

[1] It should be noted, however, that the sapphic and alcaic hendecasyllables are themselves in effect dicola, compounded of an iambo-trochaic segment and choriambic colarion $-\cup\cup-\cup-$ (blunt) or $-\cup\cup-\cup--$ (pendant). Cf. below, p. 179, n. 1.

[2] Perhaps the best explanation of the puzzling line *O.T.* 872, is that it is the same as *O.C.* 533, with resolved first syllable μέγας ἐν τούτοις θεὸς οὐδὲ γηράσκει $\cup\cup-\underset{\times}{-}-\cup\cup-\cup-\underset{\times}{-}-$.

[3] Except for chor. trim. and the asclepiad types these are clearly compounds (chor. dim.+ia. or +chor., dodrans A repeated, etc.).

− x̱ − ∪ ∪ − ∪ − ∪ − ∪ −   στηρίζει ποτὲ τᾷδ᾽ ἀγωνίῳ σχολᾷ.

Aj. 194.

x̱ − ∪ − | − x̱ − ∪ ∪ − ∪ −   ἤ που παλαιᾷ μὲν σύντροφος ἀμέρᾳ.

Aj. 624.

With more than one choriamb:

− ∪ ∪ − − ∪ ∪ − − ∪ ∪ −   chor. trim.

− ∪ ∪ − ∪ − − ∪ ∪ − ∪ −   οὐ γὰρ ἀνασχετὸν τοῦτό γ᾽ ἐλευθέρῳ.

Eccl. 941.

− x − ∪ ∪ − − ∪ ∪ − x̱ −   ἀλλ᾽ ἁ μοιριδία τις δύνασις δεινά.

Ant. 951.

(The asclepiad.)

− ∪ ∪ − ∪ − ∪ − − ∪ ∪ −   ἀρά ποτ᾽ αὖθις ἁ παλαιὰ Τροία.

Rhes. 360.

Pendant with single choriamb (= hipponactean with bacchiac prefix).[1]

∪ − − − ∪ − − ∪ ∪ − ∪ − −   ἐρώτων δ᾽ ἐρώτων ἀπέπαυσεν, ὤμοι.

Aj. 1206.

With more than one choriamb:

x̱ − ∪ ∪ − − ∪ ∪ − ∪ − −   τὰν οὔθ᾽ ὕπνος αἱρεῖ ποθ᾽ ὁ παντογήρως.

Ant. 606.

x̱ − ∪ − ∪ ∪ − − ∪ ∪ − −[2]   ψαλμοῖσι καὶ κυλίκων οἰνοπλανήτοις.

Rhes. 363.

Lengths of more than twelve syllables can always be represented as dicola, though they continue to expand syllable by syllable up to

[1] The Sapphic ἔχει μὲν ᾽Ανδρομέδα καλὰν ἀμοιβάν ∪ − ∪ − ∪ ∪ − ∪ − ∪ − − (Heph. 47) does not seem to occur in drama. It is equivalent to a phalaecean with an extra syllable at the beginning. Similarly, Alcaeus' ἰόπλοκ᾽ ἀγνὰ μελλιχόμειδε Σαπφοῖ ∪ − ∪ − x̱ − ∪ ∪ − ∪ − −, which is the sapphic hendecasyllable with an extra initial syllable, is not found in the tragedians, though *Aj.* 1206 here quoted is in analogous relation to another form of − x − x − ∪ ∪ − ∪ − −, e.g. *Ant.* 806 ὁρᾶτ᾽ ἔμ᾽, ὦ γᾶς πατρίας πολῖται.

[2] Hephaestion's 'epionic trimeter' (see above, p. 128). These two cola are enlargements of choriambic enoplia A and B respectively by insertion of an extra choriamb on the same principle as in the glyconic-asclepiad series: − − ∪ ∪ − ∪ − −   − − ∪ − ∪ ∪ − −

− | − ∪ ∪ − | − ∪ ∪ − ∪ − −   − − ∪ | − ∪ ∪ − | − ∪ ∪ − −

sixteen along exactly the same lines, as (thirteen syllables) *P.V.* 397
στένω σε τᾶς οὐλομένας τύχας Προμηθεῦ × – ∪ – – ∪ ∪ – ∪ – ∪ – –
= *Ant.* 839 οἴμοι γελῶμαι. τί με πρὸς θεῶν πατρῴων ia.+enneasyll.
like *O.C.* 161; *Aj.* 1221 τὰς ἱερὰς ὅπως προσείποιμεν 'Αθήνας
– ∪ ∪ – ∪ – ∪ – – ∪ ∪ – – chor. dim. A+adonean; *Vesp.* 1242
οὐδ' ἀμφοτέροισι τοῦτο γίγνεσθαι καλόν $\bar{\times}$ – ∪ ∪ – ∪ – ∪ – $\bar{\times}$ – ∪ –
a nameless skolion-compound; (fourteen syllables) *Ant.* 950 καὶ
Ζηνὸς ταμιεύεσκε γονὰς χρυσορύτους– $\bar{\times}$ – ∪ ∪ – – ∪ ∪ – – ∪ ∪ –
dodrans B+chor. dim.; *Cho.* 319 σκότῳ φάος ἀντίμοιρον· χάριτες δ'
ὁμοίως ∪ – ∪ ∪ – ∪ – – ∪ ∪ – ∪ – – tel.+arist.; (fifteen syllables)
O.T. 870 ἔτικτεν οὐδὲ μήποτε λάθα κατακοιμάσῃ ∪ – ∪ – ∪ – ∪ ∪
– – ∪ ∪ – – – which is difficult to split; (sixteen syllables) *O.T.* 483
δεινὰ μὲν οὖν, δεινὰ ταράσσει σοφὸς οἰωνοθέτας, a pure choriambic
tetrameter; *Phil.* 726 Σπερχειοῦ τε παρ' ὄχθας ἵν' ὁ χάλκασπις ἀνὴρ
θεοῖς – – – ∪ ∪ – – ∪ ∪ – – ∪ ∪ – ∪ – the 'greater asclepiad'.

The ambiguity of some of these cola with ionic is obvious. The repeated choriamb as in οὐδ' οἰκτρᾶς γόον ὄρνιθος ἀηδοῦς is often combined with an unvarying long *anceps* (οὐδ' οἰκτρᾶς – – –, not – ∪ – or ∪ – –[1]), so that the beginning of the line can be taken as a contracted ionic metron. The trouble starts with the pherecratean of the form – – – ∪ ∪ – –, which as well as being potentially σύμπτυκτοι ἀνάπαιστοι could be an ionic dimeter with contracted initial metron. A series of successive enlargements could then be built on this by adding ionic metra to the end, as in *O.C.* 701, 694 and 696

– – – ∪ ∪ – –   pher. or ion. dim.
– – – ∪ ∪ – – ∪ ∪ – –   *O.C.* 701.
– – – ∪ ∪ – – ∪ ∪ – – ∪ ∪ – –   *O.C.* 694.
– – – ∪ ∪ – – ∪ ∪ – – ∪ ∪ – – ∪ ∪ – –   *O.C.* 696.

On the other hand, in the clausula of this same stanza 705–6

λεύσσει νιν Μορίου Διὸς   – – – ∪ ∪ – ∪ –
χἁ γλαυκῶπις 'Αθάνα   – – – ∪ ∪ – –

it is hardly possible to take the second line as anything but a cratean, catalectic to the glyconic, and this same serie

---

[1] All these *could* of course be ionic initial r

built up as aeolics by the insertion of extra choriambs before the final long, on exactly the same principle as the glyconic enlargement into asclepiads (see above, p. 139) by the insertion of extra choriambs before the final ∪ −.[1]

Another series of the same type starts with dodrans B − − − ∪ ∪ − which could be represented as a catalectic ionic dimeter with initial contracted metron. Soph. *El.* 473 εἰ μὴ 'γὼ παράφρων μάντις ἔφυν − − − ∪ ∪ − − ∪ ∪ − is the next stage, and *Ant.* 950 καὶ Ζηνὸς ταμιεύεσκε γονὰς χρυσορύτους − − − ∪ ∪ − − ∪ ∪ − − − ∪ ∪ − a fourteen-syllable version.

If we admit 'major ionics'[2] we get an ambiguous series of an analogous type but as it were inverted—starting with two longs and ending in three. This is rarer, and will not provide all the intermediate steps, but a dragged telesillean of the form − − ∪ ∪ − − − *Trach.* 848 τέγγει δακρύων ἄχναν would make a major ionic dimeter, and the next line ἁ δ' ἐρχομένα μοῖρα προφαίνει δολίαν καὶ μεγάλαν ἄταν a pentameter of the same type.

In most of these series the greater simplicity of the process of accretion to be assumed if they are taken as ionics—the simple addition of metra at the end—and the fact that they do then move κατὰ μέτρον might seem at first sight to be decisive. But the progression from glyconic to asclepiads resists such treatment, and the insertion of extra choriambs is really the same process in all. Moreover, − x̄ − is very much commoner as aeolic opening than ⸚ − − as ionic (*Bacch.* 81 κισσῷ τε στεφανωθείς is one of the few undoubted examples). The problem is almost entirely confined to Sophocles, who seems here to have evolved what amounts to a special form of aeolo-ionic, using only longs and double-shorts.[3]

Euripides creates a different kind of ambiguity by occasionally

---

[1] There is no doubt that at least in *Phil.* 710 Sophocles intends us to hear the line as aeolic, as a catalectic version of the two preceding asclepiads:

οὐ φορβὰν ἱερᾶς γᾶς σπόρον, οὐκ ἄλλων　　 − − − ∪ ∪ − − ∪ ∪ − x̄ −
αἴρων τῶν νεμόμεσθ' ἄνερες ἀλφησταί,　　　 − − − ∪ ∪ − − ∪ ∪ − x̄ −
πλὴν ἐξ ὠκυβόλων εἴ ποτε τόξων.　　　　　 − − − ∪ ∪ − − ∪ ∪ − −

[2] See above, pp. 121 ff.

[3] Except in the longer asclepiad *Phil.* 714 = 726, ending in ∪ −.

using the anaclastic form of clausula ∪ ∪ – ∪ – – in ionics.[1] No other interpretation is possible in *Bacch.* 536, where at the end of a stanza which is ionic throughout he has three dimeters followed by ἔτι τοι τοῦ Βρομίου μελήσει ∪ ∪ – – – ∪ ∪ – ∪ – –. This makes it all the more difficult to be sure whether 370–85 = 386–401 is also continuously ionic or whether it goes over into aeolic at the end as a lead into the next pair. Rhetorical division in both strophe and antistrophe suggests that it does so change. Perhaps the antistrophe is the clearer:

τὸ σοφὸν δ' οὐ σοφία,	∪ ∪ – – ∪ ∪ –
τό τε μὴ θνητὰ φρονεῖν	∪ ∪ – – ∪ ∪ –
βραχὺς αἰών· ἐπὶ τούτῳ	∪ ∪ – – ∪ ∪ – –
δέ τις ἂν μεγάλα διώκων	∪ ∪ – ⌒ ∪ ∪ – –
τὰ παρόντ' οὐχὶ φέροι.	∪ ∪ – – ∪ ∪ –
μαινομένων οἵδε τρόποι	– ∪ ∪ – – ∪ ∪ –
καὶ κακοβούλων παρ' ἐμοί γε φωτῶν.	– ∪ ∪ – – ∪ ∪ – ∪ – –

The catalectic τὰ παρόντ' οὐχὶ φέροι picks up six previous catalectic dimeters in the stanza, and the effect of cutting off a catalectic choriambic pentameter at the end makes admirable rhetorical rhythm, but the whole *could* carry through in ionic to the end exactly as in 519–36 = 537–55. The poets in fact delighted in interweaving the two metres and passing from one to the other by way of ambiguous cola. Our uncertainties of colometry are aggravated by the tendency of glyconics and choriambic dimeters to link with the next line by word-overlap. Consider, for instance, *Phil.* 702–6 (antistrophe)

τότ' ἂν εἰλυόμενος,	∪ ∪ – – ∪ ∪ –
παῖς ἄτερ ὡς φίλας τιθή-	– ∪ ∪ – ∪ – ∪ –
-νας, ὅθεν εὐμάρει' ὑπάρ-	– ∪ ∪ – ∪ – ∪ –
-χοι πόρου ἀνίκ' ἐξανεί-	– ∪ ∪ – ∪ – ∪ –
-η δακέθυμος ἄτα.	– ∪ ∪ – ∪ – –

As it stands, this is aeolic (iambo-choriambic) with a first line which could be either an ionic dimeter catalectic or a dodrans with resolved

---

[1] This was a favourite closing rhythm of the lyric poetess Corinna in her ionics. Aesch. also has an instance in *P.V.* 130 προσέβα τόνδε πάγον πατρῴας, see below, pp. 162f., and cf. above, p. 128, n. 2.

first syllable. By transferring παῖς to the end of the first line, however, we can get an ionic-anacreontic series[1]

τότ' ἂν εἰλυόμενος, παῖς   ∪ ∪ – – ∪ ∪ – –

ἄτερ ὡς φίλας τιθήνας,   ∪ ∪ – ∪ – ∪ – –

ὅθεν εὐμάρει' ὑπάρχοι   ∪ ∪ – ∪ – ∪ – –

πόρου ἀνίκ' ἐξανείη   ∪ ∪ – ∪ – ∪ – –

δακέθυμος ἄτα.   ∪ ∪ – ∪ – –

This might look tempting but for the corrective of the strophe:

τόδε ⟨δ' αὖ⟩ θαῦμά μ' ἔχει,   ∪ ∪ – – ∪ ∪ –

πῶς ποτε πῶς ποτ' ἀμφιπλά-   – ∪ ∪ – ∪ – ∪ –

-κτων ῥοθίων μόνος κλύων,   – ∪ ∪ – ∪ – ∪ –

πῶς ἄρα πανδάκρυτον οὔ-   – ∪ ∪ – ∪ – ∪ –

-τω βιοτὰν κατέσχεν;   – ∪ ∪ – ∪ – –

Here the clearer rhetorical division and the colon ending at κλύων are decisive for the first alternative. The single syllable is as we saw earlier the prevailing type of word-overlap. Moreover, the linking by this kind of *enjambement* of four cola is a peculiarly frequent effect in Euripides' aeolics,[2] and in this respect as in others Sophocles' later work is showing traces of Euripidean influence. Where there are ambiguities, the colometry of each passage has to be decided on its own merits and in its own context, and often no assured decision is possible. A recurring breach of rhetorical division, however,

---

[1] There are many passages in which anacreontics (more than straightforward ionic) intermingle with aeolic cola to a baffling extent, almost as though ∪ ∪ – ∪ – ∪ – – were being regarded as a yet further shift leftwards of the double-short in enoplians, the eight-syllabled pendants. Its ionic history and provenance are, as the last chapter showed, undoubted, but the movement is of course very similar to aeolic (it is, for instance, the last part of the phalaecean). Whether this means a double line of descent or merely 'association' based on similarity of movement cannot be determined.

[2] Cf. *Heracl.* 358–61, 910–13; *Hec.* 446–9; *H.F.* 794–7; *Ion* 184–7. Cf. also *Eq.* 973–96; *Vesp.* 319–22. According to Maas (*Gr. Met.*[4] 65) this is the maximum length allowed without 'pause', i.e. the longest possible minor period. If so, then *Ag.* 447–51 is too long for a πνῖγος, and indeed both rhetorical division and the general style of Aeschylus's colometry are against it. ἀλλοτρίας διαὶ γυναικός should be left as an enneasyllable.

especially when it occurs in both strophe and antistrophe, should at once be suspect; thus the ugly series of breaks after the fifth syllable in the choriambic setting given by Wilamowitz and Schroeder to *P.V.* 397ff. ‒ ‒ ∪ ‒ ‒ | ∪ ∪ ‒ is enough to cause its rejection in favour of an anacreontic division. Where there is no doubt as to colometry and it is merely the attribution to ionic or aeolic which is uncertain a decision is perhaps not of great importance. Choriambic series and ionic series are in ἐπιπλοκή, and perhaps the best we can do is to call such passages aeolo-ionic, whether this be taken merely as a confession of our own ignorance or (as I believe) as a valid indication that such ἐπιπλοκή was objectively present in the actual choral rendering of the passages in question.

Each of the three tragedians has his characteristic use of aeolic, and comedy again shows a different emphasis from tragedy. Most striking in comedy is its development of the type κατὰ δίμετρον in the creation of various forms of dicolon which are used stichically, obviously as the equivalent of catalectic tetrameters in other metres—iambic, trochaic and anapaestic. Such are the compound 'aristophanean' ‒ ∪ ∪ ‒ ‒ ‒ ∪ ‒ ‒ ∪ ∪ ‒ ∪ ‒ ‒, the 'cratinean' ‒ ∪ ∪ ‒ ∪ ‒ ∪ ‒ ‒ ∪ ‒ ∪ ‒ ∪ ‒, and the curious 'eupolidean'[1] (*Nub.* 518–62). In lyric proper comedy makes more use of iambo-choriambic, particularly 'dimeters' with heptasyllabic clausulae, than of the more elaborate types, but shows a particular predilection for the shorter pairs, the seven-syllabled telesillean with its pendant catalectic the reizianum. Thus, for instance, *Eq.* 1111ff.

[1] This tetrameter is a compound of chor. dim. B ‒ × ‒ × ‒ ∪ ∪ ‒ and a catalectic half ‒ × ‒ × ‒ ∪ ‒. One might at first suppose that Eupolis invented, uniquely, this form of catalexis on a theory of 'final *anceps*' rather like Hephaestion's (p. 157, n. 2), ‒ ∪ ∪ ‒ giving catalexis ‒ ∪ ∪ ∧ = ‒ ∪ ⌣ by *brevis in longo*. But in the second half of the cratinean (above) no such elaborate explanation is possible; there is just a shortening achieved by the *substitution* of a cretic for a choriamb. It looks as if Eupolis simply took over this idea from the older comedian, using chor. dim. B instead of chor. dim. A.

In either half there may be inversion of the first two sylls. to × ‒ (so 529, 518) but not a double (iambic) inversion as in *Nub.* 571; in 539 there is resolution of the first long ἐρυθρὸν ⌒ ∪.

divides into two major periods of three tel.+reiz. and five tel.+reiz., and the exodos of the *Peace* is an epithalamium of popular rude form composed entirely in these two cola:

δεῦρ' ὦ γύναι εἰς ἀγρόν,	x̄ – ∪ ∪ – ∪ –
χὥπως μετ' ἐμοῦ καλὴ	x̄ – ∪ ∪ – ∪ –
καλῶς κατακείσει κτλ.	∪ – ∪ ∪ – –

The refrain is the twice-repeated reizianum Ὑμην Ὑμέναι' ὦ. A longer version of this is the glyc.+pher. Ὑμην ὦ Ὑμέναι' Ὑμην, Ὑμην ὦ Ὑμέναι' ὦ. Both these forms must be echoes of actual wedding-songs, and there is no doubt that the simpler forms of aeolic were used in ancient popular refrains. Some trace of this survives in the choice of this metre for the more seemly and thought-ful refrains—ἐφύμνια—of tragedy. In the choruses beginning *Supp.* 630ff. and *Ag.* 355ff. Aeschylus uses a six-times-repeated quatrain (with different words each time) of two phers. and a priapean or linked glyc.+pher.

οἱ δ' αὐτοῦ περὶ τεῖχος	– x – ∪ ∪ – –
θήκας 'Ιλιάδος γᾶς	– x – ∪ ∪ – –
εὔμορφοι κατέχουσιν· ἐ-	– x – ∪ ∪ – ∪ –
-χθρὰ δ' ἔχοντας ἔκρυψεν.	– x – ∪ ∪ – –

Euripides has a similar ἐφύμνιον in the cult hymn, *H.F.* 348ff., where the first two pairs of stanzas both end with a verse of three phers. and priapean and the next pair with a modified version consisting of four phers. and priapean, with some resolution in the base:

τάν τε μυριόκρανον	– ∪ – ∪ ∪ – –
πολύφονον κύνα Λέρνας	⌒ ∪ – ∪ ∪ – –
ὕδραν ἐξεπύρωσεν	– x̄ – ∪ ∪ – –
βέλεσί τ' ἀμφέβαλ' ἰόν,	⌒ ∪ – ∪ ∪ – –
τὸν τρισώματον οἶσιν ἔ-	– σ – ∪ ∪ – ∪ –
-κτα βοτῆρ' Ἐρυθείας.	– σ – ∪ ∪ – –

In *Bacch.* 877ff. = 897ff. (the first line is on no account to be emended) the refrain is repeated in words as well as in rhythm:

τί τὸ σοφόν; ἢ τί τὸ κάλλιον	∪ ⌒ ∪ – ∪ ∪ – σ[1] –
παρὰ θεῶν γέρας ἐν βροτοῖς	⌒ ∪ – ∪ ∪ – ∪ –

---

[1] Either scansion is permissible for κάλλιον in lyric.

ἢ χεῖρ' ὑπὲρ κορυφᾶς $\bar{\times} - \cup - \cup \cup -$
τῶν ἐχθρῶν κρείσσω κατέχειν; $- \bar{\times} - \bar{\times} - \cup \cup -$
ὅ τι καλὸν φίλον ἀεί.[1] $\widehat{\cup\cup} - \cup \cup - -$

Aeschylus uses rather more iambo-choriambic than pure aeolic; hence his cola contain a much larger proportion of simple choriambic and of A-dimeter $- \cup \cup - \cup - \cup -$ (B-type is comparatively rare) than do those of either Sophocles or Euripides. It is a characteristic of his to mix aeolics with dactylic or partly dactylic cola; his transitions from pendant hemiepes $- \cup \cup - \cup \cup - -$ to pherecratean $- - - \cup \cup - -$ and so to priapean have already been illustrated (p. 43); so too the blunt $- \cup \cup - \cup \cup -$ passes into the dodrans $- - - \cup \cup -$ and $- \cup \cup - - - -$ (whether dochmiac or choriambic), and the hipponactean combines with the more dactylic 'alcaic decasyllable':[2]

βροτῶν τλάμονι καὶ πανούργῳ $\cup - - \cup \cup - \cup - -$
χειρί, τοκεῦσι δ' ὅμως τελεῖται $- \cup \cup - \cup \cup - \cup - -$ (*Cho.* 384–5).

In this metre as in others Aeschylus sometimes uses short stanzas of a metrical simplicity approaching that of comedy yet achieving a high degree of tragic intensity, such as the close of the long kommos *Cho.* 315 ff., a verse of form *abbcc* (466 ff.):

ὢ πόνος ἐγγενὴς	dodrans
καὶ παράμουσος ἄτας	arist.
αἱματόεσσα πλαγά.	arist.
ἰὼ δύστον' ἄφερτα κήδη,	hipp.
ἰὼ δυσκατάπαυστον ἄλγος.	hipp.

Of all the dramatists Sophocles makes the richest and most flexible use of aeolic rhythms, especially among the longer cola. This

[1] The first line of this is not to be taken as glyconic with proceleusmatic base. A refrain is not the place for introducing so violent a metrical anomaly, particularly among orthodox aeolic cult hymn rhythms. Schroeder treats it as an ibycean (see next chapter) $\widehat{\cup} \cup \cup - \cup \cup - \bar{\cup} -$, but if so it is the only departure in these stanzas from aeolo-choriambic. It is surely simplest to regard it as a blunt enneasyllable $\cup \widehat{\cup} \cup - \cup \cup - \bar{\cup} -$, cf. *Hipp.* 525 Ἔρως Ἔρως ὁ κατ' ὀμμάτων. The first three lines then go in decreasing order—nine, eight, seven syllables.

[2] See next chapter.

flexibility tends to be obscured by the over-rigid arrangement of some of our texts, where these ignore rhetorical division in both strophe and antistrophe in a Procrustean attempt to reduce all lines to the most familiar lengths. *Ant.* 944ff. is a case in point:

944   ἔτλα καὶ Δανάας οὐράνιον φῶς   — x̄ — ∪ ∪ — — ∪ ∪ — —
       ἀλλάξαι δέμας ἐν χαλκοδέτοις αὐλαῖς·   — x̄ — ∪ ∪ — — ∪ ∪ — x̄ —
       κρυπτομένα δ' ἐν τυμβή-   — ∪ ∪ — — — —
       -ρει θαλάμῳ κατεζεύχθη·   — ∪ ∪ — ∪ — x̄ —
       καίτοι ⟨καὶ⟩ γενεᾷ τίμιος, ὦ παῖ παῖ,   — x̄ — ∪ ∪ — — ∪ ∪ — x̄ —
       καὶ Ζηνὸς ταμιεύεσκε γονὰς   — x̄ — ∪ ∪ — — ∪ ∪ —
              χρυσορύτους.   — ∪ ∪ —
950   ἀλλ' ἀ μοιριδία τις δύνασις δεινά.   — x̄ — ∪ ∪ — — ∪ ∪ — x̄ —
       οὔτ' ἄν νιν ὄλβος οὔτ' Ἄρης,   x̄ — ∪ — ∪ — ∪ —
       οὐ πύργος, οὐχ ἁλίκτυποι   x̄ — ∪ — ∪ — ∪ —
       κελαιναὶ νᾶες ἐκφύγοιεν.   ∪ — — — ∪ — ∪ — —

The last major period is iambic; it cannot be said with certainty whether there are any main divisions among the remaining six minor periods, but possibly they are grouped in twos. The first line, one of the ambiguous aeolo-ionics, is clearly meant here as in *Phil.* 710 (see above, p. 144, n. 1) to be heard in relation to the following asclepiad, like a pherecratean leading into a glyconic (cf. *Alc.* 962) or like Soph. *El.* 193–4

> οἰκτρὰ μὲν νόστοις αὐδά,
> οἰκτρὰ δ' ἐν κοίταις πατρῴαις

where there is (in dragged anapaests) a similar catalectic pendant followed by the full blunt length. The asclepiad returns in 948 and 950; 949 begins in the same rhythm but ends in a choriamb. 946–7 is of course a single minor period; whether it is a dicolon or not and what exactly to call each segment if so is not clear—I suspect a contracted choriamb in δ' ἐν τυμβή-, see Additional note, p. 155.[1]

---

[1] *I.T.* 1126 = 1141 appears to be a contraction, whether of glyc. (with dragged close) or chor. dim. B:

> συρίζων δ' ὁ κηροδέτας   — — — ∪ — ∪ ∪ —
> 1126 κάλαμος οὐρείου Πανὸς   ⌒ ∪ — ‥ — x̄ —
> κώπαις ἐπιθωΰξει.   x̄ — ∪ ∪ — x̄ —

The joyful chorus *Aj.* 693 ff. is an example of Sophocles' liking for the rarer aeolic variants and his habit of combining them curiously in dicola. After a short iambic period the rest is aeolic:

693	ἔφριξ' ἔρωτι περιχαρὴς δ' ἀνεπτόμαν.	iamb. trim.
	ἰὼ ἰὼ Πὰν Πὰν	sync. iamb. dim.
	ὦ Πὰν Πὰν ἁλίπλαγκτε Κυλ-	glyc.
	-λανίας χιονοκτύπου	+glyc.
	πετραίας ἀπὸ δειράδος	glyc.
	φάνηθ' ὦ θεῶν χοροποί' ἄναξ,	∪ – × – ∪ ∪ – ∪ –
	ὅπως μοι Μύσια Κνώσι' ὀρ-	∪ – × – ∪ ∪ – ∪ –
700	-χήματ' αὐτοδαῆ ξυνὼν ἰάψῃς.	– ∪ – ∪ ∪ – ∪ – ∪ – –
	νῦν γὰρ ἐμοὶ μέλει χορεῦσαι.	– ∪ ∪ – ∪ – ∪ – –
	Ἰκαρίων δ' ὑπὲρ πελαγέων	× ⌣ – ⊽ – ∪ ∪ –
	μολὼν ἄναξ Ἀπόλλων	∪ – ∪ – ∪ – –
	ὁ Δάλιος εὔγνωστος	∪ – ∪ ∪ – × ⌣
	ἐμοὶ ξυνείη διὰ παντὸς εὔφρων.	∪ – ∪ – – ∪ ∪ – ∪ – –

Both blunt enneasyllable 699 and octosyllable 702 are unusual, and still more their linking, the one with a phalaecean, the other with a catalectic iambic dimeter. The form of the latter pair gives it the effect of an extension of the phalaecean rhythm, both choriambic and iambic segments being prolonged. The dragged telesillean with Pause (*brevis in longo*) marks a penultimate close, leaving the final clausula detached in a highly characteristic Sophoclean manner.

After the rhythmic subtlety of Sophocles, aeolic in the Euripidean manner is apt to appear sometimes formless and monotonous, the reason being probably that Euripides needs his accompanying music more. His fondness for choriambic dimeter B and for the blunt heptasyllable which is the equivalent of a headless form of it gives, especially in his later plays (from the *Ion* onwards), a curious sameness to the ends of his cola, which together with the frequency of the resolutions in the base produces a wholly different kind of rhythm from Aeschylean or Sophoclean aeolic. The following stanza (*I.A.* 543–57) is typical of many, the opening rhythms and the second colon of the clausula being glyc.-pher. with the choriamb switched further back and the middle portion giving no clue to divide it into periods; it is in fact probably written as a πνῖγος:[1]

---

[1] See below, ch. XII, p. 200.

543 μάκαρες οἳ μετρίας θεοῦ

μετά τε σωφροσύνας μετέ-

-σχον λέκτρων Ἀφροδίτας,

γαλανείᾳ χρησάμενοι

μανιάδων οἴστρων, ὅθι δὴ

δίδυμ' Ἔρως ὁ χρυσοκόμας

τόξ' ἐντείνεται χαρίτων

τὸ μὲν ἐπ' εὐαίωνι πότμῳ

τὸ δ' ἐπὶ συγχύσει βιοτᾶς,

ἀπενέπω νιν ἁμετέρων

Κύπρι καλλίστα θαλάμων.

εἴη δέ μοι μετρία

μὲν χάρις, πόθοι δ' ὅσιοι,

καὶ μετέχοιμι τᾶς Ἀφροδί-

-τας, πολλὰν δ' ἀποθείμαν.

The penultimate line has the same form as *Aj.* 702, being here a variant of the earlier ⌒ ⏑ – ⏑ form of base. Even in Euripides' earlier plays, where the strophic construction is often simple, this initial tribrach resolution is common; the ἀμοιβαῖον of Andromache and her child (*Andr.* 501–14), sung wholly in glyconics and pherecrateans, contains three such resolved bases. The complete resolution of the base of chor. dim. B πότνια πότνια σεμνοτάτα ⌒ ⏑ ⌒ ⏑ – ⏑ ⏑ – appears more than once in Sophocles too (e.g. *Aj.* 1185, *Ant.* 108), but the frequent recurrence of this dimeter in *Ran.* 1309 ff., Aristophanes' parody of an aeolic ode in Euripidean style, suggests that he associated it with Euripides. The notorious anapaestic base of περίβαλλ' ὦ τέκνον ὠλένας is repeated, together with a startling resolution, in a pherecratean of the cock-stealing monody (1337)

φόνια φόνια δερκόμενον,   ⌒ ⏑ ⌒ ⏑ – ⏑ ⏑ –

μεγάλους ὄνυχας ἔχοντα[1]   ⏑ ⏑ – ⌒ ⏑ ⏑ – ⏑

and again 1347 προσέχουσ' ἔτυχον ἐμαυτῆς ⌒ – ⌒ ⏑ ⏑ – –. There is no parallel pherecratean extant in Euripides, but *H.F.* 640–1 (unfortunately the antistrophe is corrupt) does appear to give *some* basis for the libel:

ἐπὶ κρατὶ κεῖται βλεφάρων   ⌒ – ⏑ – – ⏑ ⏑ –   chor. dim. B

σκοτεινὸν φάος ἐπικάλυψαν   ⏑ – – ⏑ ⏑ ⌒ ⏑ – –   hipp.

[1] The line would be more orthodox (and could be paralleled) as an ionic dimeter, but there is no trace of ionic in the context.

There is no echo in the *Frogs* of the resolution in the final syllable which is rather a favourite effect of Euripides:

ὑπολελειμμένα μοι δάκρυα   ⌣⌣ ∪ – ∪ ∪ – ∪⌣⌣

μέλεα παιδὸς ἐν οἴκοις   ⌣⌣ ∪ – ∪ ∪ – –   (*Supp.* 971),

perhaps because Aristophanes was saving that up for the iambics 1353 f.

ἐμοὶ δ' ἄχε' ἄχεα κατέλιπε
δάκρυα δάκρυά τ' ἀπ' ὀμμάτων.

Additional note

W. S. Barrett in his edition of Eur. *Hipp.* Appendix 1, p. 422, has a diagrammatic formula for the varieties in drama of the commoner aeolo-choriambic cola which is clear and serviceable: they are 'lengths taken from the sequence

A   B

$$\ldots \times \,–\, \times \,–\, \times \,–\, \times \,–\, \cup \cup \,–\, \times \,–\, \times \,–\, \times \,–\, \times \ldots$$

beginning not later than A... and ending not earlier than B'. This needs a few qualifications, however. The pre-A sequence has different habits from the post-B:

(*a*) Resolution of either one or two longs, normally carrying short-*anceps* with it, is confined to the left of A (except that in later Eur. there is occasional resolution at colon-end in the first long after B, ...B ∪ ⌣⌣ |; Eur. may also resolve A or B, at some risk of structural damage).

(*b*) There may be inversion before A, i.e. | – × A... is quite commonly turned to | × – A..., and occasionally | – × – × A... to | × – – × A... (S. *Ant.* 1145). Responsion is usually strict, i.e. ∪ – may correspond to ⨯̶ – but rarely to – ∪ (see however S. *Phil.* 1125–6 ∼ 1148–9). Double inversion always takes the form of an iambic metron, i.e. | × – ∪ – A... (with heptasyll. | – ∪ – A...), never | × – × – A.... Aeolics here shade off into iambo-choriambic.

(*c*) Long-*anceps* is very common to the left of A, very rare to the right of B, except for 'dragged close' ...B ⨯̶ – | (blunt) in both Soph. and Eur. (And, of course, any pendant close ends in *anceps* (p. 26).) Eur., exceptionally, has drag in a pendant close *Hipp.* 70

χαῖρέ μοι ὦ καλλίστα – ∪ ∪ – x̄ – –. I do not now believe, however, that 70–1 should be written with double drag in 70

χαῖρέ μοι ὦ καλλίστα καλ-   – ∪ ∪ – x̄ – x̄ / –

-λίστα τῶν κατ᾽ Ὄλυμπον   – x̄ / – ∪ ∪ – –

giving a unique colon with an ugly shape of overlap. καλλίσ-|-τα would have been a different matter, as the single-syll. overlap is common; but the real trouble is in the end of the line x̄ / –, where the expectation of Pause after the long-*anceps* with word-end is overwhelming. Soph., more adventurous than Eur. with long aeolo-chor. lengths, is careful in this, cf. *Aj.* 693 ff. (p. 151), where twice he has this unusual word-division between dicola, at 695–6 = 708–9 ἁλίπλαγκτε̆ / Κυλ-|-λανίας = λευκὸν / εὐ-|-άμερον (short-*anceps*), and 699–700 = 712–13 Κνωσΐ᾽ / ὀρ-|-χήματ᾽ = θέσμΐ / ἐξ-|-ήνυσ᾽ (short-*anceps* with elision). I would therefore write *Hipp.* 70–1

χαῖρέ μοι ὦ καλλίστα   – ∪ ∪ – x̄ – – ||

καλλίστα τῶν κατ᾽ Ὄλυμπον   x̄ – x̄ – ∪ ∪ – –

in accord with the word-rhythm. The unusual dragged aristophanean carries the ceremonial repetition of καλλίστα.

Normal cola, then, continuing to the right after B do so with … ∪ –, … ∪ – –, … ∪ – ∪ –, … ∪ – ∪ – –, and only one 'drag', in the first of these, is a *common* form of *anceps* in the series. Soph., however, appears to have a clausular ending … B ∪ – x̄ – *Aj.* 1191 = 1198, and 598, 604 = 610, 615, *O.C.* 520 = 533. It is curious that in each case the last word has three long sylls., Ἑλλάνων, ἀνθρώπους, εὐδαίμων, ὤμοι μοι, εὐνῶμαι, ηὕρηται, προσχρήζεις, ὠδῖνος. But all these are in long and rare cola, the blunt enneasyll. × – ∪ ∪ – ∪ – x̄ – and blunt hendecasyll. × – × – ∪ ∪ – ∪ – x̄ –, where the corresponding forms without drag (ending … B ∪ – ∪ –) are still rarer—if indeed they exist at all (*Aj.* 399 οὔθ᾽ ἀμερίων ἔτ᾽ ἄξιος is isolated in iambo-dochmiac context and might possibly be of the same category itself). It is conceivable that Soph. has here, instead of 'drag', created a new clausular suffix, an 'overrun' of two true longs ('spondee')—or perhaps only the last syllable is strictly an 'overrun'. Only *Tr.*

949 = 952 δύσκριτ' ἔμοιγε δυστάνῳ – ‿ ‿ – ‿ – $\underset{\times}{}$ – has a corresponding regular form without drag (chor. dim. A), but even this could be the usual clausular catalexis (aristophanean)+overrun of one long syllable. The same would apply to the blunt decasyll., not self-contained but the end of a compound, forming the clausula *Ant.* 816 = 833, and the blunt decasyll. Eur. *I.T.* 1093 = 1110, since no undragged form seems to occur. The hendecasyll. *Ion* 1237 (p. 141) is an isolated freak, but *may* be a dragged form of the phalaecean two lines below.

Barrett's diagram is of course confined to forms of aeolic with a single choriamb. Only Soph. of the dramatists assimilates the Lesbian asclepiads, with their repeated choriambs, to choral use, and he does so with great elaboration and finesse, especially in *Aj.* 221ff., 624ff., 1199ff., *Ant.* 604ff., 944ff., *El.* 473ff., 823ff., *Phil.* 676ff., 707ff., *O.C.* 510ff., 694ff. Some of his variations leave us guessing. The dicolon *Aj.* 231–2

κελαινοῖς ξίφεσιν βοτὰ καὶ   ‿ – – ‿ ‿ – ‿ ‿ –
βοτῆρας ἱππονώμας   ‿ – ‿ – ‿ – –

clearly echoes the rhythm of 223–4 above

ἀνέρος αἴθονος ἀγγελίαν   – ‿ ‿ – ‿ ‿ – ‿ ‿ –   dact. tetr. cat.
ἄτλατον οὐδὲ φευκτάν   ‿ – ‿ – ‿ – –

(followed by dact. pent. cat.). Should one, in view of the 'aeolic base' of 231, label it a freak glyconic with 'anapaestic' end instead of ‿ – or $\underset{\times}{}$ –? (ὁρᾷς τὸν πόδα τοῦτον; ὁρῶ.) Or is – ‿ ‿ – ‿ ‿ – παρὰ προσδοκίαν for – ‿ ‿ – – ‿ ‿ – of the three preceding cola? And what are we to make of *Ant.* 946–7 (the stanza is analysed p. 150)? 944–50 are clearly a series of long aeolics with repeated choriambs, which could be grouped in three pairs: (*a*) asclep. cat., asclep.; (*b*) 946–7, asclep.; (*c*) 949, asclep. Now 949 can be described as base (prefix)+three choriambs: – $\underset{\times}{}$ – ‿ ‿ – | – ‿ ‿ – | – ‿ ‿ –; could 946–7 be the same kind of thing in reverse, with the middle choriamb contracted?

κρυπτομένα δ' ἐν τυμβήρει θαλάμῳ κατεζεύχθη
   – ‿ ‿ – | – ∺ – | – ‿ ‿ – | ‿ – – –

three chor.+suffix? (The latter may end in the Sophoclean 'spondee' described above, here with a tetrasyllabic word in str.; ant. has again the trisyllabic ἐν δεσμῷ.) This is to assume that careful quantitative delivery, perhaps assisted by the stepping of the dance, can distinguish between the alternatives ἐν τυμβή- $\overline{\times} - \overline{\times}$ and $- \overline{\overset{..}{\times}} - = - \cup \cup -.$

X

AEOLIC: (2) PROSODIAC-ENOPLIAN

'Aeolic base' in Lesbian rhythms of non-choriambic form—Prosodiacs
and enoplians in drama—Various affinities—Prosodiac pendant clausulae
to dactylic rhythms: aristophanean, alcaic decasyllable, praxillean—
Corresponding forms of enoplian—Blunt and dragged series of prosodiacs
and enoplians—Affinity with aeolo-choriambic and with dochmiac—
Forms with more than one single-short and with no single-short:
affinities with dactylo-anapaestic and dactylo-epitrite—Dicola.

The type of aeolic metre considered in the last chapter had always a
choriambic nucleus; sometimes this meant that a colon could be
analysed into tetrasyllabic component parts of which the choriamb
was one, as in iambo-choriambic, sometimes that it could be placed
in a series of cola enlarged or diminished either by single syllables
at beginning or end, leaving the choriamb intact, or by the insertion
or removal of whole choriambs, whether at the extremities or (more
commonly) contiguously in the middle. This accounts for the great
majority of all Lesbian metres adopted into the drama, doubtless for
the sake of easy association with the other metres of dramatic lyric,
in which tetrasyllabic forms predominate.[1]

The variable 'aeolic base', sometimes adopted by the dramatists
for this choriambic aeolic, has in Sappho and Alcaeus, however,
another common use in what are usually, though with dubious
propriety,[2] called 'aeolic dactyls'. These begin in × × and end in

---

[1] Even the non-tetrasyllabic forms, the dactylic and anapaestic, are often
approximated to iambics and trochaics by being made to run κατὰ
δίμετρον, see above, chs. III and IV.

[2] The notion of a final 'dactyl' of the form – ∪ ⌣ is a perversion of the
principle of final *anceps*. A final long has licence to shorten before a pause,
because short+Pause has the effect of a long; and an *anceps* (as in
trochaic) in final position may take its short form; but we cannot speak
of the lengthening of a final short because no 'Vers' (minor period) *can*
end in a final short; thus when Hephaestion calls a line like Ἄτθι, σοὶ
δ' ἔμεθεν μὲν ἀπήχθετο a 'dact. tetram. acatalectic', i.e. divides it

∪ – like the glyconic and asclepiad, but the middle part of the line instead of being choriambic has the form – ∪ ∪ – ∪ ∪ – like a blunt hemiepes, or – ∪ ∪ – ∪ ∪ – ∪ ∪ – like a dact. tetram. cat.:

Ἔρος δηὖτέ μ' ὁ λυσιμέλης δόνει.   x x – ∪ ∪ – ∪ ∪ – ∪ –
ἠράμαν μὲν ἔγω σέθεν Ἄτθι πάλαι ποτά.

                              x x – ∪ ∪ – ∪ ∪ – ∪ ∪ – ∪ ⌣

Now it is clear that the middle of the glyconic itself – ∪ ∪ – can be treated as a length—the shortest possible—in the same series, and this in fact is what Sappho appears to do in a poem (94 L.–P.) of three-line stanzas, the first two lines being glyconic and the third like Ἔρος δηὖτέ μ' ὁ λυσιμέλης δόνει:

> τὰν δ' ἔγω τάδ' ἀμειβόμαν·
> 'χαίροισ' ἔρχεο κἄμεθεν
> μέμναισ', οἶσθα γὰρ ὥς σε πεδήπομεν.'

In the drama this dual nature of the glyconic is not exploited in this form, because the 'aeolic base' is almost confined to aeolo-choriambic and such lines as x x – ∪ ∪ – ∪ ∪ – ∪ – rarely occur;[1] *I.A.* 792 πατρίδος οὐλομένας ἀπολωτιεῖ in choriambic context is a possible instance with resolved base ⌒ ∪ (see p. 134). But there are in tragedy a number of cola which begin in dactylic movement (with no 'base') and turn at the close to single-short, whether blunt

x x | – ∪ ∪ | – ∪ ∪ | – ∪ ∪, he fails to realize that -ήχθετο is simply – ∪ ⌣ in the sense in which the final metron of an iambic trimeter may be ⌣ – ∪ ⌣. Again, such lines as ἦρος ἄγγελος ἱμερόφωνος ἀήδων are not to be reckoned as (aeolic) dactylic pentameters x x | – ∪ ∪ | – ∪ ∪ | – ∪ ∪ | – – but as catalectic versions of x x – ∪ ∪ – ∪ ∪ – ∪ ∪ – ∪⌣ ἠράμαν μὲν ἔγω σέθεν Ἄτθι πάλαι ποτά, just as x x – ∪ ∪ – – (pher.) is a catalectic version of x x – ∪ ∪ – ∪ – (glyc.).

It was Hephaestion's erroneous notion of 'final *anceps*' that led him (xv, 93) to accept δυσπαιπάλους (? for δυσπαίπαλος) in Archil. frag. 116D.[2]

Additional note: The above (n. 2) is perhaps too dogmatically expressed; for a more cautious statement see *Observations on Dactylic* (above, p. 25, n. 1). I am however still in two minds about the whole subject; in any case, whatever the truth about 'aeolic dactyls', the problem lies outside drama.

[1] *Vesp.* 1234–5 does not count, being a quotation from Alcaeus.

or pendant, such as – ∪ ∪ – ∪ ∪ – ∪ –, – ∪ ∪ – ∪ ∪ – ∪ – –, or begin in rising movement ⏓ – ∪ ∪ – ∪ ∪ – ∪ –, etc. Some of these cola are found in Lesbian lyric, others seem more reminiscent of the western lyric poets Stesichorus and Ibycus. Those in falling movement I have called prosodiacs, those in rising movement enoplians; this use of the names is somewhat arbitrary, but while the two were used interchangeably in antiquity they have been applied in a variety of ways by modern writers on metric.

Though prosodiacs and enoplians taken altogether do not bulk very large in the drama, yet their variety of form is so great and their associations with other kinds of metre so multifarious that it is difficult to get any clear impression of them; there are not enough of any one sort for their habits to be observed very closely, and we have to ask ourselves whether we are merely making a rag-bag collection of odd cola which seem to be misfits in other categories or whether they do form a coherent group with a characteristic movement and related contexts. One difficulty is that so many of the cola have ambiguous connections; the same sequence of syllables may be an ordinary form of X or a resolved form of Y or a rare variant of Z, and a whole context and its colometry may be susceptible of different interpretations according to the choice of X, Y or Z here.

A basis of classification commonly used by metricians—at least for what I have called enoplians—is the number of long syllables; the cola are divided into 'Dreiheber' such as × – ∪ ∪ – ∪ ∪ – and 'Vierheber' such as ⏓ – ∪ ∪ – ∪ ∪ – – or × – ∪ ∪ – ∪ – – or ∪ ∪ – ∪ ∪ – ∪ – ∪ –, the intervening spaces between these 'Hebungen' (the longs) being filled by all possible[1] combinations of single- and double-short. This method of classification was prompted by the paroemiac,[2] since from among the mass of proverbs of 'Vierheber' form a few can be selected which resist emendation to the regular ⏓ – ∪∪ – ∪∪ – – and appear to show an occasional

---

[1] This is in fact not the case; forms such as ∪ ∪ – ∪ – ∪ ∪ – ∪ – or ∪ – ∪ ∪ – ∪ – ∪ ∪ –, changing from double- to single-short and back, or *vice versa*, do not occur, a point which considerably weakens the theory.

[2] See above, p. 33.

single-short, as in ἀδελφὸς ἀνδρὶ παρείη ∪ – ∪ – ∪ ∪ – – or ἐπὶ σαυτῷ τὴν σελήνην ∪ ∪ – – – ∪ – –. On the strength of this a theory is built up of a primitive 'Urvers' which like some old German metres had a constant number of 'Hebungen' with an indeterminate number of 'Senkungen'. Further, Wilamowitz actually classes the blunt 'Vierheber' as 'free iambics'. I have not followed these lines of classification, because in the first place I am not convinced of the truth of the theory (whatever the aberrations of some few of the παροιμίαι each was an isolated phrase; they were not recited continuously κατὰ στίχον and therefore need not constitute *a* metre in the ordinary sense, nor do we know anything about their origins or how they were added to) and in the second place there is absolutely no evidence (such as free responsion) in the drama that e.g. × – ∪ ∪ – ∪ ∪ – –, × – ∪ ∪ – ∪ – –[1] and × – ∪ – ∪ – – were ever regarded as interchangeable variants of the same rhythm, and in default of such evidence there are no grounds for transferring the iambic and choriambic phrases from their proper place; thirdly, such a 'horizontal' classification obscures the relation to phrases both longer and shorter than the various forms of 'Drei-' and 'Vierheber', and to other metres with which they associate. But while as a basis of classification the theory is both unsound and too narrow, some of the facts to which it calls attention are relevant, as will be seen in the course of this chapter.

In the lyrics of drama various lines of affinity can be traced for prosodiacs and enoplians, affinity with dactyls, anapaests and dactylo-anapaests, with aeolo-choriambic, with dactylo-epitrite, and with dochmiac. This last is peculiarly characteristic of Euripides, and it is chiefly in this connection that something distinct emerges which might be called prosodiac-enoplian movement; this is mostly con-

[1] The overworked Ἐρασμονίδη Βάθιππε, τῶν ἀωρολείων (Crat. frag. 10 K. from his Ἀρχίλοχοι) is of course a reminiscence of Archilochus's Ἐρασμονίδη Χαρίλαε, χρῆμά τοι γελοῖον, but this can hardly be used as evidence for a 'popular' metre in which ∪ – ∪ ∪ – ∪ ∪ – ∪ was regarded as in effect the 'same' as ∪ – ∪ ∪ – ∪ – ∪. Still less need we suppose (with Hephaestion) that Cratinus did not realize he was using a different metre from the original. The resemblance was near enough for the purpose of Cratinus' parody.

fined to the long passages of astrophic ἀπολελυμένα which form an increasingly important part of the lyric content of later fifth-century drama.

Dactylic rhythms in lyric, since they cannot run to a close in – ∪ ∪, usually end blunt – ∪ ∪ –, or pendant – ∪ ∪ – –, but occasionally their final phrase is a colon which begins – ∪ ∪ and ends as it were more elaborately in – ∪ – –. Such at least is the effect of hearing a colon of this type after a run of dactyls, and even the short aristophanean – ∪ ∪ – ∪ – – has this effect when it breaks the uniform dactylic rhythm of the first song of the Clouds (*Nub.* 286, see above, pp. 32 f.). The prosodiac known as the 'alcaic decasyllable' because it forms the last line of the alcaic stanza, – ∪ ∪ – ∪ ∪ – ∪ – –, is an extended version of the aristophanean in this aspect, and in the clausula of *P.V.* 160ff. it ends the run of dactylo-anapaests:

πρὶν ἂν ἢ κορέσῃ κέαρ ἢ παλάμᾳ τινὶ
τὰν δυσάλωτον ἕλῃ τις ἀρχάν.

It is also used fairly freely, at least by Aeschylus, as a clausula among mixed rhythms, cf. *Ag.* 1482, 1496, and especially in aeolo-choriambic as in *Supp.* 662. The next larger size – ∪ ∪ – ∪ ∪ – ∪ ∪ – ∪ – –, called 'praxillean' after the poetess Praxilla of Sicyon, closes in much the same way a run of dactylo-anapaests in Ar. *Thesm.* 1159

εἰ καὶ πρότερόν ποτ' ἐπηκόω ἤλθετε,
νῦν ἀφίκεσθ' ἱκετεύομεν ἐνθάδ' ἡμῖν.

So too *Or.* 1299–1300, in a dactylic run:

ὦ Διὸς ὦ Διὸς ἀέναον κράτος,
ἔλθ' ἐπίκουρος ἐμοῖσι φίλοισι πάντως.

In *Ag.* 1547 a praxillean is followed by an aristophanean, which repeats its latter segment, and an iambic line closes:

τίς δ' ἐπιτύμβιον αἶνον ἐπ' ἀνδρὶ θείῳ
σὺν δακρύοις ἰάπτων
ἀλαθείᾳ φρενῶν πονήσει;

It is found elsewhere with aeolo-choriambics (*Ant.* 134–5, *Med.* 432, *Tro.* 1070), and in *Eum.* 996 as an introduction to lekythia.

This, then, is one little pendant prosodiac series which is sometimes set in related contexts:

$$- \cup \cup - \cup - - \quad \text{aristophanean}$$
$$- \cup \cup - \cup \cup - \cup - - \quad \text{alcaic decasyllable}$$
$$- \cup \cup - \cup \cup - \cup \cup - \cup - - \quad \text{praxillean}$$

There is a parallel series of pendants in the rising enoplian rhythm:

$$\overset{\cup}{\underset{\cup}{}}^{1} - \cup \cup - \cup - -$$
$$\overset{\cup}{\underset{\cup}{}} - \cup \cup - \cup \cup - \cup - -$$
$$\cup \cup - \cup \cup - \cup \cup - \cup \cup - \cup - -$$

The first of these in the form $\times - \cup \cup - \cup - -$ is the 'choriambic enoplian A' of the last chapter; with initial double-short it closes a series of anapaests in Aristophanes' *Tagenistae* (frag. 502 K.)

φέρε παῖ ταχέως κατὰ χειρὸς ὕδωρ,
παράπεμπε τὸ χειρόμακτρον

just as the alcaic decasyllable closes a dactylic run; it is in effect a headless form of that prosodiac. The next size (with initial ∪ ∪ like a headless praxillean) closes the first major period of *Ant.* 354–64 = 365–75:

κ020αὶ φθέγμα καὶ ἀνεμόεν $\quad \overline{\cup} - \cup \cup - \cup \cup -$
φρόνημα καὶ ἀστυνόμους $\quad \cup - \cup \cup - \cup \cup -$
ὀργὰς ἐδιδάξατο καὶ δυσαύλων $\quad \overline{\cup\cup} - \cup \cup - \cup \cup - \cup - -$

(in the antistrophe with initial double-short); the rest of the stanza is iambic. In Aesch. *Supp.* 524ff. it follows precisely the same colon, to which in effect it adds a bacchiac:

ἄναξ ἀνάκτων, μακάρων $\quad \cup - \cup - - \cup \cup -$
μακάρτατε καὶ τελέων $\quad \cup - \cup \cup - \cup \cup -$
τελειότατον κράτος, ὄλβιε Ζεῦ. $\quad \cup - \cup \cup - \cup \cup - \cup - -$

(This colon $\underset{\cup}{\smile} - \cup \cup - \cup \cup -$ is as we shall see itself to be reckoned with the enoplians.) In *P.V.* 135 it picks up an earlier alcaic decasyllable (l. 132) in an ionic-anacreontic stanza:[2]

---

[1] Where this symbol is used it should be understood that ∪ may correspond to – and – to ∪ ∪, but not ∪ to ∪ ∪.

[2] See above, p. 129.

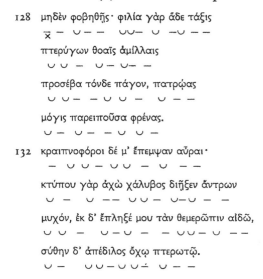

128 μηδὲν φοβηθῇς· φιλία γὰρ ἅδε τάξις

⨯ – ∪ – – ∪∪– ∪ –∪ – –

πτερύγων θοαῖς ἀμίλλαις

∪ ∪ – ∪ – ∪– –

προσέβα τόνδε πάγον, πατρῴας

∪ ∪ – – ∪ ∪ – ∪ – –

μόγις παρειποῦσα φρένας.

∪ – ∪ – – ∪ ∪ –

132 κραιπνοφόροι δέ μ' ἔπεμψαν αὖραι·

– ∪ ∪ – ∪ ∪ – ∪ – –

κτύπου γὰρ ἀχὼ χάλυβος διῆξεν ἄντρων

∪ – ∪ – – ∪ ∪ – ∪–∪ – –

μυχόν, ἐκ δ' ἔπληξέ μου τὰν θεμερῶπιν αἰδῶ,

∪ ∪ – ∪ – ∪ – – ∪ ∪ – ∪ – –

σύθην δ' ἀπέδιλος ὄχῳ πτερωτῷ.

∪ – ∪ ∪ – ∪ ∪ –· ∪ – –

The third and longest of this series, known as the archebulean, is not common in drama, but is used by Euripides in the *Heracleidae* (l. 356 = 365) among aeolo-choriambics and in *H.F* 1198 πολυμοχθότερον πολυπλαγκτότερόν τε θνατῶν in one of those long astrophic passages with which dramatic lyric was then beginning to experiment.

It is arguable that a still smaller size in these enoplians ∪ ∪ – ∪ – – should be recognized as a colarion, though hardly as an independent one. It is of course an ionic clausular rhythm, and is probably to be so interpreted in *P.V.* 134 above, being added to the anacreontic μυχόν, ἐκ δ' ἔπληξέ μου τὰν θεμερῶπιν αἰδῶ[1] (l. 130 is clearly also ionic). *Ant.* 609 should almost certainly make a single minor period with 610 κατέχεις 'Ολύμπου μαρμαρόεσσαν αἴγλαν ∪ ∪ – ∪ – – – ∪ ∪ – ∪ – –. This colarion seems in fact to be in much the same case as the dodrans – ∪ – ∪ ∪ – which is only semi-independent.[2]

---

[1] Alternatively this might be divided—more easily rhetorically—μυχόν, ἐκ δ' ἔπληξέ μου (cat. anac. or enoplian, see below)+τὰν θεμερῶπιν αἰδῶ. It is in any case a dicolon, though a single minor period.

[2] Our texts are apt to give ∪ ∪ – ∪ – – as a separate line in places where it would be better absorbed into a single minor period, as, for instance, *Alc.* 244 οὐράνιαί τε δῖ- ναι νεφέλας δρομαίου – ∪ ∪ – ∪ – | – ∪ ∪ –

The groups of cola so far discussed have all been pendant and therefore often clausular. There are in both prosodiacs and enoplians a number of cola which are blunt forms and 'dragged' forms catalectic in relation to the previous series; thus, first

$$-\cup\cup-\cup\cup-\cup-$$
$$-\cup\cup-\cup\cup-\cup\cup-\cup-$$
$$-\cup\cup-\cup\cup-\cup\cup-\cup\cup-\cup-$$

Of these prosodiacs only the first is at all common in drama; it is sometimes called 'ibycean' from the opening line ἦρι μὲν αἵ τε Κυδώνιαι of a poem of Ibycus of Rhegium. *Alc.* 243 ff. begins:

Ἅλιε καὶ φάος ἁμέρας $-\cup\cup-\cup\cup-\cup-$
οὐράνιαί τε δῖναι νεφέλας δρομαίου. $-\cup\cup-\cup--\cup\cup-\cup--$

The second line, a dicolon of dodrans A+aristophanean, shows clearly enough a possible relation between $-\cup\cup-\cup-$ and the ibycean, and the dodrans might be prefixed to this series as its shortest colarion, just as the aristophanean is in one aspect related to the corresponding pendants. The ibycean is identical in form with one version of the glyconic: that which (in drama only) resolves a base $--$ into $-\cup\cup$. As the ibycean, like most prosodiacs

$\cup--$, not $-\cup\cup-\cup--\mid\cup\cup-\cup--$. *Alc.* 252–6 should I think be three long minor periods (synartete dicola):

ὁρῶ δίκωπον ὁρῶ σκάφος ἐν   λίμνᾳ· νεκύων δὲ πορθμεύς
ἔχων χέρ' ἐπὶ κοντῷ Χάρων   μ' ἤδη καλεῖ 'τί μέλλεις;
ἐπείγου· σὺ κατείργεις'· τάδε τοί   με σπερχόμενος ταχύνει.

It may simplify matters metrically to delete ἐν λίμνᾳ, but it is inexplicable how the words should have got there spuriously; her vision is precise in detail—the Styx, the two-oared boat, the boatman with his pole. The antistrophe on the other hand is easy to muddle and has conflicting versions. λίμνᾳ in responsion with ὁρᾷς is no difficulty in the opening syllable of a choriambic enoplian.

If $\cup\cup-\cup--$ is a semi-detachable colarion, this might help to explain the baffling line Aesch. *Supp.* 167 χαλεποῦ γὰρ ἐκ πνεύματος εἶσι χειμών. This might be two equal phrases $\cup\cup-\cup--\mid\cup\cup-\cup--$, but more probably it works analogously to such an iambic line as ἐπεὶ δ' ἀνάγκας ǀ ἔδυ λέπαδνον, with a catalectic $\cup\cup-\cup-$+aristophanean. It is difficult to believe that Aeschylus would at any date open an iambo-choriambic line $--\cup--\cup\cup-\cup--$ with a resolution $\cup\cup-$.

and enoplians, is liable to appear in choriambic contexts, it is not easy to decide if and where a distinction is to be drawn between the two. Eur. *El.* 150–6, for instance, is a curious 'mesodic' interlude between strophe and antistrophe

ἒ ἔ· δρύπτε κάρα· $-\ -\ -\ \cup\ \cup\ -$ ||

οἷα δέ τις κύκνος ἀχέτας $-\ \cup\ \cup\ -\ \cup\ \cup\ -\ \cup\ -$

ποταμίοις παρὰ χεύμασιν $\cup\ \cup\ \cup\ -\ \cup\ \cup\ -\ \cup\ -$

πατέρα φίλτατον καλεῖ, $\cup\ \cup\ \cup\ -\ \cup\ -\ \cup\ -$ ||

ὀλόμενον δολίοις βρόχων $\cup\ \cup\ \cup\ -\ \cup\ \cup\ -\ \cup\ -$

ἕρκεσιν, ὥς σε τὸν ἄθλιον, $-\ \cup\ \cup\ -\ \cup\ \cup\ -\ \cup\ -$

πάτερ, ἐγὼ κατακλαίομαι, $\cup\ \cup\ \cup\ -\ \cup\ \cup\ -\ \cup\ -$

which passes in the middle of a sentence into the antistrophe. Wilamowitz takes these six lines, after the dodrans which is cut off by hiatus, as all glyconic, the apparent lekythion being a 'glyconic with single-short'. But little is gained by the change of name; the modification of rhythm is not eliminated thereby, and it would be best to leave these as they stand, in two groups of three cola, *abc*, *bab*. The difference between *a* and *b* may be no more than that of initial *anceps* in the trisyllabic base; here it is impossible to say. In *I.T.* 1092 = 1109 εὐξύνετον ξυνετοῖς βοάν $\underset{\times}{}\frown -\ \cup\ \cup\ -\ \cup\ -$ actually corresponds to ὀλομένων ἐν ναυσὶν ἔβαν $\cup\frown -\ \underset{\times}{}-\ \cup\ \cup\ -$ and we can say without hesitation that the former is a glyconic variant in responsion to chor. dim. B. But in spite of many ambiguous cases the separate identity of the ibycean is unquestionable; it has its place in the series, and it occurs frequently as we shall see in typical prosodiac contexts, associated with other cola of the same category, especially its own 'dragged' variant $-\ \cup\ \cup\ -\ \cup\ \cup\ -\ \underset{\times}{}-$, and with dochmiacs of the form $-\ \cup\ \cup\ -\ \cup\ -$ and $-\ \cup\ \cup\ -\ \underset{\times}{}-$. It does also associate easily with aeolo-choriambics, and where it appears in isolation among them may well be a glyconic variant. But there are mixed contexts where the ibycean prosodiac movement seems to predominate and the glyconic is as it were pulled over into that rhythm.[1] This is perhaps the nearest approach in drama to that

---

[1] Strictly, of course, the ibycean starts with true long, the glyconic $\underset{\times}{}\frown -\ \cup\ \cup\ -\ \cup\ -$ with long *anceps*, but this could well be a case like that of the aeolic dodrans $-\ \cup\ \cup\ -\ \cup\ -$ exerting a pull on the dochmiac $\underset{\times}{}\frown -\ \cup\ -$ (p. 106, n. 2); an initial choriamb has a powerful effect.

other aspect of the glyconic which emerges from Sappho's use of it with $\times\times - \cup\cup - \cup\cup - \cup -$ as indicated at the beginning of this chapter. Take, for instance, the astrophic chorus *Thesm.* 1136–59,

Παλλάδα τὴν φιλόχορον ἐμοὶ	ibyc.
δεῦρο καλεῖν νόμος ἐς χορόν,	ibyc.
παρθένον ἄζυγα κούρην, ‖	hemiep. (ibyc. cat.)
ἢ πόλιν ἡμετέραν ἔχει	ibyc.
καὶ κράτος φανερὸν μόνη	glyc.
κληδοῦχός τε καλεῖται. ‖	pher.
φάνηθ', ὦ τυράννους στυγοῦσ' ὥσπερ εἰκός. ‖	bacch. tetram.
δῆμός τοι σε καλεῖ γυναι-	glyc.
-κῶν, ἔχουσα δέ μοι μόλοις	+glyc.
εἰρήνην φιλέορτον. ‖	pher.
1148 ἥκετ' εὔφρονες ἵλαοι,[1]	glyc.
πότνιαι, ἄλσος ἐς ὑμέτερον	glyc. ending ↶
ἀνδράσιν οὐ θεμίτ' εἰσορᾶν	ibyc.
ὄργια σεμνὰ θεοῖν ἵνα λαμπάσι	dact. tetram.
φαίνετον ἄμβροτον ὄψιν. ‖	dact. trim. (hemiep.)
μόλετον ἔλθετον ἀντόμεθ' ὦ	$\cup\cup\cup - \cup\cup - \cup\cup -$ [2]
Θεσμοφόρω πολυποτνία. ‖	ibyc.
εἰ καὶ πρότερόν ποτ' ἐπηκόω ἤλθετε,	dact. anap.
νῦν ἀφίκεσθ' ἱκετεύομεν ἐνθάδ' ἡμῖν.	prax.

Here clearly the dominant movement is the ibycean-dactylic; the glyconics have shed their choriambic, tetrasyllabic aspect and accommodate themselves to their surroundings. Only the bacchiac

[1] Possibly here the change of address should be signalized by ἥκετ⟨ε δ'⟩, giving another ibycean.

[2] This might be reckoned a freak form of glyconic like Eur. *El.* 439 = 449 κοῦφον ἅλμα ποδῶν Ἀχιλῆ $- \cup - \cup\cup - \cup\cup -$. A proper name in the strophe is sometimes the occasion of a metrical licence even where the antistrophe follows suit without a proper name. In *Thesm.* 1153 it appears to be an extension of the dactylic modification of these glyconics, and I am inclined to take this and similar lines as a form of prosodiac, one of those which begin instead of ending with the single-short (see below). *Bacch.* 112 and 115 are again of this type but with trisyllabic base, and the latter is followed by a dact. tetram. cat. (or prosodiac, see below):

Βρόμιος ὅστις ἄγει θιάσους $\cup\cup\cup - \cup\cup - \cup\cup -$
εἰς ὄρος εἰς ὄρος ἔνθα μένει. $- \cup\cup - \cup\cup - \cup\cup -$

line, the cry to Athena, arrests the quick movement and strikes a note of sudden gravity—the year was 411 B.C.

Longer blunt prosodiacs of this type are rare; *Phil.* 827 is dact. tetram. (ch. VII, Add. n. p. 117), and at *Med.* 135–6 the weakly repetitive text is probably false and we should adopt Elmsley's γόον. In *Lys.* 1279ff., a trochaic and dactylic chorus, l. 1284 is apparently a long colon of the type:

ὃς μετὰ μαινάσι Βάκχιος ὄμμασι δαίεται

$$- \cup \cup - \cup \cup - \cup \cup - \cup \cup - \cup -$$

with an ibycean 1290

ἦν ἐπόησε θεὰ Κύπρις. $- \cup \cup - \cup \cup - \cup -$

Here the blunt prosodiacs are used like the pendants of this type, to close dactylic runs. In *Ion* 1479–80, however, in ἀπολελυμένα the same colon occurs in unmistakable dochmiac-prosodiac-enoplian movement, of which more presently.

The corresponding series of enoplians starts with one which is ambiguous with the telesillean $\overset{\cup\cup}{} - \cup \cup - \cup -$, as the ibycean is ambiguous with the glyconic, but resolution of the opening syllable is very rare in purely choriambic contexts.[1] When it appears in isolation as in Eur. *Supp.* 778 τὰ μὲν εὖ τὰ δὲ δυστυχῆ, introducing a stanza which is otherwise all iambo-trochaic, it does not much matter what it is called, but there are contexts where its relation to surrounding metres cuts right across the choriamb and shows it to be enoplian. Thus *Ion* 452–71 = 472–91, a curious passage in which every line opens in rising rhythm, ends as follows:

ἱκετεύσατε δ' ὦ κόραι $\cup \cup - \cup \cup - \cup -$
τὸ παλαιὸν ᾿Ερεχθέως $\cup \cup - \cup \cup - \cup -$
γένος εὐτεκνίας χρονίου καθαροῖς $\cup \cup - \cup \cup - \cup \cup - \cup \cup -$
μαντεύμασι κῦρσαι. $- - \cup \cup - -$

The effect of the apparent anapaestic dimeter (itself a form of enoplian as we shall see) is to give the other three lines an enoplian instead of a choriambic twist, just as the dactyls of the *Thesmophoria zusae* passage quoted above affected the ibyceans. Similarly,

---

[1] See last chapter, p. 134, n. 1.

an anapaestic enoplian *Phoen.* 163 (in an astrophic duet) precedes the next larger enoplian in this series, ∪ ∪ – ∪ ∪ – ∪ ∪ – ∪ –,

ἀνεμώκεος εἴθε δρόμον νεφέλας
ποσὶν ἐξανύσαιμι δι' αἰθέρος,

and five dochmiacs follow; *Hel.* 640 ξυνομαίμονες ὤλβισαν ὤλβισαν has a similar context.

The longest of this series, ∪ ∪ – ∪ ∪ – ∪ ∪ – ∪ ∪ – ∪ –, is found in *Andr.* 487 Μενέλα· διὰ γὰρ πυρὸς ἦλθ' ἑτέρῳ λέχει in responsion to 480 κατὰ πηδαλίων δίδυμαι πραπίδων γνῶμαι, which ends on a 'drag'. As the colon in the strophe (480) is generally explained as 'anapaestic dimeter+spondee', λέχει is often written λέχεϊ in our texts or emended to λέκτρῳ. But λέχει is blameless; any prosodiac or enoplian ending in ∪ – has licence to respond to a dragged close, precisely as in dochmiacs – ∪ ∪ – ∪ – may respond to – ∪ ∪ – x̄ –. Thus *Sept.* 222 = 229 gives ibyceans as clausula to a dochmiac stanza τυφόμενον πυρὶ δαΐῳ – ∪ ∪ – ∪ ∪ – ∪ – ∼ κριμναμέναν νεφέλαν ὀρθοῖ – ∪ ∪ – ∪ ∪ – x̄ –, and *O.C.* 1564 = 1575 has enoplians νεκρῶν πλάκα καὶ Στύγιον δόμον ∪ – ∪ ∪ – ∪ ∪ – ∪ – ∼ κατεύχομαι ἐν καθαρῷ βῆναι ∪ – ∪ ∪ – ∪ ∪ – x̄ –. Forms with dragged close, however, are not merely incidental variants but common enough in this *genre* to contribute whole series on their own account, in some cases commoner than the ∪ – ending. This is especially the case in astrophic contexts in association with dochmiacs; so *Or.* 1255

φόβος ἔχει με μή τις ἐπὶ δώμασι   2 doch.
σταθεὶς ἐπὶ φοίνιον αἷμα   enop. (of paroemiac form)
πήματα πήμασιν ἐξεύρῃ   pros. – ∪ ∪ – ∪ ∪ – x̄ –

picking up the dochmiac 1248 τίνα θροεῖς αὐδάν; ∪ ∪ ∪ – x̄ –. There is little doubt that *Andr.* 274 = 284[1] is a long colon of this kind – ∪ ∪ – ∪ ∪ – ∪ ∪ – ∪ ∪ – x̄ – rather than a 'catalectic hexameter', and in the same ode 296 = 304 ὅτε νιν παρὰ θεσπεσίῳ δάφνᾳ and 298 = 306 δεκέτεις ἀλάληντο νέοι λόγχαις ∪ ∪ – ∪ ∪ –

---

[1] See above, p. 42.

∪ ∪ − ⪥ −¹ are not anapaestic dimeters but dragged enoplians, shorter lengths of l. 480 quoted above κατὰ πηδαλίων δίδυμαι πραπίδων γνῶμαι.² Again, in 825–65 of the same play, an ἀμοιβαῖον in which Hermione voices her lyrical despair in dochmiacs and prosodiacs and the Nurse tries to reason with her in iambic trimeters, ll. 841–3 (Hermione, between two trimeters) run

τί μοι ξίφος ἐκ χερὸς ἡγρεύσω;   ∪ − ∪ ∪ − ∪ ∪ − ⪥ −³
ἀπόδος ὦ φίλα, 'πόδος ἵν' ἀνταίαν   ∪ ∪ ∪ − ∪ − ∪ ∪ ∪ − ⪥ −
ἐρείσω πλαγάν· τί με βρόχων εἴργεις;   ∪ − − ⪥ − ∪ ∪ ∪ − ⪥ −

where the interrelation of dochmiacs and enoplian emerges very clearly. Another line of affinity shown by these dragged dochmiacs and prosodiacs is with the dactylo-epitrites discussed in the next chapter.

The prosodiacs and enoplians so far analysed have been in double-short movement (except in some cases of initial *anceps*) turning to one single-short, or drag, at the end. Occurring in the same contexts and undoubtedly akin are a limited number with an additional single-short (which may be dragged) at the end, and even occasionally inverted with the single-short segment first. There are also a larger number which have no single-short at all and are in some cases ambiguous with, sometimes perhaps identical with, cola already classed among dactylic and anapaestic lengths. These appear, however, so constantly among prosodiacs and enoplians, sometimes even linked with them in synartete dicola, that they also must be adopted

¹ Cf. *Hyps.* frag. 64, 77 τέκνον οἷά τε Γοργάδες ἐν λέκτροις (Wilam.'s τέκνον for τέκνα is essential on more than metrical grounds), and 81

    ἐπὶ τ' οἶδμα θαλάσσιον ὀρνίθων   ∪ ∪ − ∪ ∪ − ∪ ∪ − ⪥ −
    ἐρῆμον κοίταν.   doch.

² For further examples of this length see *Ion* 717, 1442, *Phoen.* 184, and Eur. *El.* 167 (see above, p. 137, n. 1) Ἀγαμέμνονος ὦ κόρα, ἤλυθον, Ἠλέκτρα.

³ Cf. *Phaethon*, frag. 781 N.² 61

    τάλαιν' ἐγὼ τάλαινα ποῖ   ∪ − ∪ − ∪ − ∪ −
    πόδα πτερόεντα καταστάσω;   ∪ − ∪ ∪ − ∪ ∪ − ⪥ −

into this category. There is in fact a considerable overlapping in categories between dactylo-anapaestic, dactylo-epitrite and kindred types, and prosodiac-enoplian, and these cannot be tidily sorted out.

The blunt enoplians ◡ ◡ – ◡ ◡ – ◡ – ◡ –, ◡ – ◡ – ◡ ◡ – ◡ ◡ – and their corresponding pendants ◡ ◡ – ◡ ◡ – ◡ – ◡ – – and ◡ – ◡ – ◡ ◡ – ◡ ◡ – – have one foot in this category and one in the iambo-anapaestic which as we shall see is akin to the dactylo-epitrite. The corresponding prosodiacs (– ◡ ◡ – ◡ ◡ – ◡ – ◡ – –, etc.) are best treated among the dactylo-epitrites though they occasionally appear in the contexts of this chapter. The shorter lengths ◡ ◡ – ◡ – ◡ – and – ◡ ◡ – ◡ – ◡ –, ◡ – ◡ – ◡ ◡ – and – ◡ ◡ – ◡ – –, ◡ – ◡ – ◡ ◡ – and – ◡ – ◡ – ◡ ◡ –, are mixed up with aeolo-choriambics and with anacreontics, and though theoretically they have a place here are far commoner in their choriambic and ionic associations.[1] The anacreontics at least have a double line of descent, but it is hardly possible to make any distinction between choriambic and prosodiac cola where the forms are identical; only their double affinity can be noted.

Eur. *El.* 585–95 is an astrophic chorus in dochmiac-enoplian throughout:

ἔμολες ἔμολες ὦ χρόνιος ἁμέρα,	2 doch.
κατέλαμψας ἔδειξας ἐμφανῆ	◡ ◡ – ◡ ◡ – ◡ – ◡ –
πόλει πυρσόν, ὃς παλαιᾷ φυγᾷ	2 doch.
πατρίων ἀπὸ δωμάτων τάλας	◡ ◡ – ◡ ◡ – ◡ – ◡ –
ἀλαίνων ἔβα.	doch.
θεὸς αὖ θεὸς ἁμετέραν τις ἄγει	◡ ◡ – ◡ ◡ – ◡ ◡ – ◡ ◡ –
νίκαν ὦ φίλα.	doch.
ἄνεχε χέρας ἄνεχε λόγον ἵει λιτὰς	2 doch.
εἰς θεούς, τύχᾳ σοι τύχᾳ	cr.+doch.
κασίγνητον ἐμβατεῦσαι πόλιν.	2 doch.

---

[1] *O.T.* 1209 θαλαμηπόλῳ πεσεῖν ◡ ◡ – ◡ – ◡ – after three 'hypo-dochmiacs' – ◡ – ◡ – might be noticed as a clear instance of enoplian where there is no sort of ionic-anacreontic rhythm in the context. Cf. *Hipp.* 125 ὅθι μοί τις ἦν φίλα followed by a hypodochmiac+dochmiac.

Phaethon, frag. 781 N.² 65–7, has a similar rhythm:

ἰώ μοί μοι, κακὰ φανήσεται·   2 doch.
βασίλεια τάλαινα παῖς τ' ἔσω   ∪ ∪ – ∪ ∪ – ∪ – ∪ –¹
κρυφαῖος νέκυς.   doch.

This form of enoplian was apparently so far standardized later, possibly by some Hellenistic poet, that it got a name—cyrenaic; in drama it is not common, and Euripides rather prefers its dragged form ∪ ∪ – ∪ ∪ – ∪ – $\underset{\times}{}$ –, to echo dragged dochmiacs; so *Hel.* 657 ἀδόκητον ἔχω σε πρὸς στέρνοις, and again 680–1

Hel. Πάριν ὡς ἀφέλοιτο   Men. πῶς; αὔδα.   ∪ ∪ – ∪ ∪ – ∪ – $\underset{\times}{}$ –
Hel. Κύπρις ᾧ μ' ἐπένευσεν, Men. ὦ τλάμων.   ∪ ∪ – ∪ ∪ – ∪ – $\underset{\times}{}$ –
Hel. τλάμων τλάμων ὧδ' ἐπέλασ' Αἰγύπτῳ.   2 doch.

Cf. *Hyps.* 64, 94 ἀπομαστίδιόν γ' ἐμῶν στέρνων, *Ion* 1494 ἀνὰ δ' ἄντρον ἔρημον οἰωνῶν. The pendant form ∪ ∪ – ∪ ∪ – ∪ – ∪ – – appears in *H.F.* 1080 Ταφίων περίκλυστον ἄστυ πέρσας, *Med.* 648 θανάτῳ θανάτῳ πάρος δαμείην, twice in *Alc.* 435 ff. and twice in *Rhes.* 895 ff. quoted below.

The blunt inversion ∪ – ∪ – ∪ ∪ – ∪ ∪ – is not wholly independent in its rare occurrences, but in *Alc.* 252 (see above, p. 163, n. 2) is found in a dicolon, and in *Hipp.* 1270 with dochmiacs:

1268 σὺ τὰν θεῶν ἄκαμπτον φρένα καὶ βροτῶν   ∪ – – ∪ – – ∪ ∪ – ∪ –
    ἄγεις Κύπρι, σὺν δ'   ∪ – – ∪ –
    ὁ ποικιλόπτερος ἀμφιβαλὼν   ∪ – ∪ – ∪ ∪ – ∪ ∪ –
    ὠκυτάτῳ πτερῷ.   – ∪ ∪ – ∪ –

The pendant form occurs *Med.* 206 τὸν ἐν λέχει προδόταν κακόνυμφον ∪ – ∪ – ∪ ∪ – ∪ ∪ – –, and after two dochmiacs *Phoen.* 128 γίγαντι γηγενέτᾳ προσόμοιος; possibly *Bacch.* 1190 σοφὸς σοφῶς ἀνέπτηλ' ἐπὶ θῆρα is to be reckoned with these, but the text is doubtful. Occasionally longer cola in the same style appear in these ἀπολελυμένα, as *Ion* 1466

ὅ τε γηγενέτας δόμος οὐκέτι νύκτα δέρκεται
    ∪ ∪ – ∪ ∪ – ∪ ∪ – ∪ ∪ – ∪ – ∪ – ‖
ἀελίου δ' ἀναβλέπει λαμπάσιν,   2 doch.

¹ I suspect that *Med.* 204 ff. should open with this enoplian:
    ἰαχὰν ἄϊον πολύστονον [γόων].   ∪ ∪ – ∪ ∪ – ∪ – ∪ –

cf. *Hel.* 644

τὸ κακὸν δ' ἀγαθὸν σέ τε κἀμὲ συνάγαγεν, πόσι, ||
χρόνιον ἀλλ' ὅμως ὀναίμαν τύχας.

For the cola without any single-short the close connection of prosodiac-enoplian with dactylo-epitrite is probably responsible, since all these forms are found in both categories. The link with dactyls, anapaests and dactylo-anapaests is also obvious, but the common use of a single initial *anceps* in enoplian forms (e.g. in the paroemiac × – ⏑ ⏑ – ⏑ ⏑ – –) readily differentiates them in this relation. The commonest forms are the hemiepes, blunt – ⏑ ⏑ – ⏑ ⏑ – and pendant – ⏑ ⏑ – ⏑ ⏑ – –, × – ⏑ ⏑ – ⏑ ⏑ – (the καὶ φθέγμα καὶ ἀνεμόεν of *Ant.* 354), and ⏕ – ⏑ ⏑ – ⏑ ⏑ – – (paroemiac). Occasionally the longer – ⏕ – ⏑ ⏑ – ⏑ ⏑ – (equivalent to a dactylic tetrameter catalectic) and ⏕ – ⏑ ⏑ – ⏑ ⏑ – ⏑ ⏑ – (equivalent to an anapaestic dimeter) are found. In shorter lengths the single choriamb occurs now and again as a semi-detachable colarion, and ⏕ – ⏑ ⏑ – –, identical in form with the reizianum, seems sometimes (e.g. *Ion* 458 and 471, see above, p. 167, *ibid.* 504 and 508) by the company it keeps to belong to this series. There is occasional contraction of the double-short into one long, usually at the beginning, so that the hemiepes – ⏑ ⏑ – ⏑ ⏑ – may appear as – ⏒ – ⏑ ⏑ – (not dodrans or dochmiac, since it is checked by responsion to – ⏑ ⏑ – ⏑ ⏑ –), and the next length as – ⏒ – ⏑ ⏑ – ⏑ ⏑ –; thus *Alc.* 89 f.

οὐ μὰν οὐδέ τις ἀμφιπόλων	– – – ⏑ ⏑ – ⏑ ⏑ –
στατίζεται ἀμφὶ πύλας.	⏑ – ⏑ ⏑ – ⏑ ⏑ –

Probably some cola containing a series of long syllables not easy to rationalize may be explained by an extension of this contraction, as, for instance, *Ion* 503

ἵνα τεκοῦσά τις	⏑ ⏑⏑ – ⏑ –	doch.
παρθένος, ὦ μελέα,	– ⏑ ⏑ – ⏑ ⏑ –	hemiep.
βρέφος Φοίβῳ πτανοῖς	⏑ – ⏒ – ⏒ –	= ⏑ – ⏑ ⏑ – ⏑ ⏑ –
ἐξώρισε θοίναν.	× – ⏑ ⏑ – –	reiz.

These purely double-short lengths appear in typical astrophic contexts both as separate cola and as ingredients in dicola. The latter is rather more common, the reason being that here again they are passing into the sphere of 'dactylo-epitrite', the essence of which is the combination of cola and colaria into compound wholes, whether of single-short+double-short, of single-short+single-short, of double-short+double-short, or of one or the other+such a mixed colon as ⏑ ⏑ – ⏑ ⏑ – ⏑ –. *Alc.* 435–44 = 445–54 is an ode constructed of straightforwardly separable prosodiac-enoplian cola, in strophic stanzas:

ὦ Πελίου θύγατερ,	– ⏑ ⏑ – ⏑ ⏑ –
χαίρουσά μοι εἰν ᾿Αίδαο δόμοις	×̅ – ⏑ ⏑ – ⏑ ⏑ – ⏑ ⏑ –
τὸν ἀνάλιον οἶκον οἰκετεύοις.	⏑ ⏑ – ⏑ ⏑ – ⏑ – ⏑ – – ‖
ἴστω δ᾿ ᾿Αίδας ὁ μελαγχαί-	×̅ – ⏑ ⏑ – ⏑ ⏑ – ×̅
-τας θεός, ὅς τ᾿ ἐπὶ κώπᾳ	– ⏑ ⏑ – ⏑ ⏑ – ×̅
πηδαλίῳ τε γέρων	– ⏑ ⏑ – ⏑ ⏑ –
νεκροπομπὸς ἵζει	– ⏑ – ⏑ – – ‖
πολὺ δὴ πολὺ δὴ γυναῖκ᾿ ἀρίσταν	⏑ ⏑ – ⏑ ⏑ – ⏑ – ⏑ – – ‖
λίμναν ᾿Αχεροντίαν πορεύ-	×̅ – ⏑ ⏑ – ⏑ – ⏑ –
-σας ἐλάτᾳ δικώπῳ.	– ⏑ ⏑ – ⏑ – –

Of similar elements, and of an almost un-Euripidean simplicity, is the Muse's lament for her son, *Rhes.* 895 ff.

ἰαλέμῳ αὐθιγενεῖ	⏑ – ⏑ ⏑ – ⏑ ⏑ –
τέκνον σ᾿ ὀλοφύρομαι, ὦ	⏑ – ⏑ ⏑ – ⏑ ⏑ –
ματρὸς ἄλγος, οἵαν	– ⏑ – ⏑ – –
ἔκελσας ὁδὸν ποτὶ Τροίαν,	⏑ – ⏑ ⏑ – ⏑ ⏑ – –
ἦ δυσδαίμονα καὶ μελέαν	– ⏓̈ – ⏑ ⏑ – ⏑ ⏑ –
ἀπὸ μεμφομένας ἐμοὶ πορευθείς,	⏑ ⏑ – ⏑ ⏑ – ⏑ – ⏑ – –
ἀπὸ δ᾿ ἀντομένου πατρὸς βιαίως.	⏑ ⏑ – ⏑ ⏑ – ⏑ – ⏑ – –
ὤμοι ἐγὼ σέθεν, ὦ φιλία	– ⏑ ⏑ – ⏑ ⏑ – ⏑ ⏑ –
φιλία κεφαλά, τέκνον, ὤμοι.	⏑ ⏑ – ⏑ ⏑ – ⏑ ⏑ – –

The penultimate couplet here (⏑ ⏑ – ⏑ ⏑ – ⏑ – ⏑ – – *bis*) is as we saw of enoplians to which the corresponding prosodiac is – ⏑ ⏑ – ⏑ ⏑ – ⏑ – ⏑ – –. Both are types of phrasing which come under the heading 'dactylo-epitrite and kindred metres', the second being sometimes called 'encomiologus' or 'elegiambus' from its component colaria the dactylic (elegiac) hemiepes – ⏑ ⏑ – ⏑ ⏑ – and the iambic penthemimer × – ⏑ – ×. These elements in reverse order form the 'iambelegus' which is again found in dochmiac-prosodiac-enoplian ἀπολελυμένα, as in the kommos between the Chorus, Creusa and the πρεσβύτης, *Ion* 763–99. After an opening dochmiac passage it continues

P. μήπω στενάξῃς – C. ἀλλὰ πάρεισι γόοι.   ⏓–∪–⏓ –∪∪–∪∪–
P. πρὶν ἂν μάθωμεν – C. ἀγγελίαν τίνα μοι;   ∪–∪–∪ –∪∪–∪∪–

This division of a compound between two speakers is found again in *H.F.* 1185 f. Theseus is questioning in trimeters and Amphitryon answers and mourns in dochmiacs, so Theseus gets the steadier iambic half and Amphitryon finishes it in a dragged prosodiac ‒∪∪‒∪∪‒⏓ ‒.

T. εὔφημα φώνει.   A. βουλομένοισιν ἐπαγγέλλῃ.
T. ὦ δεινὰ λέξας.   A. οἰχόμεθ᾽ οἰχόμεθα πτανοί.
T. τί φῃς; τί δράσας; A. μαινομένῳ πιτύλῳ πλαγχθεὶς
ἑκατογκεφάλου βαφαῖς ὕδρας,[1]   ∪∪‒∪∪‒∪‒⏓‒

(the dragged enoplian of ἀπομαστίδιόν γ᾽ ἐμῶν στέρνων, see above). This same dicolon occurs in *Phoen.* 121, and again in *Ion* 714 ff. after a long dragged enoplian:

ἰὼ δειράδες Παρνασοῦ πέτρας	2 doch.
ἔχουσαι σκόπελον οὐράνιόν θ᾽ ἕδραν	2 doch.
ἵνα Βάκχιος ἀμφιπύρους ἀνέχων πεύκας	∪∪‒∪∪‒∪∪‒∪∪‒⏓‒
λαιψηρὰ πηδᾷ νυκτιπόλοις ἅμα σὺν Βάκχαις,	⏓‒∪‒⏓ ‒∪∪‒∪∪‒⏓‒

the rest being dochmiac.

When the segments of a dicolon are not synartete it is not always possible to say whether they really form a single minor period or should be counted as two separate cola and therefore potentially as two minor periods. The question is treated more fully in the next chapter; here it may be pointed out that they tend constantly to be so juxtaposed that they *could* combine naturally into a single running rhythm. Just as in iambo-trochaics *anceps* ‒ ∪ ‒ × at colon-ends is never followed by *anceps* at the beginning of the next colon but always by long, so a paroemiac or pendant hemiepes is not followed by enoplian (unless there is Pause) but always by prosodiac, while blunt ends are mostly taken up by enoplians. Thus in *H.F.* 1028 ff.

---

[1] There is very possibly a lacuna somewhere in the text here, but this line should not be emended.

when the inner stage is revealed with the dead bodies and the bound
Heracles, the Chorus chant (the exclamations are *extra metrum*):

φεῦ φεῦ·
ἴδεσθε διάνδιχα κλῇθρα   ∪ – ∪ ∪ – ∪ ∪ – ∪
κλίνεται ὑψιπύλων δόμων.   – ∪ ∪ – ∪ ∪ – ∪ –
ἰώ μοι·
ἴδεσθε δὲ τέκνα πρὸ πατρὸς   ∪ – ∪ ∪ – ∪ ∪ – ∪
ἄθλια κείμενα δυστάνου.   – ∪ ∪ – ∪ ∪ – x̄ –

This combination of paroemiac+prosodiac occurs so often that it
is clearly to be taken as a dicolon. In *Andr.* 826–7 and 830–1
(synartete), *Or.* 1256–7 = 1276–7, and *Tr.* 266–7 it is unmistakably
a single minor period. Now as in *all* these instances the final syllable
of the paroemiac is short, so that the run-on in unbroken rhythm
is more easily taken, it follows (if further proof were needed)
that this enoplian paroemiac is quite distinct from the *catalectic*
anapaestic dimeter, where a shortening of the final syllable indicates
pause. The final syllable here is in fact a true *anceps* like the *anceps*
of iambo-trochaic, and the colon should strictly be written
∪̆∪̆ – ∪ ∪ – ∪ ∪ – ×. Probably the same applies to some of the
other combinations of similar kind, such as *Phoen.* 146 f. (paroem.+
lekyth.)

καταβόστρυχος ὄμμασι γοργὸς   ∪ ∪ – ∪ ∪ – ∪ ∪ – ∪
εἰσιδεῖν νεανίας   – ∪ – ∪ – ∪ –

and 191 f.

χρυσεοβόστρυχον ὦ Διὸς ἔρνος   – ∪ ∪ – ∪ ∪ – ∪ ∪ – ∪
Ἄρτεμι δουλοσύναν τλαίην.   – ∪ ∪ – ∪ ∪ – x̄ –

So too the three hemiepe *H.F.* 1199 ff.

αἰδόμενος τὸ σὸν ὄμμα   – ∪ ∪ – ∪ ∪ – ∪
καὶ φιλίαν ὁμόφυλον   – ∪ ∪ – ∪ ∪ – ∪
αἷμά τε παιδοφόνον,   – ∪ ∪ – ∪ ∪ –

where the second and third lines form a recognized dicolon
known as the 'choerilean'[1] – ∪ ∪ – ∪ ∪ – × – ∪ ∪ – ∪ ∪ – but the

[1] See above, p. 42.

whole appears here to make a tricolon, like the three prosodiacs, *Or.* 202 ff.

βίου τὸ πλέον μέρος ἐν   ∪ – ∪ ∪ – ∪ ∪ –
στοναχαῖσί τε καὶ γόοι-   ∪ ∪ – ∪ ∪ – ∪ –
-σι δάκρυσί τ᾽ ἐννυχίοις.   ∪ – ∪ ∪ – ∪ ∪ –

Some of these dicola have ancient names, like the 'iambelegus', the 'choerilean', and the 'archilochean' Ἐρασμονίδη Χαρίλαε, χρῆμά τοι γελοῖον ∪ – ∪ ∪ – ∪ ∪ – × – ∪ – ∪ – – because they are relatively common and often synartete (the *Wasps* ends with seven archilocheans κατὰ στίχον) or because one of the earlier lyrists or some later Hellenistic poet took up such a compound and used it stichically. Others still remain nameless. Thus, for instance, the astrophic passage *Ion* 1439–1509 ends in three long compound cola:

1504 δεινὰ δὲ καὶ τάδ᾽ · ἑλισσόμεσθ᾽ ἐκεῖθεν   elegiambus
ἐνθάδε δυστυχίαισιν εὐτυχίαις τε πάλιν,   choerilean
μεθίσταται δὲ πνεύματα. ‖   +iamb. dim.
μενέτω· τὰ πάροιθεν ἅλις κακά· νῦν δὲ γένοιτό τις οὖρος
ἐκ κακῶν ὦ παῖ.   – ∪ – – –

Each of these begins in double-short and passes into single-short, the first with blunt hemiepes + iambic penthemimer, the second with pendant + blunt hemiepes + iamb. dim., the last with an enoplian like an immensely elongated paroemiac + a sequence – ∪ – – – which is a recognized colarion in dactylo-epitrite.[1] The whole series belongs as much to the dactylo-epitrite-iambo-anapaestic purlieu as to the prosodiac-enoplian and is an illustration of Euripides' tendency to mingle the two categories inextricably. The mixture is in fact characteristic of these monodies, duos, and kommoi in which the rhythm changes constantly with the rhetorical phrasing and the emotions of the singers. It was the 'modern music' of the last two decades of the fifth century, and Euripides was in the forefront of the movement.

Additional note

Many cola which the ear must be able to grasp as whole patterns of sound have no generally agreed name and are not 'lengths' of any

[1] See below, pp. 181 f.

recurring movement. This applies particularly to the prosodiacs and enoplians of this chapter; the generic name needs further definition before it can identify a given colon, or serve for oral reference. I have suggested elsewhere ('The Metrical Units of Greek Lyric Verse', *C.Q.* 1950–1) a system of notation which I have found to work quite well in practice; even beginners can pick it up easily, especially in oral teaching, and recognize extended phrases without having to memorize any more names. It is most useful in its simplest forms, which I summarize here:

d = double-short, **s** = single-short, enclosed between longs, – ∪ ∪ –, – ∪ –. These may be prolonged: – ∪ ∪ – ∪ ∪ – (hemiepes) = **dd**, – ∪ – ∪ – (hypodochmiac) = **ss**, – ∪ ∪ – ∪ – (dodrans) = **ds** or in 'dragged' form **d̄s** ('**d** dragged **s**'), – ∪ ∪ – ∪ ∪ – ∪ – (ibycean) = **dds**, etc. *Anceps* fore and aft is written in the long form, taken as including the short, and spoken as 'dash', thus the alcaic decasyll. (= '**dds** dash **dds** –'). Enoplians opening ∪ ∪ – or ∪ – are e.g. (cyrenaic) ∧ **ddss** ('headless **ddss**'), or ∧ **ssdd**. In compounds link-*anceps* is always written – ('dash'); thus iambelegus = – **s** – **dd**. The resemblance in type between iambelegus and – ∪ – × – ∪ ∪ – ∪ ∪ – – on the one hand and alcaic and sapphic hendecasylls. on the other is much easier to see in this form: thus n. 1 on p. 179 might read: 'The relation of the nameless **s** – **dd** – to the iambelegus – **s** – **dd** is like that of the sapphic to the alcaic hendecasyll. **s** – **ds** – and – **s** – **ds** . . . the final period of the sapphic stanza is **s** – **ds** – **d** – and that of the alcaic – **s** – **s** – **dds** –.

I have kept Maas's notation for the dactylo-epitrites of ch. XI because its use is widespread, but pupils brought up on **d** and **s** find it simpler to call *D* **dd** and *e* **s**. *E* is not common enough in drama to be useful, and can always be replaced by **s** – **s**. Where there is no link-*anceps* a short vertical line indicates the break in smooth continuity, e.g. *Aj.* 173 (p. 182) is **dd**, **s** – **s** ('**dd** cut **s** dash **s**'). I have added **ds** notation to analyses in the synopsis p. 216 where it gives a convenient short handle for identification and spoken reference.

XI

DACTYLO-EPITRITE AND
KINDRED METRES

Compound cola of dual movement—Maas's notation—Dactylo-epitrite of drama freer and more varied than in lyric poets, especially Pindar— Special clausular phrasing—Other variations—Epitrite a special form of iambo-trochaic—General canons observed in word-end; possible reasons —Instances of free responsion—Kindred metres; dactylo-iambic and iambo-anapaestic.

Dactylo-epitrites have now emerged from the fog of controversy which obscured them for so long while Blass and Schroeder endeavoured to explain them in tetrasyllabic terms.[1] The licences of responsion in Pindar and Bacchylides which were believed to support this theory were drastically pruned by Maas's scrutiny of the text, and the attempt to reduce these mixed metres to a uniform type of movement with a multi-variable metron-unit of four syllables has been generally abandoned. The name 'dactylo-epitrite' reflects Hermann's observations on the nature of this metre, which had remained unrecognized and unnamed by the ancient metricians. It rightly indicates the dual movement which is the essence of all metres of this class—the compound of double-short and single-short ingredients. 'Dactyl' has to be loosely interpreted for the double-short element; 'epitrite' refers to the ratio ἐπίτριτος (4:3) of the χρόνοι in the form $-\overset{3}{\smile} \mid -\overset{4}{}-$ of the unit of single-short movement. This again is too narrow a definition since the unit can have other forms, but the name is well-established and will serve.

Those of Pindar's and Bacchylides' odes which are composed in dactylo-epitrites have no admixture of any other metre. The dactylic and epitrite units respectively are mostly uniform in type but variously grouped in compounds of varying length. These com-

[1] Based on the metrical theories of Pindar's scholiast who, like Hephaestion, sees nothing inorganic in such an analysis as $- \smile \smile - \mid \smile \smile - - =$ chor.+ionic.

pounds (in German called 'Verse' though, because of the different meaning of 'verse' in English, I prefer to continue using the term 'minor periods') are easily defined in this choral lyric with its triadic scheme of stanzas several times repeated, which at ambiguous points sooner or later throws up the *brevis in longo* or the hiatus which betrays period-close. In the lyrics of drama, where there is at most the single repetition of the antistrophe, the length of minor periods is often impossible to determine. The colon-units are more varied than in Pindar, and there is often admixture of kindred or even quite different metres within the same stanza.

P.V. 887–93 = 894–900 is the only ode in drama which confines its colon-units to those found in the commonest and most straightforward of Pindar's dactylo-epitrites. The irreducible unit of 'dactyl' is the hemiepes – ∪ ∪ – ∪ ∪ –, of 'epitrite' the cretic – ∪ –. These may have *anceps* prefixed in initial position or added in final position in the period, or interposed as a 'link'-syllable between colon-units. *Anceps* may not follow *anceps* except where there is period-close and pause. This *anceps* is much more often long than short, possibly as a make-weight to counterbalance the preponderance of shorts caused by the greater length of the dactylic unit. Thus, for instance, the 'iambelegus', a simple form of ready-made dactylo-epitrite compound ⏒ – ∪ – ⏒ – ∪ ∪ – ∪ ∪ –, gives initial *anceps*, epitrite, link *anceps*, hemiepes; the common but unnamed – ∪ – ⏒ – ∪ ∪ – ∪ ∪ – –[1] gives epitrite, link *anceps*, hemiepes, final *anceps*; and the 'choerilean' – ∪ ∪ – ∪ ∪ – ⏒ – ∪ ∪ – ∪ ∪ – gives hemiepes, link *anceps*, hemiepes. Maas uses a convenient form of notation for this straightforward type, letting D stand for – ∪ ∪ – ∪ ∪ –, *e* for – ∪ –, and E for the common double epitrite with link

---

[1] The relation of this dicolon to the iambelegus is like that of the sapphic to the alcaic hendecasyllable – ∪ – × – ∪ ∪ – ∪ – – and × – ∪ – × – ∪ ∪ – ∪ –. These Lesbian phrases are in effect dicola of similar type to the common dactylo-epitrite dicola, with the dodrans – ∪ ∪ – ∪ – as ingredient in place of the hemiepes – ∪ ∪ – ∪ ∪ –; so too the final period of the sapphic stanza – ∪ – × – ∪ ∪ – ∪ – × – ∪ ∪ – – is a tricolon and that of the alcaic × – ∪ – × – ∪ – × – ∪ ∪ – ∪ ∪ – ∪ – – a dicolon of similar formation, i.e. iambo-trochaic + prosodiac. See ch. x, Additional note, p. 177.

syllable, $e \smile e$. The iambelegus could thus be written $\smile e \smile D$, and *P.V.* 887ff. has the following scheme:

ἤ σοφὸς ἤ σοφὸς ἦν	$D - e - D - D \smile$
ὃς πρῶτος ἐν γνώμᾳ τόδ' ἐβάστασε καὶ γλώσ-	
-σᾳ τόδ' ἐμυθολόγησεν,	
ὡς τὸ κηδεῦσαι καθ' ἑαυτὸν ἀριστεύει μακρῷ	$e - D - e$
καὶ μήτε τῶν πλούτῳ διαθρυπτομένων	$- e - D$
μήτε τῶν γέννᾳ μεγαλυνομένων	$e - D$
ὄντα χερνήταν ἐραστεῦσαι γάμων.	$E - e$

It should be noted that the only evidence available for determining period-close in all this stanza is rhetorical pause and the familiarity from many other contexts of these particular lengths of colon-compound.

The most striking departure of the tragedians from the Pindaric model is their admission of varied clausulae, even where the rest of the ode can be expressed in Maas's notation. The commonest of such clausulae is the ithyphallic $- \cup - \cup - -$, which clearly has the effect of an elongated epitrite with added final *anceps*. In the *Medea*, which has four stasima containing dactylo-epitrite stanzas, three[1] of these are composed of regular D and e elements, with an ithyphallic clausula. 410 ff., for instance, runs as follows:

ἄνω ποταμῶν ἱερῶν χωροῦσι παγαί,	$\smile D - e -$
καὶ δίκα καὶ πάντα πάλιν στρέφεται.	$e - D$
ἀνδράσι μὲν δόλιαι βουλαί, θεῶν δ'	$D - e D \smile$
οὐκέτι πίστις ἄραρε·	
τὰν δ' ἐμὰν εὔκλειαν ἔχειν βιοτὰν στρέψουσι φᾶμαι·	$e - D - e \smile$
ἔρχεται τιμὰ γυναικείῳ γένει·	$E - e$
οὐκέτι δυσκέλαδος φάμα γυναῖκας ἕξει.	$D -$ ithyph.

In Ar. *Eq.* 1264–73 = 1290–9 again the clausula Πυθῶνι δίᾳ μὴ κακῶς πένεσθαι, $- e -$ ithyph., is the only break in D and e construction. The strophe is a parody of a Pindaric προσόδιον, but the ithyphallic is not found in any of Pindar's extant dactylo-epitrite. The rhythm of Πυθῶνι δίᾳ μὴ κακῶς πένεσθαι (identical in form with an iambic trimeter catalectic) recalls the πολλὴν κατ' ἀχλὺν ὀμμάτων ἔχευεν of Archilochus (frag. 112 D.[2]) which alternates with a com-

---

[1] Reading λαβοῦσα l. 981 and assuming a lacuna in the antistrophe.

pound consisting of dactylic tetrameter+ithyph., τοῖος γὰρ φιλό-
τητος ἔρως ὑπὸ καρδίην ἐλυσθείς (Horace's 'solvitur acris hiems').
There is, as we shall see, a good deal in the freer dactylo-epitrites
and kindred metres of drama which appears to recall Archilochus.
The 'archilochean' dicolon mentioned before, Ἐρασμονίδη Χαρίλαε,
χρῆμά τοι γελοῖον, is itself a form of ready-made dactylo-epitrite
compound, ⌣ *D* ⌣ ithyph. Nor is the ithyphallic confined to final
clausulae; in *Rhes.* 224ff. it appears at the close of the first period
Θυμβραῖε καὶ Δάλιε καὶ Λυκίας ναὸν ἐμβατεύων, ⌣ *e D* ithyph., as
well as at the end of the stanza.

Eur. *El.* 859ff. has at the end of conventional dactylo-epitrites the
singular clausula καλλίνικον ᾠδὰν ἐμῷ χορῷ, which appears to be a
repeated hypodochmiac – ⌣ – ⌣ – – ⌣ – ⌣ –. Here again the
effect sought seems to be that of a prolonged epitrite, a length of
single-short corresponding to the normal double-short hemiepes
– ⌣ ⌣ – ⌣ ⌣ –. More often the clausula is a colon familiar in other
contexts and of a type of movement according easily with dactylo-
epitrites; thus *Med.* 824ff. ends in a hipponactean – ⤬ – ⌣ ⌣ – ⌣ – –
ξανθὰν Ἁρμονίαν φυτεῦσαι. The hemiepes itself is occasionally contracted to the form – ∺ – ⌣ ⌣ –, as in *Andr.* 773–4 τιμὰ καὶ κλέος·
οὔτοι | λείψανα τῶν ἀγαθῶν *D* – | *D*, where the *D* – takes the form
of a pherecratean; thus the hipponactean with long *anceps* syllable
(as in *Med.* 832 just quoted) is easily assimilated in dactylo-epitrite.
The alcaic decasyllable – ⌣ ⌣ – ⌣ ⌣ – ⌣ – –, as an equivalent uncontracted form, is also found in clausular position, in *Rhes.* 537 =
556 compounded with an epitrite:

546 καὶ μὴν ἀίω· Σιμόεντος ἡμένα κοίτας	⌣ *D* ⌣ *e* – –
φοινίας ὑμνεῖ πολυχορδοτάτα	*e* – *D*
γήρυϊ παιδολέτωρ μελοποιὸν ἀηδονὶς μερίμναν.	dact. tetram.+ithyph.
ἤδη δὲ νέμουσι κατ’ Ἴδαν	– *D* –
ποίμνια· νυκτιβρόμου	*D*
σύριγγος ἰὰν κατακούω.	– *D* –
θέλγει δ’ ὄμματος ἕδραν	*D* – (pherecratean?)
ὕπνος· ἅδιστος γὰρ ἔβα βλεφάροις πρὸς ἀοῦς.	*e* – alc. decas.

The dicola here include some of the freer type of dactylo-epitrite
compounds. The first ends in – ⌣ – – –; this should probably not

be reckoned as a syncopated ithyphallic, since it appears in Pind. *Pyth.* IX, 2 σὺν βαθυζώνοισιν ἀγγέλλων *E* − −, and Pindar does not deal in ithyphallics; the spondee should in fact be recognized as a rare but regular dactylo-epitrite ingredient.[1] The second is the common *e − D*; the third is the 'solvitur acris hiems' in synartete form. Of the four hemiepe[2] which follow, the last has the contracted 'pherecratean' form. The final *e −* alcaic decasyllable has a parallel in *Ant.* 585 οὐδὲν ἐλλείπει γενεᾶς ἐπὶ πλῆθος ἕρπον, which closes the first major period (in dactylo-epitrites) of the stanza 582ff., the rest being iambic.

Soph. *Aj.* 172ff. begins with a dactylic tetrameter and ends with a choriambic enneasyllable similar to the hipponactean, the rest being composed of regular *D* and *e*:

ἦ ῥά σε Ταυροπόλα Διὸς Ἄρτεμις,	dact. tetram.
ὦ μεγάλα φάτις, ὦ μᾶτερ αἰσχύνας ἐμᾶς,	*D E*
ὥρμασε πανδάμους ἐπὶ βοῦς ἀγελαίας,	*− e − D −* ‖
ἦ πού τινος νίκας ἀκάρπωτον χάριν,	*− E − e* ‖
ἦ ῥα κλυτῶν ἐνάρων	*D*
ψευσθεῖσ᾽ ἀδώροις εἴτ᾽ ἐλαφαβολίαις;	iambel.
ἦ χαλκοθώραξ εἴ τιν᾽ Ἐνυάλιος	iambel.
μομφὰν ἔχων ξυνοῦ δορὸς ἐννυχίοις	iambel.
μαχαναῖς ἐτείσατο λώβαν;	*− ∪ − ∪ − ∪ ∪ − −*

It is quite usual for the dactylo-epitrites of drama to disintegrate, as it were, at some point in the stanza into separate dactylic and iambic or trochaic cola, often reassembling into orthodox compounds in a subsequent period. Thus *Tro.* 799–807 throws up a hexameter at 803, and *Pax* 775–96, in part a parody of Stesichorus, has a more elaborate break-away in the middle period:

775 Μοῦσα σὺ μὲν πολέμους ἀπωσαμένη μετ᾽ ἐμοῦ	choerilean
τοῦ φίλου χόρευσον, ‖	ithyph.
κλείουσα θεῶν τε γάμους ἀνδρῶν τε δαῖτας	*− D − e −*

---

[1] Whether as syncopated cretic (epitrite) or as suffix formed by overrun, cf. ch. IX, Additional note, p. 154; also above, p. 176 and *O.T.* 1097. The phrase *− ∪ ∪ − ∪ ∪ − − −* appears in Pind. *Pyth.* I, 2 and Simon. *P.M.G.* 581, 4 ἀντία θέντα μένος στάλας.

[2] My reasons for not treating these as two dicola (as Wilamowitz, *G.V.* p. 589) are given on p. 187 below.

780 καὶ θαλίας μακάρων· σοὶ γὰρ τάδ' ἐξ ἀρχῆς μέλει. $D - E$
      ἦν δέ σε Καρκίνος ἐλθὼν $D -$
      ἀντιβολῇ μετὰ τῶν παίδων χορεῦσαι, $D - e -$
785 μήθ' ὑπάκουε μήτ' ἔλ- $- \cup \cup - \cup - -$
      -θης συνέριθος αὐτοῖς· $- \cup \cup - \cup - -$
      ἀλλὰ νόμιζε πάντας $- \cup \cup - \cup - \underset{}{\cup}$
      ὄρτυγας οἰκογενεῖς γυλιαύχενας ὀρχηστὰς $- \cup \cup - \cup \cup - \cup \cup$
                                                                          $- \cup \cup - \underset{x}{-} -$
790 ναννοφυεῖς σφυράδων ἀποκνίσματα μηχανοδίφας. dact. hexam.
      καὶ γὰρ ἔφασχ' ὁ πατὴρ ὃ παρ' ἐλπίδας   dact. tetram.
      εἶχε τὸ δρᾶμα γαλῆν τῆς ἑσπέρας ἀπάγξαι. D – ithyph.

Three linked aristophaneans are treated as if they were orthodox hemiepe $D \cup$ (in the antistrophe they are in synaphea with the preceding elegiambus); a dragged prosodiac is followed by a dactylic hexameter, and then a tetrameter leads into an orthodox dactylo-epitrite clausula. For the occasional aeolo-choriambic colon substituted for a double-short element we might compare Soph. *O.T.* 1095–7 (the whole stanza is in dactylo-epitrite):

ὡς ἐπὶ ἦρα φέροντα τοῖς ἐμοῖς τυράννοις. $- \cup \cup - \cup \cup - \cup \quad - \cup - \cup - -$
ἰήϊε Φοῖβε, σοὶ δὲ ταῦτ' ἀρέστ' εἴη. $\cup - \cup \cup - \cup - \cup \quad - \cup - -$

The orthodox dicolon is followed by a variant in which one short syllable is omitted from each segment. The association of prosodiac-enoplian aeolic with dactylo-epitrite (ll. 788–9 of *Pax* quoted above) has parallels in Euripides, as in *Alc.* 597ff.:

καὶ νῦν δόμον ἀμπετάσας $- D$
δέξατο ξεῖνον νοτερῷ βλεφάρῳ $e - D$
τᾶς φίλας κλαίων ἀλόχου νέκυν ἐν δώμασιν ἀρτιθανῆ· $e - D D$
τὸ γὰρ εὐγενὲς ἐκφέρεται πρὸς αἰδῶ.
$\cup \cup - \cup \cup - \cup \cup - \cup - - \quad ||$
ἐν τοῖς ἀγαθοῖσι δὲ πάντ' ἔνεστιν σοφίας. ἄγαμαι.
$- - \cup \cup - \cup \cup - \cup - D$
πρὸς δ' ἐμᾷ ψυχᾷ θάρσος ἧσται θεοσεβῆ
$e - - e - \mathrel{\overset{\frown}{\cup}} \cup -$ ithyph.
φῶτα κεδνὰ πράξειν.

(The occasional resolution in the epitrite element $\overset{\frown}{\cup} \cup -$ θεοσεβῆ with the still rarer $- \cup \overset{\frown}{\cup}$, is analogous to the occasional contraction in the dactylic.)

The line quoted above, ἢ πού τινος νίκας ἀκάρπωτον χάριν (*Aj.* 176), which is the equivalent of an iambic trimeter with heavy *anceps*, is typical of Sophocles' tendency to normalize his epitrite series in iambic lengths. *Tr.* 94–102 ends with a series of this kind:

ὃν αἰόλα νὺξ ἐναριζομένα	‿ e D
τίκτει κατευνάζει τε φλογιζόμενον, ‖	– e – D
Ἅλιον Ἅλιον αἰτῶ	D –
τοῦτο καρῦξαι, τὸν Ἀλκμήνας πόθι μοι πόθι παῖς	E – D – e – D
ναίει ποτ', ὦ λαμπρᾷ στεροπᾷ φλεγέθων, ‖	
ἢ ποντίας αὐλῶνας, ἢ δισσαῖσιν ἀπείροις κλιθείς,	– E – E
εἴπ' ὦ κρατιστεύων κατ' ὄμμα.	– E –

– *E* – *E* is an iambic tetrameter, and the clausula is the iambo-trochaic alcaic enneasyllable.[1] The heavy epitrite movement gives these lines a characteristic rhythm, even though formally there is nothing to distinguish them from iambo-trochaic. Iambics and trochaics in lyric, as distinct from stichic, tend to use the short *anceps*, though it is true that Sophocles more than the other trage-dians[2] tends to write 'heavy' iambo-trochaics even where there is nothing in the context which can be unequivocally described as dactylo-epitrite, as for instance in *O.T.* 883ff., where there are indeed dicola of mixed movement but not characteristically dactylo-epitrite type.

To the whole question whether the 'epitrite' of dactylo-epitrite is in fact simply iambo-trochaic it is not easy to give a straightforward answer. Perhaps the closest definition possible is the somewhat question-begging statement that this is the type of iambo-trochaic used in dactylo-epitrite compounds and dactylo-epitrite contexts. Its characteristics are the preponderance of long *anceps* and the comparative rarity of syncopation. But there is a further point. Careful analysis of responding stanzas in dactylo-epitrite shows that there is in this metre an altogether unusual degree of coincidence in word-end between strophe and antistrophe, and the reason for this is the strong tendency to avoid ending a word on a link-*anceps* where

---

[1] See above, p. 70.
[2] See Denniston, 'Lyric Iambics in Greek Drama', in *Greek Poetry and Life*, Oxford, 1936.

this syllable is long.[1] *Med.* 627–34 = 635–42 is a typical example of the stricter type:

627 ἔρωτες ὑπὲρ μὲν ἄγαν ⫶ ἐλθόντες οὐκ εὐδοξίαν   ⌣ *D* – *E*
635 στέργοι δέ με σωφροσύνα, ⫶ δώρημα κάλλιστον θεῶν ·

     οὐδ' ἀρετὰν παρέδωκαν ἀνδράσιν · εἰ δ' ἅλις ἔλθοι   *D* ⌣ *D* –
     μηδέ ποτ' ἀμφιλόγους ὀργὰς ἀκόρεστά τε νείκη

     Κύπρις, οὐκ ἄλλα ⫶ θεὸς εὔχαρις οὕτως ·   *e* – *D* –
     θυμὸν ἐκπλήξασ' ⫶ ἑτέροις ἐπὶ λέκτροις

     μήποτ' ὦ δέσποιν' ἐπ' ἐμοὶ χρυσέων τόξων ἐφείης   *e* – *D* – *E* –
     προσβάλοι δεινὰ Κύπρις, ἀπτολέμους δ' εὐνὰς σεβίζουσ'   ithyph.

     ἱμέρῳ ⫶ χρίσασ' ἄφυκτον οἰστόν.
     ὀξύφρων ⫶ κρίνοι λέχη γυναικῶν.

It will be noted that the second of these periods is the only one where there is a divergence of word-end at a colon-link, and here in the strophe the *anceps* is short (παρέδωκᾰν), so that the pattern is *D* ⌣ ⫶ *D* – (strophe) but *D* ⫶ – *D* – (antistrophe). The majority of dactylo-epitrite odes in the drama observe this rule throughout, but there are several in which it is broken once, and in three or four there are two or more infringements. Most of these instances, however, are iambelegi, which admit ⌓ – ⌣ – ⌓ ⫶ – ⌣ ⌣ – ⌣ ⌣ – (or the equivalent pendant dicolon ⌓ – ⌣ – ⌓ ⫶ – ⌣ ⌣ – ⌣ ⌣ – –); so, for instance, in *Aj.* 178 and 179 quoted above. Doubtless the familiarity of the opening phrase ⌓ – ⌣ – ⌓ in iambic trimeters acted as a powerful analogy. It is significant that in the unnamed dicolon *e* – *D* – there is no instance of *e* – ⫶ *D* –;[2] *e* – ⫶ *e*... at the beginning of a period is likewise not found, and with one exception no period ends in *e* – ⫶ *e* (–). In other words, the embargo placed by tragedians and iambographers, following Archilochus, upon this rhythm in

---

[1] Cf. Maas, *Philol.* LXIII, 297ff. and Snell's formulation of the 'Lex Maasiana', *Bacchyl.* Praefatio, p. 29. The canons observed in the older lyric poets and to a considerable extent by Pindar and Bacchylides are more complicated but also more susceptible of formulation owing to the greater average length of the minor periods as compared with dramatic lyric, which runs largely in dicola. On this whole subject of word-end in dactylo-epitrites see now L. P. E. Parker, 'Porson's Law Extended', *C.Q.* XVI, 1966, pp. 4–10.

[2] For *O.T.* 1090, however (*e* – ⫶ *D* – ⫶ *e*), see below, p. 188.

iambics and trochaics[1] is carried through in dactylo-epitrites. The exception is *Pax* 802, where Aristophanes is parodying Stesichorus:

796 τοιάδε χρὴ Χαρίτων δαμώματα καλλικόμων $D \smile D$ ithyph. ‖
      τὸν σοφὸν ποιητὴν
   ὑμνεῖν ὅταν ἠρινὰ μὲν φωνῇ χελιδών $- D - e -$
   ἐϡομένη κελαδῇ, χορὸν δὲ μὴ 'χῃ Μόρσιμος. $D \smile e - \vdots e$

The sudden descent into comic sentiment and rhythm is obviously simultaneous. Whether this rule should be regarded as a strong piece of evidence that the epitrite rhythm is in fact ordinary iambo-trochaic or whether again analogy has played a part is uncertain. It is not altogether easy to see how this particular observance fits in with the *general* tendency to avoid word-end on a long *anceps*, at any point in the period and after the dactylic hemiepes. This is rather more liable to exceptions, though some of these may be only apparent, and due to our uncertainties about period-end. Possibly in the dactylic hemiepes analogy is again at work, from the familiar opening of the hexameter which allows $- \cup \cup - \cup \cup - \vdots$ or $- \cup \cup - \cup \cup - \cup \vdots$ but not $- \cup \cup - \cup \cup - - \vdots$. *Andr.* 766–76 =777–87 is worth considering on this subject of exceptions:

766 ἢ μὴ γενοίμαν ⋮ ἢ πατέρων ἀγαθῶν   iambel.
777 κρεῖσσον δὲ νίκαν ⋮ μὴ κακόδοξον ἔχειν

   εἴην πολυκτήτων τε δόμων μέτοχος.   iambel.
   ἢ ξὺν φόβῳ σφάλλειν δυνάμει τε δίκαν.

   εἴ τι γὰρ πάσχοι τις ἀμήχανον, ἀλκᾶς $e \smile D \smile$
   ἡδὺ μὲν γὰρ αὐτίκα τοῦτο βροτοῖσιν,

   οὐ σπάνις εὐγενέταις, D
   ἐν δὲ χρόνῳ τελέθει

   κηρυσσομένοισι δ' ἀπ' ἐσθλῶν ⋮ δωμάτων $- D - e$
   ξηρὸν καὶ ὀνείδεσιν ἔγκειται δόμων.

   τιμὰ καὶ κλέος· οὗτοι $D -$ (pherecratean)
   ταύταν ᾔνεσα ταύταν

   λείψανα τῶν ἀγαθῶν D
   καὶ φέρομαι βιοτάν,

[1] See above, p. 71.

ἀνδρῶν ἀφαιρεῖται χρόνος· ἁ δ᾽ ἀρετὰ   iambel.
μηδὲν δίκας ἔξω κράτος ἐν θαλάμοις
καὶ θανοῦσι λάμπει.   ithyph.
καὶ πόλει δύνασθαι.

Here one of the three iambelegi has the diaeresis $\bar{\times} - \cup - \bar{\times}$ ⫶. It
should be remembered that this particular dicolon is common
outside strictly dactylo-epitrite contexts, and the difference between
l. 766 and l. 767 may have been felt simply as a question of synartete
or asynartete dicolon, just as in archilocheans in Ar. *Vesp.* 1531–2,
in a context of seven of these compounds used κατὰ στίχον,

καὐτὸς γὰρ ὁ ποντομέδων ἄναξ πατὴρ προσέρπει
ἡσθεὶς ἐπὶ τοῖσιν ἑαυτοῦ ⫶ παισὶ τοῖς τριόρχοις,

the first is synartete, the second asynartete. In l. 771 = 782 of the
Andromache passage the antistrophe is regular while the strophe
gives $- D - $ ⫶ e. If the avoidance of $D - $ ⫶ is partly governed by
analogy from the hexameter, as suggested above, then $- D - $ ⫶ may
have been felt less liable to objection. The most difficult problem is
that of the two following lines, which also involves that of *Rhes.*
551–4 previously quoted. If these are all to be taken as dicola, the
most likely assumption is that the diaeresis works like that of
the trochaic tetrameter catalectic, dividing the complete from the
catalectic half. A curious parallel can be found in Antiphanes'
Ὅμοιοι (frag. 174 K.), which mixes trochaic tetrameters and choeri-
leans κατὰ στίχον:

εἶτ᾽ ἐπεισῆγεν χορείαν ⫶ ἢ τράπεζαν δευτέραν   troch.
καὶ παρέθηκε γέμουσαν ⫶ πέμμασι παντοδαποῖς.   choer.
ὡς δ᾽ ἐδείπνησαν, συνάψαι ⫶ βούλομαι γὰρ τὰν μέσῳ, troch.
καὶ Διὸς σωτῆρος ἦλθε ⫶ θηρίκλειον ὄργανον,   troch.
τῆς τρυφερᾶς ἀπὸ Λέσβου ⫶ σεμνοπότου σταγόνος   choer.
πλῆρες, ἄφριζον, ἕκαστος ⫶ δεξιτερᾷ δ᾽ ἔλαβεν.   choer.

But such an effect is more likely in this particular context and κατὰ
στίχον than in lyric, and I am inclined to believe that the hemiepe in
the *Rhesus* passage are separate minor periods (like οὐ σπάνις
εὐγενέταις *Andr.* 770).

On the whole it seems most likely that the general avoidance of
word-end on long link-*anceps* in dactylo-epitrites is designed to give

as much synartete effect as possible to these compounds, and if this is so it follows that the colon-ingredients were in general conceived as (⌣) – ⌣ – ⌣̲ and (⌣̲) – ⌣ ⌣ – ⌣ ⌣ – ⌣̲, with the 'link'-syllable the last of the colon before it, not the first of the following one. It is impossible to say what effect, if any, was intended in the extraordinary series of violations of this observance, *O.T.* 1088–91. The antistrophe is unfortunately corrupt, but it appears certain from a comparison of the two stanzas that the whole of this passage is in two minor periods as follows:

οὐ τὸν Ὄλυμπον ἀπείρων, ⦙ ὦ Κιθαιρών, ⦙ οὐκ ἔσῃ τὰν αὔριον D – ⦙ e – ⦙ E
πανσέληνον, ⦙ μὴ οὐ σ' ἐμὲ καὶ πατριώταν ⦙ Οἰδίπου. e – ⦙ D – ⦙ e

As far as we can tell from the uncertainties of the text, none of these diaereses is repeated in the antistrophe.

   The instances of free responsion in dactylo-epitrite, which formed such a difficult problem in the text and metric of the lyric poets, are very limited in the drama, but sufficiently puzzling even so. Our text of *P.V.* 535 = 543 gives

535   ἀλλά μοι τόδ' ἐμμένοι καὶ μήποτ' ἐκτακείη.
543   ἰδίᾳ γνώμᾳ σέβῃ θνατοὺς ἄγαν, Προμηθεῦ,

i.e. – ⌣ – ⌣ *e* – ithyph. ∼ ⌣ ⌣ – – *e* – ithyph. This is often emended away, either by Hermann's μάλα μοι τοῦτ' in 535, or by some invented substitute for ἰδίᾳ such as αὐτόνῳ. The latter can be rejected at once, not only because of the great superiority of ἰδίᾳ to any substitute but because of the appropriate position of this well recognized rhythmical variant, which is just like the instance in Pind. *Ol.* vii, 9 παρεόντων θῆκέ νιν ζαλωτὸν ὁμόφρονος εὐνᾶς ⌣ ⌣ – – *e* – *D* –, the final period of the strophe, and again *Ol.* viii, 6 (the penultimate) ἀρετὰν θυμῷ λαβεῖν ⌣ ⌣ – – *e*, followed by the final *E*. Pindar in fact uses ⌣ ⌣ – as a rare dactylo-epitrite ingredient, just as he uses the spondee, but whereas the spondee is generally the closing rhythm of a colon this is a gambit. ἰδίᾳ γνώμᾳ then in its combination of required meaning and idiomatic metre is in too strong a position to be rejected. The curiosity here is the responsion to

‒ ᴗ ‒ ᴗ, which has no parallel in the lyric poets.[1] There is no reason other than metrical for emending the strophe to give ᴗ ᴗ ‒ ‒ or ᴗ ᴗ ‒ ᴗ (a long syllable in the last place here is as unnecessary metrically as τοῦτ' is for τόδ' grammatically). The equation ᴗ ᴗ ‒ ‒ = ‒ ᴗ ‒ ᴗ is familiar in ionic-anacreontic context; are we to concede to Schroeder that dactylo-epitrite can be 'ionicized'? A more startling series of such responsions occurs in comedy, *Vesp.* 273–80 = 281–9.

273 τί ποτ' οὐ πρὸ θυρῶν φαίνετ' ἄρ' ἡμῖν ὁ γέρων οὐδ' ὑπακούει;
281 τάχα δ' ἂν διὰ τὸν χθιζινὸν ἄνθρωπον, ὃς ἡμᾶς διεδύετ'

μῶν ἀπολώλεκε τὰς ἐξαπατῶν καὶ λέγων	‒ ᴗ ᴗ‒ ᴗ̲ ᴗ ‒
ἐμβάδας ἢ προσέκοψ' ἐν ὡς φιλαθήναιος ἦν καὶ	‒ ᴗ ᴗ ‒ ᴗ̲ ᴗ ‒ ‒
τῷ σκότῳ τὸν δάκτυλόν που, ‖ τὰν Σάμῳ πρῶτος κατείποι,	‒ ᴗ ‒ ‒ ‒ ᴗ ‒ ‒
εἶτ' ἐφλέγμηνεν αὐτοῦ διὰ τοῦτ' ὀδυνηθεὶς	ᴗ̄ ᴗ ‒ ᴗ̄ ᴗ ‒ ‒
τὸ σφυρὸν γέροντος ὄντος; εἶτ' ἴσως κεῖται πυρέττων.	‒ ᴗ ‒ ᴗ̲ ‒ ᴗ ‒ ‒
καὶ τάχ' ἂν βουβωνιῴη. ‖ ἔστι γὰρ τοιοῦτος ἀνήρ.	‒ ᴗ ‒ ᴗ̲ ‒ ᴗ ‒ ‒

The remaining lines form two straightforward dactylo-epitrite periods ‒ *D* ‒ *e* ᴗ̲ | *D* ᴗ̲ *D* ‒ *E* ‒ with an ionic clausula ᴗ ᴗ ‒ ‒ ᴗ ᴗ ‒. The first four lines here form a single minor period, which starts off in indubitable ionic. Though at first sight the strophe appears to diverge, startlingly enough, into dactylo-epitrite for the rest of the period, a comparison with the antistrophe makes it clear, I think, that these three lines and the following three are really built in dimeters, of which the first and fourth are syncopated. Aristo-

---

[1] Bacchyl., frag. 4 ἀραχνᾶν ἰστοὶ πέλονται ~ παιδικοί θ' ὕμνοι φλέγονται is rejected by Snell as not being in responding stanzas (the fragment is not long enough to give any certain check on the triadic scheme), and by Maas on the grounds that such an adjective as παιδικοί is an unparalleled form in older lyric.

phanes has played on the identity of the epitrite or heavy trochee – ⏑ – – with the anacreontic metron, creating a hybrid passage in which – ⏑ ⏑ – appears by a sort of anaclasis for ⏑ ⏑ – – and – ⏑ – – – ⏑ – – for ⏑ ⏑ – – – ⏑ – –. The fourth dimeter again wavers between ionic and epitrite. The whole is one of those characteristically comic licences of responsion by which the number of syllables is kept constant but 'irrational' lengthening in strophe or antistrophe is allowed to change the rhythm, just as in *Av.* 333–4 ~ 349–50 metra of ⏑ ⏑ ⏑ ⏑ are made to correspond to metra of – ⏑ ⏑ ⏑.[1] It is hardly possible to deduce from such a passage anything about the general conception among fifth-century poets of the nature of dactylo-epitrite rhythm or its relation to ionic.

The responsion of *P.V.* 535 = 543 remains a riddle. If the text be kept we can only recall the curious mixed aeolic-anacreontic of the earlier choruses of this most baffling play, and suppose that there is an echo here of such rhythms as δακρυσίστακτον δ' ἀπ' ὄσσων ~ μεγαλοσχήμονά τ' ἀρχαί, ⏑ ⏑ – – ⏓ ⏑ – –.[2] Both ⏑ ⏑ – and – ⏑ – are in order at the opening of a dactylo-epitrite period and perhaps the poet chose to let them stand in responsion as if they were in ionics.

Since Pindar's dactylo-epitrite odes are always homogeneous we can isolate his few unusual colon-ingredients and speak of them without more ado as rare dactylo-epitrite elements. In dramatic lyric, dactylo-epitrite like every other metre has its penumbra which shades off into other metrical types, and metrical transitions may be made in the middle of a stanza, so that we cannot classify with the same precision. It has been shown, however, that Pindar's – –, ⏑ ⏑ –, and pherecratean – – – ⏑ ⏑ – – are all found in drama, and his prosodiac – ⏑ ⏑ – ⏑ ⏑ – ⏑ – (*Ol.* VI, str. 5) has analogies in Euripides' enoplians quoted above. The prolongation of clausular rhythms seems peculiar to drama; it might be described as the substitution of a final ⏑ – – for the simple –, as in the ithyphallic – ⏑ – ⏑ – – for – ⏑ – – (*e* –), the alcaic decasyllable – ⏑ ⏑ – ⏑ ⏑ – ⏑ – – for – ⏑ ⏑ – ⏑ ⏑ – – (*D* –), and the hipponactean – – – ⏑ ⏑ – ⏑ – – for the pherecratean – – – ⏑ ⏑ – –. The choriamb

[1] See above, pp. 56f.

[2] See above, p. 121, n. 1.

which Pindar now and again uses as a short form of $- \cup \cup - \cup \cup -$[1]
(and sometimes apparently as a sort of anaclasis of $- \cup - \underset{\smile}{\smile}$[2]) is rare
in drama, but there is a clear instance in *O.T.* 1086 εἴπερ ἐγὼ μάντις
εἰμὶ καὶ κατὰ γνώμαν ἴδρις $- \cup \cup - e \cup E$. For the prolonged double-
short colon $- \cup \cup - \cup \cup - \cup \cup - \cup \cup -$ (as in *Pyth.* III, str. 4) the
dramatic poets generally prefer acatalectic dactylic lengths, usually
tetrameters or hexameters. More difficult is the question whether
drama has anything really corresponding to the rare $\cup \cup - \cup \cup -$ of
Pyth. III, ep. 9 μεταμώνια θηρεύων ἀκράντοις ἐλπίσιν $\cup \cup - \cup \cup - - E$.
This is here obviously an irregularity of dactylo-epitrite, a headless
hemiepes, but where the sequence appears in this kind of context in
drama[3] it appears rather to belong to an ill-defined, nearly related
class of metres which might be called iambo-anapaestic.

When Sophocles in *Tr.* 94 writes ὃν αἰόλα νὺξ ἐναριζομένα, though
this can be represented in normal dactylo-epitrite terms as $\cup e D$,
the effect of the short *anceps* and the absence of link-syllable is
to make this line sound like a lyric iambic metron+hemiepes.
Similarly, Euripides begins *Hel.* 1137–50 with the phrase ὅτι θεὸς ἢ
μὴ θεὸς ἢ τὸ μέσον $\cup \widehat{\cup \cup} \cup - - \cup \cup - \cup \cup -$, and repeats the same
sequence five lines further on. The strophe ends with a wholly
iambic period, much resolved (trim. dim. trim. cat.), and though the
rest is dactylo-epitrite with heavy *anceps* the epitrite phrases all end
blunt, so that they could be expressed in terms of iambic metra.
Such a rhythm might more properly be described as dactylo-iambic.
Bacchylides (e.g. frag. 19) sometimes writes in a metre which is
given that name, though the division into metra cannot always be
carried through and there is no *anceps* in the 'iambic', only short
and long: the rhythms are in fact more akin to aeolic. But besides

---

[1] E.g. *Ol.* VI, ep. 17.   [2] So perhaps *Ol.* VI, str. 2.
[3] In *Ant.* 1115 = 1126 Nauck's transposition is unnecessary. πολυώνυμε,
Καδμείας νύμφας ἄγαλμα $\sim$ σὲ δ' ὑπὲρ διλόφου πέτρας στέροψ ὄπωπε is
a dicolon $\cup \cup - \cup \cup - \doteq - | \, \widehat{\cup} \, | - \cup - | \cup$ in which one double-short
has contracted to accommodate the proper name (followed as often by
ant.). The opening is 'anapaestic' instead of dactylic, longer than
Pindar's headless *D*, and the varying *anceps* has its normal position. The
metre then modulates into aeolo-choriambic.

dactylo-iambic there are various forms of an iambo-anapaestic metre used by all three tragedians,[1] which often runs in compounds very much in the dactylo-epitrite manner. Such odes, however, are too few in number and too varied in detail to afford a clear conception of this metrical type, which is not self-supporting throughout a stanza like much of dactylo-epitrite but appears in scattered periods, major or minor, and takes up, or passes into, other more orthodox metres, usually regular dactylo-epitrite or aeolic.

Thus *Med.* 643 ff., after a pair of dactylo-epitrite stanzas, mingles aeolic and iambo-anapaestic, mostly in long compounds:

ὦ πατρίς, ὦ δώματα, μὴ δῆτ' ἄπολις γενοίμαν	chor. tetram. cat.
τὸν ἀμηχανίας ἔχουσα δυσπέρατον αἰῶν'	∪∪‒∪∪‒∪‒∪‒∪‒‒
οἰκτροτάτων ἀχέων·	‒∪∪‒∪∪‒
θανάτῳ θανάτῳ πάρος δαμείην	∪∪‒∪∪‒∪‒∪‒‒
ἀμέραν τάνδ' ἐξανύσασα μόχ-	‒∪‒‒‒∪∪‒∪‒
-θων δ' οὐκ ἄλλος ὕπερθεν ἢ	‒‒‒∪∪‒∪‒
γᾶς πατρίας στέρεσθαι.	‒∪∪‒∪‒‒

Here the second period could be represented in the same terms as Pindar's μεταμώνια θηρεύων ἀκράντοις ἐλπίσιν with the addition of ‒ *D*, and the third as ∪∪‒∪∪‒∪ *e* ‒. But the Euripidean phrases have the light *anceps* characteristic of iambo-anapaests, and the third period is in fact also a recognized form of enoplian.[2]

Trach. 497 ff. is in a different style:

μέγα τι σθένος ἁ Κύπρις ἐκφέρεται νίκας ἀεὶ
∪∪‒∪∪‒∪∪‒∪∪‒ŭ‒∪‒

καὶ τὰ μὲν θεῶν
e ‒   ‖

παρέβαν, καὶ ὅπως Κρονίδαν ἀπάτασεν οὐ λέγω
∪∪‒∪∪‒∪∪‒∪∪‒∪‒∪‒   ‖

οὐδὲ τὸν ἔννυχον ῎Αιδαν
D ‒

ἢ Ποσειδάωνα τινάκτορα γαίας·
e ‒ *D* ‒

‒‒‒‒‒‒‒‒‒‒‒‒‒‒‒‒‒

[1] Aristophanes has something similar in *Av.* 451 ff. and 1313 ff.
[2] See above, p. 171.

ἀλλ' ἐπὶ τάνδ' ἄρ' ἄκοιτιν

$D - \ ||$

τίνες ἀμφίγυοι κατέβαν πρὸ γάμων;

◡ ◡ − ◡ ◡ − ◡ ◡ − ◡ ◡ −

τίνες πάμπληκτα παγκόνιτά τ' ἐξ-

◡ − − − ◡ − ◡ − ◡ −

-ῆλθον ἄεθλ' ἀγώνων;

− ◡ ◡ − ◡ − −

The first and third lines are a compound of anapaestic enoplian+
iambic metron; at the end of the stanza a similar enoplian is followed
by a dicolon of syncopated iambic trimeter+aristophanean; the
remainder is dactylo-epitrite.

The first line of *P.V.* 553–60 (this pair of stanzas like *Med.* 643 ff.
follows a regular dactylo-epitrite pair) is a pendant version of
παρέβαν κτλ. just quoted. The absence of *anceps* in these lines is
much more marked:

ἔμαθον τάδε σὰς προσιδοῦσ' ὀλοὰς τύχας, Προμηθεῦ.

◡ ◡ − ◡ ◡ − ◡ ◡ − ◡ ◡ − ◡ − ◡ − −

τὸ διαμφίδιον δέ μοι μέλος προσέπτα

◡ ◡ − ◡ ◡ − ◡ − ◡ − ◡ − −

τόδ' ἐκεῖνό θ' ὅ τ' ἀμφὶ λουτρὰ καὶ λέχος σὸν ὑμεναίουν

◡ ◡ − ◡ ◡ − ◡ − ◡ − ◡ − ◡ − ◡ − −

ἰότατι γάμων ὅτε τὰν ὁμοπάτριον ἕδνοις

◡ ◡ − ◡ ◡ − ◡ ◡ − ◡ ◡ − ◡ − −

ἄγαγες Ἡσιόναν πιθὼν δάμαρτα κοινόλεκτρον.

$D \smile e \smile e -$

The single-short lengths in the first three periods here increase in
terms of iambic from penthemimer to catalectic dimeter and then to
catalectic trimeter. But it is impossible to say whether this analysis
means anything; we might prefer to divide periods two and three,
for instance, ◡ ◡ − ◡ ◡ − ◡ − ◡ | − ◡ − −, and ◡ ◡ − ◡ ◡ − ◡ − ◡ |
− ◡ − ◡ − ◡ − −. The enoplian colon ◡ ◡ − ◡ ◡ − ◡ − ◡ is a
prominent element in Euripidean examples of iambo-anapaestic:
thus *Hipp.* 752 ff. after an aeolo-choriambic period continues:

ἐπόρευσας ἐμὰν ἄνασσαν ὀλβίων ἀπ' οἴκων

◡ ◡ − ◡ ◡ − ◡ − ◡   − ◡ − ◡ − −

κακονυμφοτάταν ὄνασιν · ἤ γὰρ ἀπ' ἀμφοτέρων

⏑ ⏑ − ⏑ ⏑ − ⏑ − ⏑   − ⏑ ⏑ − ⏑ ⏑ −

ἀ Κρησίας ἐκ γᾶς δύσορνις κτλ.

x̄ − ⏑ − x̄ − ⏑ − ⏒

and ends with a further πνῖγος of seven epitrites+ithyphallic. Here the enoplian is compounded first with an ithyphallic and then with a hemiepes; this latter combination occurs, *Andr.* 1014 = 1022,[1] after regular dactylo-epitrites, and again in *Tro.* 82off. = 84off., which is perhaps the most comprehensive mixture we possess of all the metres described in this chapter, dactylo-epitrite, dactylo-iambic, iambo-anapaests and separate iambic and trochaic cola. Period-end and division into cola are alike difficult to determine, but the general rhythmic effect is clear. The text of the antistrophe perhaps contains fewer uncertainties than the strophe:

Ἔρως Ἔρως ὅς τὰ Δαρδάνεια μέλαθρά ποτ' ἦλθες	⏑ *e e* ⏑ *D* ⏝ *D*
οὐρανίδαισι μέλων,	
ὡς τότε μὲν μεγάλως Τροίαν ἐπύργωσας θεοῖσι	*D − E* ⏝ *D*
κῆδος ἀναψάμενος.	
τὸ μὲν οὖν Διὸς οὐκέτ' ὄνειδος ἐρῶ ·	⏑⏑−⏑⏑−⏑⏑−⏑⏑− ‖
τὸ τᾶς δὲ λευκοπτέρου	sync. iamb. tetram.
φίλιον Ἀμέρας βροτοῖς	
φέγγος ὀλοὸν εἶδε γαῖαν,	troch. tetram. ‖
εἶδε Περγάμων ὄλεθρον	
τεκνοποιὸν ἔχουσα τᾶσδε	⏑ ⏑ − ⏑ ⏑ − ⏑ − ⏑ *D*
γᾶς πόσιν ἐν θαλάμοις,	
ὅν ἀστέρων τέθριππος ἔλαβε χρύσεος ὄχος	iamb. tetram.
ἀναρπάσας	
ἐλπίδα γᾷ πατρίᾳ	*D*
μεγάλαν · τὰ θεῶν δὲ φίλτρα φροῦδα Τροίᾳ.	⏑⏑−⏑⏑−⏑−⏑−−−

The clausula is the same sequence as *P.V.* 555 τὸ διαμφίδιον δέ μοι μέλος προσέπτα, and there is the same preponderance of short *anceps*, with the lightness carried further here by resolution. The general similarity of *P.V.* 546ff. to this group of Euripidean iambo-anapaestic odes is in fact one more puzzling element in the riddle of this play's choral lyric.

[1] With either − ⏑ ⏑ − ⏑ ⏑ − or − ⏑ ⏑ − ⏑ ⏑ − ⏑; the reading is uncertain.

XII

STROPHIC CONSTRUCTION

No complete and systematic account practicable—Difficulty of defining subordinate periods within the stanza—'Systematic' and 'periodic' grouping of cola in comedy and tragedy.

It is impossible to give a coherent and detailed account of the principles of structure in the lyric stanzas of drama, partly because there is so much that we cannot understand, partly because the poet invented a fresh scheme for each song, and these are rarely reducible to type in any orderly or convincing way. Strophic construction appears a manageable subject for generalization and discussion only so long as the field of inquiry is the whole of Greek poetry; one can begin with the rudimentary strophe as seen in the elegiac distich (*ab*) or the trochaic tetrameter catalectic (*aa'*), and work up through the gradually increasing complexities of Archilochus and the Lesbians to the shorter and simpler of Aeschylean or Aristophanean stanzas; but once the stage is reached where the complexity of the strophe is such that its structure is not immediately obvious—in fact where elucidation is really needed—the honest inquirer begins to falter, has to admit alternative possibilities, or at best produces a scheme which may fit the verse in question but has rarely any applicability outside it. A further misfortune is that where scholars adopt the terms of the metrical scholiasts and ancient grammarians the meagre results of systematization are altogether overweighted with portentous terminology: thus the little iambic stanzas in *Ran.* 420ff. (βούλεσθε δῆτα κοινῇ κτλ.) are summed up as a 'monostrophic octad of epodic triads'. It is simpler to call them eight stanzas of *aab*, and in any case the casual reader can see that for himself. As this book has attempted throughout to present the various cola in their periodic context rather than as isolated metrical fragments, I shall in this chapter do little more than raise some questions of principle and illustrate the difficulties of close structural analysis.

In a complex lyric stanza the only elements within the whole στροφή or περίοδος which can be distinguished with some degree of certainty are the cola. Alexandrian texts almost certainly distinguished nothing else. For an understanding of the rhythm the cola are of fundamental importance, but for the actual structure of the stanza we need to know the grouping of the cola into subordinate περίοδοι, and it is here that our understanding is deficient.

It is usually assumed that the strophe of drama is built up in the same way as Pindar's, where, although the traditional text still transmitted only the colometry, we can in most cases, thanks to the larger number of strophic repetitions, see where there is Pause and where merely diaeresis at the colon-ends, since Pause is sooner or later put beyond doubt by the occurrence of hiatus or *brevis in longo*. This means that the cola can be grouped into minor periods which run to a pause and contain a varying number of cola, usually one, two, or three. Even so, it is not usually very easy to see any general principles at work in the size and arrangement of these minor periods; they occasionally appear so to group themselves into larger, 'major' periods that the whole strophe can be seen, let us say, as a piece of dyadic or triadic construction, but in general we can discern little beyond the poet's arbitrary choice for this particular ode.

Turning to drama, we find most tragic choruses composed of stanzas repeating *a a b b* ... with an occasional epode that does not repeat at all. The 'periodic' groupings of cola are therefore much harder to verify, and in particular diaeresis is apt to be indistinguishable from Pause; it is sometimes impossible to allot a single Pause with certainty throughout a whole strophe. Comedy occasionally repeats its stanzas *a a a*..., but such stanzas are mostly of the simpler sort which hardly contain ambiguities. In comedy, moreover, there are unmistakable signs of a principle of grouping quite different from the Pindaric; and even in tragedy this principle is discernible, though of more restricted application. It is a principle very like that on which metrical 'systems' are built.

Recitative anapaests, as was explained in chapter IV, are composed in 'systems': that is to say, the dimeters though separated by diaeresis are in synaphea (i.e. they run into one another in a series without final *anceps* or hiatus, unlike metres set κατὰ στίχον), until at irregular intervals the series is broken by the paroemiac, which gives catalexis. There was probably in delivery a slight pause at the end of each colon, but this was not the recognized, technical Pause which marks the end of a minor period or στίχος. The πνῖγος of anapaestic dimeters which rounds off the tetrameters of the comic parabasis was rattled off by the singer without noticeable pause for breath, and doubtless the same 'choke' was often applied in other passages and other metres as part of the comic effect (in iambics, for instance, by Strepsiades in *Nub.* 1386ff.). But as a metrical technique, as distinct from a style of delivery, the πνῖγος or run of homogeneous metra finally stopped by catalexis is very common up and down the lyrics as well as the recitative of comedy, and there can be no doubt that the majority of simple comic stanzas are constructed on the 'systematic' rather than the 'periodic' principle; or perhaps this could be better expressed by saying that each of the little 'systems' combined in such a strophe as *Ran.* 534ff. forms a 'major period' rather than a 'minor period' or 'Vers' in the German sense:

> ταῦτα μὲν πρὸς ἀνδρός ἐστι
> νοῦν ἔχοντος καὶ φρένας καὶ
> πολλὰ περιπεπλευκότος, ‖
> μετακυλίνδειν αὑτὸν ἀεὶ
> πρὸς τὸν εὖ πράττοντα τοῖχον
> μᾶλλον ἢ γεγραμμένην ‖
> εἰκόν᾽ ἑστάναι, λαβόνθ᾽ ἓν
> σχῆμα· τὸ δὲ μεταστρέφεσθαι
> πρὸς τὸ μαλθακώτερον ‖
> δεξιοῦ πρὸς ἀνδρός ἐστι
> καὶ φύσει Θηραμένους.

These trochaic dimeters fall into the number-scheme 3, 3, 3, 2 (what the Scholiast would call an 'epodic tetrad', or *aaab*) marked off by the lekythia which give catalexis. In the three repetitions of the strophe three or four of the dimeters (besides the second here) show up as linked by word-overlap, for some of these little intra-strophic πνίγη differ from recitative anapaests in that the cola are not always separated by diaeresis (and it should be noted that absence of strict correspondence between diaeresis and caesura at colon-end is characteristic for this type of grouping). But this clearly does not mean that there is any difference of structure between clusters of dimeters which in one strophe or another can show instances of overlap and those which have diaeresis all through. The run-on is of the same nature in each case. If these periods were to be labelled 'Verse' it would mean that the strophe consisted of three trochaic hexameters followed by a tetrameter. But a 'trochaic hexameter' is hardly a recognized 'Vers', and it is clear that the number of linked cola is decided by the shape that the poet has seen fit to give to the whole strophe, not by starting from the conception of a single 'line' or 'Vers' which is to be a trochaic hexameter. 1482ff. is a similar trochaic stanza with the number-scheme (in dimeters) 1, 1, 1, 2, 4, and this last is not a 'trochaic octameter', but merely a rather longer πνῖγος; 1099ff. similarly runs 2, 4, 3, 5. The iambic Phales-song in the *Acharnians*, whether it be written out in mixed dimeters and trimeters as the traditional text is or in dimeters throughout (as White),[1] has an unbroken run of 30 metra, ll. 266–78, ending this time not in catalexis but *brevis in longo*; this is merely an exaggeration of the same technique, unrestricted here by considerations of strophic responsion.

It is merely a variation of 'systematic' structure when the clausula of such a πνῖγος instead of being marked simply by catalexis or *brevis in longo* is in a slightly different rhythm, though one which can tack on to the preceding line as a recognized dicolon. So the thrice repeated iambic strophe *Ach.* 836ff. ends with three dimeters in synaphea, and to the last is added a reizianum, making a dicolon of the type called *versus reizianus*:[2]

> ἐν τἀγορᾷ καθήμενος·
> κἄν εἰσίῃ τις Κτησίας
> ἢ συκοφάντης ἄλλος, οἰ-
> -μώζων καθεδεῖται.

Not only may any metre which moves κατὰ μέτρον run on in a πνῖγος—cf. the dactyls in *Nub.* 277–85 and the paeonic πνίγη in the

---

[1] *The Verse of Greek Comedy*, § 90. Probably the traditional arrangement is to be preferred, as a trimeter ending on *brevis in longo* is so familiar, and there could well be in this song some *rapprochement* to stichic iambics.   [2] See above, p. 80.

Acharnians—but aeolo-choriambics are also clearly susceptible of the same arrangement: thus in *Knights* 551 ff.

> ἵππι' ἄναξ Πόσειδον, ᾧ
> χαλκοκρότων ἵππων κτύπος
> καὶ χρεμετισμὸς ἁνδάνει
> καὶ κυανέμβολοι θοαὶ
> μισθοφόροι τριήρεις ‖
> μειρακίων θ' ἅμιλλα λαμ-
> -πρυνομένων ἐν ἅρμασιν
> καὶ βαρυδαιμονούντων, ‖
> δεῦρ' ἔλθ' ἐς χορὸν ὦ χρυσοτρίαιν' ὦ
> δελφίνων μεδέων Σουνιάρατε, ‖
> ὦ Γεραίστιε παῖ Κρόνου,
> Φορμίωνί τε φίλτατ' ἐκ
> τῶν ἄλλων τε θεῶν Ἀθη-
> -ναίοις πρὸς τὸ παρεστός

the four major periods are obvious at a glance, the first two of five and three A-type choriambic dimeters respectively, closing in aristophanean catalexis, and the fourth of three glyconics+pherecratean. In the antistrophe nearly all these are linked by word-overlap. It is impossible to tell whether the two aeolo-ionics of the third period are also in synaphea or should be accounted two minor periods. Similarly, *Ran.* 449 ff. divides into two major periods of two and four telesillea with reizianum catalexis.

In tragedy we are on more uncertain ground. Πνίγη are both less common and less long than in comedy, which is another way of saying that the lyric of comedy is metrically more homogeneous and its structure simpler. It is clear that dactyls, dochmiacs and ionics frequently run in πνίγη; in the last two indeed a whole strophe may be in effect a single 'system'. This latter technique was more easily applicable in the short stanzas of many of the Aeschylean choruses, and only Aeschylus uses ionics in this way. Sophocles does not often compose strophically in this style, but in the ἀπολελυμένα of the *O.C.* and to a less extent in *Phil.*, he has long dactylic πνίγη which run out in iambic cola or colaria, and the shorter ones in *El.* 121 ff. are of the same type. Euripides returns to the Aeschylean technique in his later plays, and in his own longer stanzas it becomes more remarkable. Thus, for instance, the whole of *Bacch.* 977ff. is a single dochmiac system;[1] and most characteristic of all is his new development of the trochaic πνῖγος. Aeschylus has a modest three dimeters in *P.V.* 415–17, but in *Hel.* 191ff. the last six dimeters are in synaphea, and in an astrophic song (ll. 348ff.) there is a πνῖγος of seven. Long iambic πνίγη seem to be confined to comedy; in tragedy their sequence is usually broken up by catalexis, so that blunt ends may be varied by pendants. The shorter periods are usually ambiguous; for instance, *O.T.* 203–5

> Λύκει' ἄναξ, τά τε σὰ χρυ-
> -σοστρόφων ἀπ' ἀγκυλᾶν
> βέλεα θέλοιμ' ἂν ἀδάματ' ἐνδατεῖσθαι

could be either a major period of two dims.+trim. in synaphea, or two minor periods (dim.+dim., trim.). It is arguable that we should assume a general principle, that a sequence of cola in the same metre runs without pause to a catalexis or hiatus or final *anceps*, but there is no way of proving this. Finally, in aeolo-choriambics the sequence of three glyconics+pherecratean seems, as pointed out in chapter IX, a fixed form of πνῖγος, and though it does not much matter whether this be called a minor or major period the latter seems more appropriate to its length. In this metre again it is the later Euripidean plays which develop the technique of 'systematic' construction, as in the *I.A.* chorus (543ff.) quoted on p. 152, containing a πνῖγος of eight choriambic dimeters.

A considerable part of tragic lyric, however, appears to be composed in the 'periodic' style of Pindar, with the minor period, usually colon or dicolon but sometimes (especially with the short cola of dactylo-epitrite and kindred metres) extending to three or four cola, forming a structural element intermediate between the colon and the major period or, where major periods are not distinguishable,

---

[1] It should not be broken, as in most of our texts, between 987 and 988:

> ἐς ὄρος ἐς ὄρος ἔμολ' ἔμολεν ὦ Βάκχαι;
> τίς ἄρα νιν ἔτεκεν; οὐ γὰρ ἐξ αἵματος κτλ.

τίς ἄρα νιν ἔτεκεν; οὐ is one of the 'long dochmiacs' (see above, pp. 115–16), like ἢ σκόλοπος ὄψεται above.

between the colon and the strophe. Enough has been said in the chapter on the subject to show that dactylo-epitrite stanzas work, as one would expect, on this principle, and, as there pointed out, it is probable that a good deal of prosodiac-enoplian is to be taken as structurally akin, so that there too it must be remembered that final *anceps* in a pendant close does not necessarily imply Pause. In most polymetric stanzas, however, it is possible to put up a good case for a mixture of 'periodic' and 'systematic' structure, and there are many where such a mixture seems certain. A relatively straightforward iambic strophe and antistrophe from the *Agamemnon* (367ff.) will illustrate the ambiguities of the subject; the stanzas may be set out in a series of minor periods:

367 Διὸς πλαγὰν ἔχουσιν εἰπεῖν, 385 βιᾶται δ' ἁ τάλαινα πειθώ,	1. sync. trim. cat.
πάρεστιν τοῦτό γ' ἐξιχνεῦσαι. προβούλου παῖς ἄφερτος ἄτας,	2. sync. trim. cat.
ἔπραξεν ὡς ἔκρανεν. οὐκ ἔφα τις ἄκος δὲ πᾶν μάταιον. οὐκ ἐκρύφθη	3. trim. cat.
θεοὺς βροτῶν ἀξιοῦσθαι μέλειν πρέπει δὲ φῶς αἰνολαμπὲς σίνος·	4. sync. trim.
ὅσοις ἀθίκτων χάρις κακοῦ δὲ χαλκοῦ τρόπον	5. sync. dim.
πατοῖθ'· ὁ δ' οὐκ εὐσεβής. τρίβῳ τε καὶ προσβολαῖς	+sync. dim.
πέφανται δ' ἐγγόνοις μελαμπαγὴς πέλει	6. sync. dim.
ἀτολμήτων ἔρον δικαιωθείς, ἐπεὶ	+sync. dim.
πνεόντων μεῖζον ἢ δικαίως, διώκει παῖς ποτανὸν ὄρνιν,	7. sync. trim. cat.
φλεόντων δωμάτων ὑπέρφευ πόλει πρόστριμμα θεὶς ἄφερτον.	8. sync. trim. cat.
ὑπὲρ τὸ βέλτιστον· ἔστω δ' ἀπή- λιτᾶν δ' ἀκούει μὲν οὔτις θεῶν,	9. sync. trim.

-μαντον ὦστ' ἀπαρκεῖν   +ithyph.
†τὸν δ' ἐπίστροφον τῶν†¹
εὖ πραπίδων λαχόντι.   10. arist.
φῶτ' ἄδικον καθαιρεῖ.

(The four-line ἐφύμνιον may be omitted here.) Periods 5 and 6 could each be made into two separate periods, in which case every colon except the two penultimate would stand as a minor period. But it is obvious that the whole structure might be given a very different appearance by taking periods 4–7 inclusive as a single πνῖγος; the stanza would then consist of three minor periods, πνῖγος, two minor periods, final clausula.

To take next a polymetric stanza, *O.T.* 463 ff.

463 τίς ὄντιν' ἁ θεσπιέπει-	1. iambo-chor. dim.
473 ἔλαμψε γὰρ τοῦ νιφόεν-	
-α Δελφὶς εἶπε πέτρα	+iamb. dim. cat.
-τος ἀρτίως φανεῖσα	
ἄρρητ' ἀρρήτων τελέσαν-	2. chor. dim. B
φάμα Παρνασσοῦ τὸν ἄδη-	
-τα φοινίαισι χερσίν;	+iamb. dim. cat.
-λον ἄνδρα πάντ' ἰχνεύειν. ‖	
ὦρα νιν ἀελλάδων	3. tel.
φοιτᾷ γὰρ ὑπ' ἀγρίαν	
ἵππων σθεναρώτερον	+tel.
ὕλαν ἀνά τ' ἄντρα καὶ	
φυγᾷ πόδα νωμᾶν.	+reiz.
πετραῖος ὁ ταῦρος,	
ἔνοπλος γὰρ ἐπ' αὐτὸν ἐπενθρῴσκει	4. anapaestic enoplian
μέλεος μελέῳ ποδὶ χηρεύων,	
πυρὶ καὶ στεροπαῖς ὁ Διὸς γενέτας,	+do.
τὰ μεσόμφαλα γᾶς ἀπονοσφίζων	
δειναὶ δ' ἅμ' ἕπονται	5. reiz.
μαντεῖα. τὰ δ' αἰεὶ	
Κῆρες ἀναπλάκητοι.	6. ithyph.
ζῶντα περιποτᾶται.	

¹ Wilamowitz τῶνδ' ἐπίστροφος δὲ, but the short *anceps* is improbable here.

I have given here what seems to me the most likely articulation; the shape would then be (in major periods) *ABCD*, with *A* = 1, 2; *B* = 3; *C* = 4, 5; *D* = 6 (clausula). Hiatus, *anceps* and catalexis put the first two minor periods beyond doubt; the little tel.-reiz. 'system' is very probable, since at least the last two cola must be run together; the last four lines give no technical clue to distinguish between Pause and diaeresis, and our only guide is probability.

The variety of problems and the degrees of uncertainty in this subject are legion. Sense and punctuation are occasionally pointers to a solution, though always to be used with caution. The strophe of drama (unlike Pindar's) is almost always a rounded period in thought as well as in metrical form, but its inner structure has a widely varying degree of this correspondence. Strong punctuation in *both* strophe and antistrophe usually, though not always, coincides with the end of a major or a minor period, and sometimes sense and metrical phrasing move parallel for the whole or part of a stanza. But in other cases, as so often in Pindar's poetic technique, the two may each go their independent ways.

Note

Those who feel that the attempt to face the problems of strophic construction is here tamely abandoned almost before it has begun should consult W. Kraus, *Strophengestaltung in der griechischen Tragödie, I. Aischylos und Sophokles*, Vienna, 1958, which, working on careful principles, endeavours to reduce the multifarious phenomena to a limited number of stanza-shapes. I find parts of it more convincing than others.

XIII

SOME NOTES ON PERFORMANCE

Antistrophic music probably in responsion and the melody therefore ignored pitch-accent—Dionysius of Halicarnassus on a passage of the *Orestes*—Possibility of a special kind of musical accompaniment for some types of comic chorus—Recitative and singing perhaps mixed in some lyrics of tragedy, especially in Euripides: the *Orestes* papyrus-fragment—Dancing: the cordax and emmeleia—Relation of dance to metre: arsis and thesis—Antistrophic dancing not always in strict responsion.

Of the meagre fragments that remain to us of Greek music, only the one which gives a mutilated piece of ll. 338–44 of the *Orestes* can claim to be music of the great century of tragedy. This is probably the music which Euripides himself composed, since Dionysius of Halicarnassus writing at a later date assumes without question (*Comp. Verb.* 11) that his score of the *Orestes* is authentic Euripides. The same fragment is the only one which is certainly antistrophic. Unfortunately so little of the notation remains that it gives no answer to the question whether antistrophic music is noticeably unlike other kinds in the degree to which it ignores the tonic accent of the words. While none of the other fragments shows a melodic line which follows the word-pitch throughout, in most of them, though in rather differing degrees, there is an obvious tendency to make the two coincide. But since strophe and antistrophe pay no attention to correspondence of word-accent, either the melody here must also have ignored word-accent or the melody of the strophe was not repeated in the antistrophe.

It is one of the most curious and deplorable gaps in our understanding of classical lyric that we do not know which of these alternative suppositions is correct. The former is the more generally assumed, and on *a priori* grounds appears the more likely. But some scholars point to the length of Pindar's fourth Pythian, and ask if it would have been tolerable to listen to twenty-six repetitions of the music of the strophe and antistrophe and thirteen of the epode. And

it is certainly odd at first sight that Dionysius in the passage above
referred to should so single out a particular ode of Euripides to
illustrate how sometimes in sung poetry the words are subordinated
to the music if *all* antistrophic poetry was equally bound to show
this characteristic. The passage runs:

(music. . .) τάς τε λέξεις τοῖς μέλεσιν ὑποτάττειν ἀξιοῖ καὶ οὐ τὰ μέλη ταῖς
λέξεσιν, ὡς ἐξ ἄλλων τε πολλῶν δῆλον καὶ μάλιστα ἐκ τῶν Εὐριπίδου μελῶν,
ἃ πεποίηκεν τὴν Ἠλέκτραν λέγουσαν ἐν Ὀρέστῃ πρὸς τὸν χορόν·

> σῖγα σῖγα, λευκὸν ἴχνος ἀρβύλης
> τίθετε,[1] μὴ κτυπεῖτ'.
> ἀποπρόβατ' ἐκεῖσ', ἀποπρό μοι κοίτας.

He says the first six syllables here are all sung to one note, though
each of the words has high and low pitch, that in ἀρβύλης the third
syllable is as high as the middle one, that in τίθετε[1] the first syllable
is lower and the other two on the same higher note, that the circum-
flex in κτυπεῖτ' is ignored since both syllables have the same pitch,
and that in ἀποπρόβατε the raised pitch of the third syllable is trans-
ferred to the fourth. He shows no consciousness of any problem of
response, but this might mean either that the point is not relevant
here or that he had never thought about it. As for his singling out
of this particular passage, the καὶ μάλιστα here may well mean no
more than that he has selected a popular and much read play and
turned up the first lyric in it—'yes, here is a good example'. The
one thing that is clear from this passage is that Dionysius is not an
author whose evidence can be pressed in detail on a technical
question of this kind. Either the text he was using was a bad one
(cf. λευκὸν for λεπτὸν and the attribution to Electra instead of to
the Chorus) or he was misreading his copy. Editors disguise the fact
by emending his accents to the best textual tradition of Euripidean
MSS, but it is quite clear from his comments that he was reading,
not σῖγα σῖγα and ἀποπρὸ βᾶτε, but σίγα σίγα and ἀποπρόβατε, so
that the pitch accents he is discussing are mostly beside the mark,
and since he is so heedless about the metre any notion of a responding

[1] The MSS vary between τιθεῖτε and τίθεται. The criticism which follows
is not appropriate to τιθεῖτε, but whether we are justified in assuming
that D. could not have read τίθεται I am not at all sure.

antistrophe was clearly far from his mind. Further, he goes on to say that music behaves in just the same way about quantities; it shortens the naturally long and lengthens the naturally short to such an extent that it often inverts their relations. Whatever the applicability of this to the music of Dionysius' own time, such wholesale inversion is unthinkable for fifth-century music. It seems then that we need not take too seriously the *obiter dicta* of Dionysius in a consideration of classical music, and his silence on the subject of antistrophic response in music does not mean that it did not respond. As for the repetitiveness of the fourth Pythian, we cannot judge with any certainty what the Greeks would or would not find tolerable in music, and in any case it does not seem to me impossible that different conventions of response prevailed in long triadic compositions and the comparatively restricted parallels in drama.[1]

On the whole, then, there is no cogent reason for rejecting the assumption, with its *a priori* likelihood, that the music repeated from strophe to antistrophe in the choruses of drama. Antistrophic verse would thus acquire an added formality in that unlike astrophic it took no account at all of the rise and fall of pitch in the same words delivered in the speaking voice. The further assumption (made by White, for instance) that parallel subordinate periods within the strophe repeated the same music is more speculative, though of course not impossible. It would apply particularly to comedy, which repeats its subordinate periods to a far greater degree than tragedy. The amount of repetition involved would in some cases appear rather excessive, but this problem is swept up into the whole gigantic question-mark of Greek music in Greek dramatic choruses. It is impossible to imagine how music at all resembling that of the fragments we possess, to our ear so strangely formless and lacking in 'themes', in musical balance and logic, can have been fitted to the shapes of choral songs, especially the simple, well-defined metrical structures of comedy. It is indeed tempting to suppose that all but the more formal and elaborate of the songs in comedy were sung to a different kind of music altogether, and perhaps rendered with something less than the full singing voice, in a delivery nearer to

[1] See above, ch. I, pp. 2–3 and p. 5, n. 1.

recitative, a sort of 'patter' which did not require a filled-in melody but was kept in time and tune by a more intermittent form of accompaniment, possibly one which marked the metra. This might make it easier to account for the peculiar form of *approximate responsion* found in Aristophanes—the omission of whole tetrameters, or dimeters, or metra, or the correspondence of a full to a catalectic metron.[1] Such instances of omission, always in neat segments and always in metres which run κατὰ μέτρον, where the sense runs on perfectly, are far too numerous to admit of wholesale emendation, and they do suggest a somewhat different type of music for these songs.

In tragic choruses another question as to the manner of delivery is raised by the *Orestes* papyrus-fragment. The line

κατέκλυσεν δεινῶν πόνων ὡς πόντου

shows a curious group of three signs ƆΓƆ before and after δεινῶν πόνων, possibly a piece of accompaniment since they are symbols of notation, but on a level with the text instead of above it. There are no notes above the words δεινῶν πόνων, and there is a gloss τὸ δὲ δεινῶν πόνων ἐν μέσῳ ἀναπεφώνηται. The effect of this would be to give a cross-rhythm overlaying the two dochmiacs κατέκλυσεν δεινῶν | πόνων ὡς πόντου, dividing the line into three syncopated iambic metra, the last a molossus: κατέκλυσεν | δεινῶν πόνων | ὡς πόντου. The corresponding line in the strophe would lend itself to similar treatment: μανιάδος | φοιταλέου | φεῦ μόχθων. No satisfactory explanation has ever been given of the musical symbols, which appear as it were to bracket the unsung words; whether they were to be played, and in what relation to the words, cannot be determined. But the phenomenon of the words δεινῶν πόνων declaimed in the middle of a song might be taken in connection with one of the *Problems* of Aristotle (XIX, 6) διὰ τί ἡ παρακαταλογὴ ἐν ταῖς ᾠδαῖς

---

[1] To give some examples, see the omissions in *Nub.* 1309, *Vesp.* 647, *Eccl.* 487 (iambic metron), *Ach.* 231 (paeonic metron), *Vesp.* 309 (ionic metron), *Pax* 491 (anap. metron), *Ran.* 592, 993 (troch. metron), *Vesp.* 469 (two troch.-paeonic dims.), *Pax* 585 (troch. tetram.), *Vesp.* 1284 (paeonic tetram.), *Lys.* 332 (chor. dim.), and resp. of cat. to complete troch. metron in *Av.* 1560 and *Ran.* 1495.

τραγικόν; ἢ διὰ τὴν ἀνωμαλίαν; παθητικὸν γὰρ τὸ ἀνωμαλὲς καὶ ἐν μεγέθει τύχης καὶ λύπης· τὸ δὲ ὁμαλὲς ἔλαττον γοῶδες. The 'irregularity' should surely imply that 'recitative in songs' means bits of recitative in the middle of singing, the intrusion of the speaking voice for emotional effect. Now there is evidence of a tradition of such mixed delivery in tragic iambics, descending, according to Plutarch, *de musica* (1140), from Archilochus: ἔτι δὲ τῶν ἰαμβείων τὸ τὰ μὲν λέγεσθαι παρὰ τὴν κροῦσιν τὰ δ' ἄδεσθαι, 'Αρχίλοχόν φασι καταδεῖξαι, εἶθ' οὕτω χρήσασθαι τοὺς τραγικοὺς ποιητάς. The only iambic trimeters in tragedy which seem appropriate for a mixture of singing and recitative are those which occur so often in association with dochmiacs and certain other metres, as in the lament of Theseus in the *Hippolytus* (816ff.) and of Oedipus in *O.T.* 1313ff. They are commonest in actors' lyrics and in kommoi, though they are occasionally heard from the orchestra too. But Euripides has a special group of metres which he associates in a manner peculiar to himself with this trimeter-dochmiac mixture (typical passages are *H.F.* 875–921 and 1016–85, *Ion* 1439–1509, *Hel.* 625–97); the group consists of slightly syncopated iambics of various lengths (including bacchiacs), anapaests, and prosodiac-enoplians of the type described in chapter x as assimilated to anapaests and dochmiacs. Dactyls and trochaics make a rare and fleeting appearance, but all the large aeolo-choriambic group, ionics, and dactylo-epitrites are excluded. What the special group have in common, in fact, is proximity to some recitative or spoken metre into which they can easily pass, so that a mixed style of delivery is possible without too violent a disturbance of continuity. Their use is characteristic of scenes of emotional tension, and such a song with fragments of declamation would naturally be most commonly a solo. If this interpretation of the δεινῶν πόνων in the *Orestes* papyrus is correct, Euripides sometimes sought the emotional irregularity of mixed delivery in choral lyric too.

Of the dancing which accompanied the singing of the theatre-choruses we are almost wholly ignorant. Of the three dances traditionally associated with the three types of performance—the ἐμμέλεια with tragedy, the κόρδαξ with comedy and the σίκιννις with the satyr-play—we can form rather more idea, from allusions in Aristophanes and other authors and from vase-paintings, of the κόρδαξ than of the other two. Its basic steps were the high kick, forward and back, the pirouette, the twirl with outstretched leg, and the γαστρισμός; it was considered φορτικός, suitable only for drunks, and obviously lent itself to indecency in execution. But the cordax was clearly not the staple stuff of the evolutions of the comic chorus; it was usually a *pas seul*, or at most the performance of *coryphées*, not of the *corps de ballet*. At the end of the *Wasps*, Philocleon and the three sons of Carcinus, dancing in this extravagant fashion, each lead out one of the four files of the chorus; the latter, or possibly the coryphaeus speaking for it, eggs on the soloists to wilder and faster gyrations, while speaking itself with some detachment and apparently hopping about in a more restrained fashion. The steps described are those of the cordax, but the context out of which the performance arose was a discussion of the *tragic* dance (cf. Philocleon's threat of a knuckle-emmeleia for his rival); it seems then that in this finale the cordax is substituted παρὰ προσδοκίαν for the emmeleia. This suggests that the emmeleia also was mostly an affair of steps and attitudes for the individual dancer, and so could be danced by Io or Cassandra or Agave as well as by a tragic chorus; it did not give a choreography for a ballet of fifteen performers.

What those steps and attitudes were can only be very vaguely surmised. The general style is testified to be τὸ βαρὺ καὶ σεμνόν; this is not unexpected, though a list of σχήματα τραγικῆς ὀρχήσεως given by Pollux (IV, 105) contains some which sound surprisingly vigorous for a 'grave and dignified' performance—'hollow hand', 'basket', 'passing on the club', 'tongs', 'the double', 'somersault'. 'Tongs' is somewhat confusingly included by Athenaeus among the μανιώδεις ὀρχήσεις, and would appear to have been a kind of entrechat; possibly the chorus in Eur. *El.* 859ff. which summons itself to dance ὡς νεβρὸς οὐράνιον πήδημα κουφίζουσα σὺν ἀγλαΐᾳ might have sketched such a step, but in what circumstances a somersault (κυβίστησις) could have been performed on the tragic stage is beyond our wit to imagine, and one may well suspect that Pollux is drawing from some tradition of mime which had little connection with the deportment of the chorus of classical tragedy. The tradition of choral dancing in tragedy was so completely lost after the decay of the tragic stage that the scholiasts—admittedly of unknown date— are found to have been misled by the Aristotelian term στάσιμον for all odes subsequent to the parodos or 'coming-on song'; these were 'stationary' merely in the sense that the chorus had finished its progressive movement and taken up its stance in the orchestra, but the scholiasts clearly thought that the term implied 'standing still', i.e. an ode unaccompanied by dancing. Hence, where the words of the chorus unmistakably implied that it *was* dancing (as in *Aj.* 693 ff., *Trach.* 205 ff., Eur. *El.* 859 ff.) they had to note the exception: so Σ *Trach.* 205 τὸ γὰρ μελιδάριον οὐκ ἐστὶ στάσιμον ἀλλ᾽ ὑπὸ τῆς ἡδονῆς ὀρχοῦνται. This led Eucleides, the authority followed by the Byzantine Tzetzes in his account of tragedy, to invent another εἶδος χορικοῦ besides parodos and stasimon which he called ὑπορχη-ματικόν, the 'song accompanied by dancing'. Modern commentators have sometimes taken this seriously, and label odes like the above-mentioned 'hyporchemes', but there is no distinction in kind between these choruses and any others.

The most interesting question about the dance, and the most difficult to answer, is that of its relation to metre. Was there a conventional movement for iambics, and another for dactyls, and should we be able to settle the controversy about 'choriambic' or 'logaoedic' scansion by watching a danced glyconic? Is such conventional movement to be reconciled with the mimetic requirements of some dances? The problem is not comparable to that of combining miming with musical rhythm in the modern ballet, since the rhythmical elements of modern music are so very much simpler. The crux of the matter is the real meaning of ἄρσις and θέσις; did these, as is usually assumed by modern metricians who mention them at all, correspond to the actual movements of dancers' feet when a rhythm was danced, or are they metaphorical terms applied to the metaphorical πούς, and if so what *do* they represent?

We have not the evidence to answer these questions satisfactorily, but it is certain that nothing of any value for our understanding of Greek metric or our conception of Greek rhythms has been gained from any attempt to piece together the fragmentary and often irreconcilable statements of ancient authorities on ἄρσις and θέσις or to carry such analysis further. Systems which begin with an ordered scheme of metres so divided silently drop the division before they get very far. No one knows what to do with a hipponactean in the way of ἄρσις and θέσις. The decay of a belief in 'ictus' in Greek verse and the now fairly general realization that the simple πούς is not a practical unit of analysis with which to work have left the function of ἄρσις and θέσις still more of a sinecure. The use of the στιγμή in papyrus-fragments of musical notation, with the comment of the Anonymus *de musica* (of unknown date) ἡ μὲν οὖν θέσις σημαίνεται ὅταν ἁπλῶς τὸ σημεῖον ἄστικτον ᾖ, ἡ δ' ἄρσις ὅταν ἐστιγμένον, has not thrown much light upon the subject, partly because of the lateness of the sources and the confusion caused by the contradictory uses of the words ἄρσις and θέσις at different times, partly because of the extreme textual corruptibility of such a dot. Its existence, however, proves that this distinction was not evolved by mere theorists, and its distribution in the text at least shows conclusively that it has nothing to do with such dynamic stress as marks a beat in modern music, since it can appear over two consecutive syllables, a short and a long.

My own belief, very tentatively held, is that the names arose in the first place as an expression of the duality inherent in all rhythm—motion and rest, sound and stillness, up and down, left, right, loud and soft, quick and slow. The primary unit of rhythm common to Greek word, music and dance is one of time; the smallest sequence of longs and shorts that by repetition can produce a rhythmical effect was called a πούς and its repetitive movement a βάσις. But within the foot itself there must be some kind of alternation or swing to make its rhythm perceptible, and to this were given the names of the movements of the human foot in its simplest form of progress—ἄρσις and θέσις (cf. Ar. *Probl.* v, 41 πᾶσα πορεία ἐξ ἄρσεως καὶ θέσεως συντελεῖται). When this terminology was first used is not known; Damon, according to Socrates, used ἄνω καὶ κάτω, and Aristoxenus speaks of χρόνος ὁ ἄνω and χρόνος ὁ κάτω as well as ἄρσις and θέσις. The function of the terms is the same—to denote the swing in the unit of repetition. This could be followed by the movement of the foot in dancing, but was applicable metaphorically independently of that, and it is unlikely that the dancing to any particular rhythm was bound to analyse the 'feet' in this way. The dances called δάκτυλοι, ἰαμβική, μολοσσική mentioned by Athenaeus (XIV, 629) need not be taken as simply dances suitable for those metres; they could equally well be figures consisting of, for example, one slow and two quick steps, and so on.

It is more probable that the terms were used primarily from the conductor's or instructor's point of view, and for this reason were associated with the music, to indicate the unit of repetition—the 'bar'—in metres which were divisible into metra. So long as simple 'feet' were in question, an iambic 'foot' ∪ – would naturally be represented with the short syllable as arsis and the long as thesis, and the trochaic – ∪ and dactyl – ∪ ∪ conversely would be thesis-arsis, but when the more organic 'metron' or 'colon' was in question—Aristoxenus' ποὺς σύνθετος—the division into arsis and thesis was more arbitrary and ceased to correspond in the same obvious way to any 'swing' in the time or change in syllabic quantity. But the combination of arsis and thesis still served to mark the unit of movement and so to order the sequence of 'times', whether it was indicated by hand, or foot, or dots in a text which was to be preserved on record or sent by post. It is significant that among the various forms of confusion which arose among ancient authorities as to the reference of these terms there is one which makes ἄρσις the first part of every foot and θέσις the second part. We do not know how the device was used in those cola, such as the aeolics, which contain no smaller units of recurring movement; possibly some artificial subdivision was used by musicians as well as in the metrical tradition followed by Hephaestion.

My tentative suggestion then is that ἄρσις and θέσις were in effect a conventionalized guide to the nature of a rhythm intended chiefly for the musician or the χοροδιδάσκαλος and that though they might sometimes be followed by the dancer's foot this could be, and in theatre-choruses very often was, overridden at any time for considerations of mimesis, of dramatic action. The dancing of particular

emotions, for instance joy or panic or horror, must require quite
different kinds of step even where the metre is the same; also the
chorus had sometimes to 'act' more directly. The comic chorus in
particular often had to threaten, or pursue, or caper about in a way
that was hardly compatible with the punctilious rendering of 'feet'.
Here I might mention the curious tradition which appears from time
to time in scholia that the mimesis of the chorus included expressive
dancing to the speeches of the actors, in a kind of synchronized
miming. Thus on Ar. *Ran.* 896 τίνα λόγων ἐμμέλειαν Σ remarks that
the word ἐμμέλεια is here simply the equivalent of εὐρυθμία, though
properly it should mean ἡ μετὰ μέλους τραγικὴ ὄρχησις· οἱ δέ, ἡ
πρὸς τὰς ῥήσεις ὑπόρχησις, a definition which is duly recorded in
the Suda s.v. ἐμμέλεια. And on *Nub.* 1351–2

> ἀλλ' ἐξ ὅτου τὸ πρῶτον ἤρξαθ' ἡ μάχη γενέσθαι
> ἤδη λέγειν χρὴ πρὸς χορόν· πάντως δὲ τοῦτο δράσεις

there is the comment οὕτως ἔλεγον πρὸς χορὸν λέγειν, ὅτε τοῦ
ὑποκριτοῦ διατιθεμένου τὴν ῥῆσιν ὁ χορὸς ὠρχεῖτο. λέγειν πρὸς
χορόν of course means 'tell the chorus', not 'recite to dancing'
(possibly, with Hermann, δεῖ δὴ λέγειν πρὸς τὸν χορόν). It is
probable that here the scholiast has confused two different traditions
of dancing, the χορός which danced expressively to its own song
and the synchronized mimetic dance which accompanied certain
types of solo citharoedic singing. This latter has no relation to the
circumstances of the stage, where the chorus relatively to the actor-
singers or speakers is audience, not mimetic expressionist.

A further unresolved question is the degree of correspondence in
dance-movement between strophe and antistrophe. There is no
direct evidence, but the probability of such general correspondence
is very strong. I do not think, however, that this should be assumed
an absolute rule, for sometimes the requirements of dramatic accompanying action seem to call for some modification of similar
movements—in a realistic parodos like that of the *Ion*, for instance,
where the first three of the four verses represent a sight-seeing tour
of the Delphic sculptures, while the fourth verse asks 'May we look
inside?' Strophe β', that is to say, requires quite different gestures

and movements from antistrophe β'. And in the chorus of Bacchants
977ff. the strophe is a hounding-on of the θίασος in the mountains
against the spy in woman's dress whose discovery is dramatically
imagined, while the antistrophe is reflective in tone. It is difficult
to suppose that precisely the same movements would be found
appropriate in

ἴτε θοαὶ Λύσσας κύνες, ἴτ' εἰς ὄρος

and

ὃς ἀδίκῳ γνώμᾳ παρανόμῳ τ' ὀργᾷ.

Again, the song of the women of Troy in *Hec.* 923ff. seems to call
for mimetic accompanying action: in the strophe the tiring of the
hair before the golden mirror, the sudden shout of the Greek
invader; in the antistrophe the captive departing, turning to gaze
back upon her city.

We have in our possession only the skeleton of Greek tragedy
and comedy, and cannot recreate the living performance that would
clothe it in flesh and blood. It may even be that if by some miracle
we were enabled to see and hear, instead of read, the Greek whole
we should find our understanding and appreciation still inadequate
for the reality—that we should first have to set ourselves laboriously
to acquire new idioms of music and orchestic and stagecraft no easier
than the language itself; perhaps harder, if the prejudices of our
modern aesthetic should prove to be too deeply wrought into our
consciousness.

SYNOPSIS OF TYPICAL AND COMMON COLA

Dactylic

Hexam.	– ∪ ∪ – ∪ ∪ – ∪ ∪ – ∪ ∪ – ∪ ∪ – –
Tetram. A	– ∪ ∪ – ∪ ∪ – ∪ ∪ – –
Tetram. B	– ∪ ∪ – ∪ ∪ – ∪ ∪ – ∪ ∪
Hemiepes blunt	– ∪ ∪ – ∪ ∪ –
Hemiepes pendant	– ∪ ∪ – ∪ ∪ – –
Adonean	– ∪ ∪ – –

Anapaestic

Dim.	∪ ∪ – ∪ ∪ – ∪ ∪ – ∪ ∪ –
Paroemiac	∪ ∪ – ∪ ∪ – ∪ ∪ – –
Spondaic paroemiac	– – – – – – –

Dactylo-anapaestic

∪ ∪ – ∪ ∪ – ∪ ∪ – ∪ ∪ – ∪ ∪

Iambic

Dim.	⏓ – ∪ – ⏓ – ∪ –
Sync. trim. cat., e.g.	⏓ – ∪ – – ∪ – ∪ – –
Penthemimer	⏓ – ∪ – ⏓

Trochaic

Dim.	– ∪ – ⏓ – ∪ – ⏓
Sync. dim., e.g.	– – ∪ – ∪ – ⏓

Iambo-trochaic

Lekythion	– ∪ – ∪ – ∪ –
Ithyphallic	– ∪ – ∪ – –

Cretic-paeonic

Dims.	– ∪ – – ∪ –
	– ∪ ∪ ∪ – ∪ –
	∪ ∪ ∪ – ∪ ∪ ∪ –
Dim. cat.	– ∪ ∪ ∪ – –
Bacchiac dim.	∪ – – ∪ – –
or with molossus	– – – ∪ – –

Dochmiac

Commonest regular forms	⊽ – – ⊽ –
	∪ ∪ ∪ – ∪ –
	∪ – ⌣ ∪ –
	∪⌣⌣ ∪ ⊽
	– ∪ ∪ – ⊽ –
Long doch., e.g.	∪ – ∪ – ∪ –
	∪ ∪ ∪ ∪ ∪ ∪ –

Ionic

Dim.	∪ ∪ – – ∪ ∪ – –
Sync. dim.	∪ ∪ – ∪ ∪ – –
Ionic colarion	– – ∪ ∪ – –
Anacreontic	∪ ∪ – ∪ – ∪ – –

Aeolo-choriambic

Regular chor. dim.	– ∪ ∪ – – ∪ ∪ –	
Chor. dim. A	– ∪ ∪ – ∪ – ∪ –	**d s s**
Chor. dim. B	– x – x – ∪ ∪ –	
Chor. enoplian A	x – ∪ ∪ – ∪ – –	
Chor. enoplian B	x – ∪ – ∪ ∪ – –	
Glyconic	– x – ∪ ∪ – ⊽ –	
Pherecratean	– x – ∪ ∪ – –	
Aristophanean	– ∪ ∪ – ∪ – –	**d s –**
Telesillean	x – ∪ ∪ – ∪ –	
Blunt heptasyll. B	x – x – ∪ ∪ –	
Reizianum	x – ∪ ∪ – –	
Dodrans A	– ∪ ∪ – ⊽ –	
Dodrans B	– x – ∪ ∪ –	
Chor. enneasyll. blunt	x – ∪ – ∪ ∪ – ∪ –	**– s d s**
Chor. enneasyll. pendant	– ∪ ∪ – ∪ – ∪ – –	**d s s –**
Hipponactean	– x – ∪ ∪ – ∪ – –	
Asclepiad	– x – ∪ ∪ – – ∪ ∪ – ⊽ –	
Sapphic hendecasyll.	– ∪ – x – ∪ ∪ – ∪ – –	**s – d s –**
Alcaic hendecasyll.	x – ∪ – x – ∪ ∪ – ∪ –	**– s – d s**
Phalaecean	– x – ∪ ∪ – ∪ – ∪ – –	
Chor. trim. cat.	– ∪ ∪ – – ∪ ∪ – ∪ – –	
Greater Asclepiad	– x̄ – ∪ ∪ – – ∪ ∪ – – ∪ ∪ – ⊽ –	
Dodecasyll. pendant	– – ∪ ∪ – – ∪ ∪ – ∪ – –	
Aeolo-ionic cola	– – – ∪ ∪ – –	
	▬ – – ∪ ∪ – – ∪ ∪ – – ∪ ∪ – –	

Prosodiac-enoplian

Ibycean	– ∪ ∪ – ∪ ∪ – ∪ –	**d d s**
Alcaic decasyll.	– ∪ ∪ – ∪ ∪ – ∪ – –	**d d s –**
Praxillean	– ∪ ∪ – ∪ ∪ – ∪ ∪ – ∪ – –	**d d d s –**
Other prosodiacs	– ∪ ∪ – ∪ ∪ – ∪ ∪ – ∪ –	**d d d s**
	– ∪ ∪ – ∪ ∪ – – –	**d d s̄**
Choriambic enoplian	× – ∪ ∪ – ∪ – –	**– d s –**
Other enoplians	∪ ∪ – ∪ – ∪ –	**∧ d s s**
	∪ ∪ – ∪ ∪ – ∪ –	**∧ d d s**
	× – ∪ ∪ – ∪ ∪ –	**– d d**
(paroemiac)	× – ∪ ∪ – ∪ ∪ – –	**– d d –**
	× – ∪ ∪ – ∪ ∪ – ∪ – –	**– d d s –**
(cyrenaic)	∪ ∪ – ∪ ∪ – ∪ – ∪ –	**∧ d d s s**
	∪ – ∪ – ∪ ∪ – ∪ ∪ – (–)	**∧ s s d d (–)**

Dactylo-epitrite

Iambelegus	× – ∪ – × – ∪ ∪ – ∪ ∪ –	**– s – d d**
	– ∪ – × – ∪ ∪ – ∪ ∪ – –	**s – d d –**
Encomiologus	– ∪ ∪ – ∪ ∪ – × – ∪ – –	**d d – s –**
Dactylo-iambic	∪ – ∪ – – ∪ ∪ – ∪ ∪ –	
Iambo-anapaest	∪ ∪ – ∪ ∪ – ∪ – ∪ – ∪ – –	**∧ d d s s s –**

INDEX LOCORUM

In continuous passages only the first and last lines are indexed

GENERAL INDEX

Acephalous, 18, 22 f., 138
Adonean, 29, 31, 35, 66, 140, 143, 215
Aeolic, 17, 22 f., 38, 90 f., 120 ff., IX
  passim, 190 ff.
Aeolic base, 23, 117, 133 f., 155, 157
Aeolic dactyls, 19, 30, 46, 90, 117, 157
Aeolo-choriambic, 17, 20, 23, 33, 41, 43,
  84, 106, 113, 128, IX *passim*, 158, 160 f.,
  165, 170, 183, 191, 193, 199, 208, 216
Aeolo-ionic, 128, 144, 150, 199, 216
Aeschylus, 32, 39, 42, 44 f., 49, 52, 59, 77,
  81 ff., 84 f., 92, 95, 99 f., 104, 110 f.,
  121, 126, 129, 146, 148 f., 151, 164,
  195, 199 ff.
Alcaeus, 131, 133, 141 f., 157 ff.
Alcaic decasyllable, 24, 67, 129, 149,
  161 f., 177, 181, 190, 216
Alcaic enneasyllable, 70, 95, 184
Alcaic hendecasyllable, 141, 177, 179, 216
Alcaic stanza, 141, 161, 177, 179
Alcman, 33, 37, 90, 128
ἀμοιβαῖον, 110, 152, 169, 176
Anaclasis, 10, 83, 85, 95, 105, 108, 121 ff.,
  136, 138, 140 f., 145, 191
Anacreon, 35, 121 f., 125 f.
Anacreontic, VIII *passim*, 146 f., 162, 173,
  189 f., 216
Anacrusis, 18, 22 f., 40
Anapaestic, 16, 19, 21, 24, 26, 34 ff., 38 f.,
  41, IV *passim*, 70, 76 ff., 90, 98, 103,
  105, 116 f., 143, 147, 150, 152, 160,
  167 ff., 175, 191 f., 196 f., 207 f., 215
Anaphora, 49, 105, 110
ἀντιλαβή, 28, 113
Antiphanes, 187
Antispast, 61, 96, 136
ἀπολελυμένα, 13, 39, 51, 57, 67, 111, 138,
  161, 167, 171, 174, 199
Archebulean, 163
Archilochean, 176, 181, 187
Archilochus, 21, 35, 72, 77, 158, 160, 180,
  185, 195, 208
Aristides Quintilianus, 2, 34
Aristophanean, 20, 33, 83, 106, 127, 132,
  134 ff., 139, 143, 147, 161, 164, 183,
  193, 199, 216
Aristophanes, 2, 22, 28, 42, 44 f., 55, 65,
  77, 97, 98, 112 f., 116, 134, 139, 147,
  152, 162, 186, 189, 192, 195, 207 f.
Aristotle, 69, 207, 210 f.
Aristoxenus, 2, 6, 7, 211 f.
Arsis and thesis, 2, 23, 48, 210 ff.
Asclepiad, 139, 142 ff., 150, 155, 158, 216

Astrophic, 13, 39, 47, 51, 57, 99, 101,
  110, 161, 166, 168 f., 170, 200
Asynartete πνῖγος, 35
Athenaeus, 209, 212
Autocrates, 87

Bacchiac, 3, 16, 26, 72 ff., VI *passim*, 107 f.,
  132, 142 f., 162, 166, 208, 215
Bacchylides, 24, 178, 185, 189, 191
Barrett, W. S., 153
Blass, 178
Brachycatalexis, 18, 21, 54
Bucolic diaeresis, 31, 117

Catalexis, 3, 6, 11, 18 ff., 35, 42, 48, 51,
  75 ff., 87 f., 93, 121, 124, 136, 145, 147,
  155, 158, 175, 187, 197 ff.
Catullus, 123
Choerilean, 42, 176, 179, 187
Choeroboscus, 3
Choriambic, 10, 17, 20 f., 24, 35, 38, 42 f.,
  59, 61 f., 80, 83 ff., 106, 117, 129, IX
  and X *passim*, 182, 190, 199 f., 210,
  216
Colarion, 35 f., 59, 71, 95, 103, 114 f.,
  125, 127, 133, 139, 141, 163, 172, 176
Colometry, 11 f., 39 f., 94, 108, 116, 126,
  145 ff., 196
Contraction, 24, 31, 38 f., 43, 51, 58, 62,
  84, 95, 106, 122, 143, 150, 172
Corinna, 128, 145
Correption, 25
Cratinean, 147
Cratinus, 55, 97
Cretic, 3, 16, 72 ff., 89, 91, 95, VI *passim*,
  107 ff., 117, 138, 147, 215
Cretic-paeonic, 16, 55 ff., 73, 89, 91, VI
  passim, 215
Cyclic dactyl, 5, 91
Cyrenaic, 171, 177

Dactylic, 5 f., 8, 14, 16 f., 19, 21, 24, III
  passim, 67, 83 f., 90, 95, 97, 117, 122,
  138, 149, 157 f., 161 f., 178 ff., 181,
  199, 212, 215
Dactylo-anapaestic, 40 f., 67 ff., 122,
  160 f., 170, 172, 215
Dactylo-epitrite, 12, 17, 21, 25 f., 35, 42,
  43 f., 52, 67 f., 71, 84, 93, 125, 128, 160,
  170, 172 f., 176 f., XI *passim*, 200 f.,
  208
Damon, 211
Dance, I *passim*, 208 ff.

Made in the USA
Coppell, TX
21 April 2020